D0889792

KELLY

AT HOME ON THIRD

By

KEVIN BOLAND

and

KELLY GRUBER

VIKING

VIKING
Published by the Penguin Group
Penguin Books Canada Ltd, 10 Alcorn Avenue, Toronto, Ontario, Canada
M4V 3B2
Penguin Books Ltd, 27 Wrights Lane, London W8 5TZ, England
Viking Penguin, a division of Penguin Books USA Inc., 375 Hudson Street, New
York, New York 10014, USA
Penguin Books Australia Ltd, Ringwood, Victoria, Australia
Penguin Books (NZ) Ltd, 182-190 Wairau Road, Auckland 10, New Zealand

Penguin Books Ltd, Registered Offices: Harmondsworth, Middlesex, England

First published 1991

10 9 8 7 6 5 4 3 2 1

Copyright © Kevin Boland and Kelly Gruber, 1991

All rights reserved. Without limiting the rights under copyright reserved above,
no part of this publication may be reproduced, stored in or introduced into a
retrieval system, or transmitted in any form or by any means (electronic,
mechanical, photocopying, recording or otherwise), without the prior written
permission of both the copyright owner and the above publisher of this book.

Every effort has been made to locate holders of copyright for the photographs
contained herein. If you have any information pertaining to such copyright not
already credited here, please contact the publisher immediately.

Printed and bound in Canada on acid free paper ♽

Canadian Cataloguing in Publication Data
Boland, Kevin
    Kelly: at home on third

ISBN 0-670-83900-0

1. Gruber, Kelly, 1962-   . 2. Baseball players—
Canada—Biography. 3. Toronto Blue Jays (Baseball
team)—Biography. I. Gruber, Kelly, 1962-
II Title.

GV865.G78B65 1991   796.357'092   C91-093516-5

Printed and bound in Canada by John Deyell Company

*For my wife Lynn
and our baby boy Kody
K.W.G.*

*For Katie and Michael
and their tiny, perfect mom
K.J.B.*

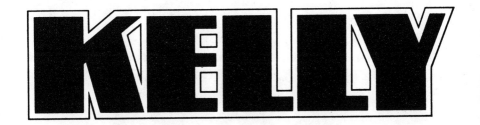

CONTENTS

◆ PREFACE

Funny, isn't it, the kind of snapshot the mind's eye will take all on its own, for no reason apparent at the time, and store away for years until the detail that was captured takes on its own very special meaning.

The images that crowd my thoughts today were made over a period of seven years, beginning with that first "snap" on as fine a morning in March as there ever will be.

For two hours beneath a sky as high as a pop fly, with not a cloud to be seen from Tampa to Havana, the Toronto Blue Jays of 1984 had been working up a sweat at the Cecil P. Englebert Complex on the northeast side of Dunedin, Florida. The vets would get the rest of the afternoon off, to go golfing or fishing or shopping, but the rookies would be back in an hour to pay another instalment for the sin of being young.

The clubhouse crew had outdone itself in whipping up a three-star, four-course luncheon—bread rolls, chicken noodle soup, five-alarm chili, jelly doughnuts—and the brave were wolfing their way through it when a clutch of newspaper guys gathered at the locker of the large and gregarious Cliff Johnson.

Right off the mark he got a laugh when he said his idea of spring training was to find the biggest shade tree on the grounds and developing the "mental toughness" to will himself to sleep between trips to the batting cage.

Click.

It was at that moment that I first set eyes on Kelly Gruber, out of the corner of one of them at that. As I study that hazy image now, what strikes me about it is how alone he seemed to be on that bench at the far side of the clubhouse. Cap pushed back off his forehead, hunched over with his elbows on his knees, a battered set of spikes beside his stockinged feet, he had just squirted shave cream into his infielder's glove and was working the lather into the pocket. It gave the rookie something to do, I figured, while he cased the clubhouse for a friendly face that first week of camp.

Neither of us had an inkling of it at the time, of course, but it just might have been book at first sight.

As well as any newspaper scribbler can, I got to know him over the next couple of months of his first season in the major leagues. In the process I can hardly lay claim to being the big brother he never had, but I do remember helping Kelly Gruber through a couple of rough spots instead of heeding my spit-disturbing sports editor's admonishment to "dig up a little dirt" on the Blue Jays.

One of those situations involved me breaking the news to him that the club had made a deal to ship him out to their top farm club in Syracuse. The Cleveland Indians, from whom the Blue Jays had claimed Gruber the previous December, were granted rights to backup catcher Geno Petralli in exchange for permission to send Gruber down to a lower level of baseball. They hoped this would enable him to develop into the player they thought he could be. Had the Indians chosen to do so, they could have forced the Blue Jays to keep him on their bench the entire season.

At first, the deal for Petralli was couched in terms of a straight sale (no terms disclosed) to the Indians, but one call to the right telephone in the Cleveland front office revealed the essence of the transaction. Blue Jays manager

Bobby Cox had no choice but to confirm for me what had happened. Would he tell the kid, or should I?

"Ahhh, fudge," (or something like that), said Cox. "Go ahead."

Click.

I can see Gruber now, on a chair before his locker in the visitors' clubhouse at Memorial Stadium in Baltimore, working at a crossword puzzle in the back pages of *The Sun*. He looks up as I approach. What's a six-letter word for a team named after native leaders indigenous to North America? Hint: Starts with a C. Hint: Plays in upstate New York. Hint: Just acquired paleface third baseman.

Gruber stayed with the big club for another week, until first baseman Willie Aikens arrived to take his spot on the roster, and his leave-taking in Minneapolis that afternoon is as fresh in my memory as if it had happened yesterday.

Click.

There he is, high up in the seats behind home plate at the Metrodome in Minneapolis, squirming in pressed civilian clothes while his former mates gambol on the green carpet beneath him. God, but he looks out of place—a shavetail waiting by the side of the road for the bus that will take him to boot camp; hating to go, but knowing he must; already ticking off the days and the hours until he would be back home again. That evening, when the team boards the charter back to Toronto, Gruber is left holding his bags to wait for the flight to Syracuse and Triple A baseball.

"Don't worry, pal," they say. "You'll be back in no time at all." It's what they'd tell a guy if he'd lost an arm and broken both of his legs.

We kept in touch over the next couple of years, I even made a couple of trips to Syracuse to see how he was making out, but my mind's eye seems to have pawned its slide projector where Gruber was concerned. Then it came out of hock for the Blue Jays' home opener against the New York Yankees in 1988. Just in time, too.

There had been talk all that spring that Gruber, who had failed to live up to his high promise, would be available if "the right deal" came along. This could be as little as a bag of broken bats, a couple of warm bodies in the minors, or a low pick in the June draft of high school players.

So little did his employers think of his ability to contribute that the year before, during a seven-game losing streak to end the season, they employed flyweight Garth Iorg and aging veteran Rance Mulliniks while the Blue Jays blew the East Division flag to the Tigers.

"It hurt," Gruber admits, recalling some of the darkest moments in franchise history. "A lot of games, we were down a run and I knew I was capable of hitting it out. You take those seven games, maybe I could've popped one. Why wasn't I playing?"

Call it destiny, but before a throng of 45,185 at Exhibition Stadium for the 1988 home opener, fate took a hand in the making of Kelly Gruber.

Rickey Henderson, the great one, changed the course of Blue Jays history in the first inning when he led off with a single against starter Mike Flanagan. He stole second base and then lit out for third. His theft of that base, accomplished when he rammed into Rance Mulliniks, turned the key in the door to Kelly Gruber's future.

Mulliniks, pain etched on his face, was gripping his knee on the dirt cutout at third base. As he limped off the field, Gruber trotted from the dugout and took his place. The job at third has been his ever since.

Like most who have been forced to sit and wait in the major leagues, Gruber had felt there was no hope for him to reach his potential as long as his bosses thought of him as part-time personnel. Now he had his chance to prove them wrong. Put up or shut up.

Click.

He went 4-for-6 that afternoon, belted two home runs and collected five RBIs as the Blue Jays trashed the Yankees 17-9 with a 20-hit barrage off half a dozen New York pitchers.

"For the first time up here," Mulliniks would say later, "he was in there every day. No way out. Bad day today, bad day tomorrow, Kelly knew they wouldn't be running Mulliniks or Iorg right back out there. It's what he needed."

Gruber's view cuts closer to the bone.

"I knew they had their doubts, but they couldn't look inside and see if I was made of tin or steel," he says. "You can only put the guys out there you think can win. I got the chance—who knew if it was going to be my last one?—so I made up their minds for them."

There have been occasions for lots of "pictures" since then, but there are three that I'd put on the jacket of this book if I could.

They were taken, click-click-click, at the SkyDome on a September weekend when the Blue Jays took on the Baltimore Orioles in a series that meant a lot at the time in the 1990 pennant drive.

With two out in the seventh inning of one game, score 6-3 in favour of Baltimore, Gruber lined a pitch from Jeff Ballard off the wall in left-centre field to score runners Manny Lee and Junior Felix.

RBIs 100 and 101, delivered at a pivotal point in the season, brought 50,000 out of their seats to bawl a chorus of The Standing O.

Gruber was surprised.

"I waited for it to die down," he told me later. "It was getting embarrassing. For one, we're still behind a run. For another, it wasn't like I just got my 2,000th hit. Then, the way I looked at it, if they thought it was something, I guess I had to tip my cap."

Considering the sweat and toil and tears that went into the making of it, it was a picture worth 100,000 words.

But not nearly so engaging as the one an hour or so later. Gruber, alone after holding court for the media mob, was about to close up shop at his locker when I wandered by.

"On your shoulder," I said, "is that baby barf or is tie-dye back in style?"

"What!?" said Gruber, craning to inspect a couple of white patches near the collar of his powder-blue T-shirt. "Hmmm. Looks like it. Hmmm. Smells like it. Sure is. Su-r-r-re is!"

Like all who have been humbled by the swift-changing eddies of this game, Gruber is not one to spurn a perfectly good omen, especially after a night when he was 4-for-5 at the plate, collected RBIs 100 and 101 and slid home with the tying run in the ninth inning of what became an 8-7 win over Baltimore. No, he did not wear that T-shirt until all the luck was beaten out of it, as many another might have done. He did, however, tuck it away at the bottom of his locker.

For me, fine sights though that night had provided, none was the picture that truly captured the essence of Kelly Gruber. That came in the ninth inning of a game a couple of nights later when, with none out and Tony Fernandez on second base, Gruber skipped a ball to first that became an easy out. It brought Fernandez to third and, after a walk to Freddie McGriff, set the table for George Bell's game-winning flare to right.

The cynics might suggest Gruber squibbed a ball he wanted to drive nine miles for the winning run—and, with many players, they would have been correct. Not this night.

In the dugout before the game, we had talked for a while about a player "giving himself up" and how seldom it was done efficiently.

"This turf," Gruber noted, trying to alibi for some of his mates, "it's awful tough to bunt on it. For me, anyway, it's a whole lot easier to trickle one down the right side. When the team needs it, you do it."

Ruth's called shot it wasn't, but that little bleeder in the ninth had the same result. Winning, and there need not be a batting average attached to it, is what it's all about.

Kevin Boland
August 1991

CHAPTER 1

 THE TWILIGHT ZONE

It is 12:56 AM, December 10, 1983.

Overhead, in the main room of an apartment on the top floor of the Hotel Slide—the winter home away from home for *Norte Americanos* who play with the Café Universale baseball club—a fan is clicking. The swirl of the blades has no effect on the heat.

Windows are always open wide in the Hotel Slide, but there is no breeze in Baranquilla to cut the stillness, the cloying humidity that has fallen on this port city of 900,000 on the Magdalena River delta in the Caribbean Lowlands of Colombia.

On a bed in one of the two rooms in the back of the apartment, beneath a single sheet and stewing in his own sweat, is the Toronto Blue Jays' newest recruit. The team recently has become a true contender in the East Division of the American League.

Five days earlier, when the Cleveland Indians failed for some reason to protect their once-prized prospect by retaining him on their forty-man winter roster, the Blue Jays swooped in to claim the twenty-one-year-old kid they hoped would become their third baseman of the future.

At the moment, that future means nothing to Kelly Gruber. He is listening to the thud of his heart.

"I could feel the blood being pumped from my heart and I could feel it travelling through my body," he recalled one afternoon in Chicago late in the summer of 1990. "It was the weirdest moment in my life, for sure, but I felt very in tune with everything that was going on.

"I could see my heart beating, really see it on the ceiling even though it was pitch-black in the room. It was like a row of blips on one of those monitors they have in a hospital.

"It couldn't have been more real."

He pauses in the narrative, takes off his Blue Jays cap and sets it on a forty-five-foot roll of tarpaulin by the box seats behind first base at the old Comiskey Park. The wind picks up and races across the outfield grass. He crosses his arms, spits and searches the sea of emerald green seats glistening in the bleachers in far-off left field. Comiskey Park is empty and quiet now except for a couple of coaches tossing a ball around while they wait for the young pups to show for early batting practice. This will be one of the last times Gruber has a minute to take in Comiskey Park before the wreckers make a shambles of the place. Old Comiskey has more than its share of ghosts, including at least a dozen White Sox loyalists who have had their ashes scattered across the outfield grass in the past decade.

"All of a sudden," says Gruber, his thoughts back in that pitch-black room in the Hotel Slide, "everything started closing down. The heart beat was real slow. My thoughts, too. Then, as soon as it got so slow that it was about to stop, something from me was lifted away. Something just leaves. My spirit? My soul? I don't know."

As he drifted into sleep that night, an altogether new kind of hunger was at work within him. He knew something bad had happened.

At that moment, 1,976 miles to the northeast in Austin, Texas, only hours after his last letter home had been read to her, Vita Evelyn Watkins-Hunt took one last, laboured breath. She was seventy-nine years old, and for the final eighteen months of her life—fifteen years after leukemia had been diagnosed—she had fought the good fight against the disease.

"It is as if she had been holding on to make sure I was on my way to the big leagues," Kelly Gruber says. "I don't know that I would have been a baseball player without her." He glances around the empty park again, as if to invite the spirits therein to listen.

Regarded as a "baseball palace" when it was built in 1910 by franchise founder Charles A. Comiskey, the joint is in its final days after eighty-one summers in the American League. In its shadow, just across the way at the confluence of the Dan Ryan Expressway and 35th Street, the concrete shell of the new Comiskey Park is taking shape and will be ready in plenty of time for Opening Day of 1991.

To suggest the old "palace" will be missed may be wishful thinking. The wrinkles are clear, the sags pronounced, the colours faded and caked with grime. Rickety is the term that came to mind in the last few years but now, now that she is about to be abandoned, the old crone looks downright shabby.

There were few ball parks better than this old crock for turning over memories. For generations, it had been a place where dreams went to die. Chief among them is the Black Sox Scandal, in which Joe Jackson and seven other players on the White Sox were banned for life after conspiring with gamblers to fix the 1919 World Series.

"Say it ain't so, Joe . . . say it ain't so,"
Pleaded the crippled newsie, tugging at the sleeve of his idol.

"I'm afraid it is, kid . . . I'm afraid it is,"
Said Shoeless Joe, tears fresh on his cheeks,
After the legal boys had done with him.

Not until 1959, four decades after The Scandal, was there another World Series there and the "Go-Go Sox" blew that one 4-2 to the Los Angeles Dodgers. There was a sniff of glory again in 1983, when the ChiSox won their division by twenty games, but the Baltimore Orioles buried them 3-1 in the best-of-five play-off for the pennant.

Comiskey Park was also the site of the first All-Star Game in 1933, won 4-2 by the American League when The Great Ruth walloped a two-run home run off Bill Hallahan in the third inning. Half a century later, Dave Stieb of the Blue Jays was the American League starter and, after three innings of near-perfection, they had enough to put that one in the win column, too.

Good things come. Good things go. For all these things, there is a season. As it is in baseball, so it is in life.

When Gruber left Texas to polish his talents in the Colombian winter league in the autumn of 1983, his grandmother's cancer seemed to have been in check. At a time when her grandson was about to realize her greatest ambition for him, the leukemia "took hold and snow-balled."

His devotion to her was fuelled by the fact that Vita and Archie Hunt had raised the boy in that vital period between two and four years of age when a person's character traits are formed and set for life.

Kelly Gruber's natural father is Claude King, a running back with the Chicago Bears of the National Football League, New England Patriots and Houston Oilers of the rival American Football League in the mid-sixties before he wound up his career with a two-month fling with the Saskatchewan Roughriders of the Canadian Football

League. He left the family when Kelly was in diapers. Then his mother, a former Miss Texas who was once part of a moderately successful singing trio called The Lee Sisters, married a real estate executive, David Gruber. Kelly King as a toddler had a difficult time accepting his new father. For years, theirs was a tempestuous relationship.

Part of the problem, one that any single mother can appreciate, was that Gloria Gruber had to return to work as a secretary to support Kelly and his older sister, Claudia. The Hunts, who moved to Houston from Corpus Christi to help out, also had to make their living. With a maid caring for the children during the day, discipline was lax. When David Gruber adopted the children during his first year of marriage to their mother, Kelly suddenly acquired a father figure who drew a hard line on domestic law and order.

"Unfortunately, I was only twenty-six or twenty-seven at the time and didn't know how to handle a strong-willed child," David Gruber, now a financial adviser, said over brunch one day at the family's townhouse on the outskirts of Austin. "I was trying to get him to conform. He was probably wondering who the hell this new guy thought he was. It was a clash of wills. Iron wills."

There were beatings—too many of them, David Gruber sees now. Then the parents hit upon a disciplinary plan that defused the confrontations while inadvertently grooming the child for his future in baseball.

"We had a long block in front of the house in Houston where we first lived," says David Gruber. "Instead of whipping him so much, I'd get him to run it whenever he acted up. He'd burn off energy, release his frustrations and improve his speed."

Certainly Kelly Gruber was a difficult youngster.

"It was the result of no discipline, no identification with a strong father figure," says David Gruber. "His grandfather was a prince of the world, but not a strong father figure. His grandmother was the major influence in his early years. Kelly was trying to establish himself. I was trying to get him to conform with acceptable behaviour.

"If I had it to do over, I would have disciplined him a lot less. There would have been less anger and afterward a lot of love. The idea would be to show him not who was right, but the difference between good and bad. I've talked with him many times since then, saying how sorry I was for not understanding."

It also came as a surprise to David Gruber to learn one of the most basic reasons for the boy's recalcitrant ways.

"I wasn't the son I should have been," Kelly Gruber said that day in Comiskey Park, "because I thought he might leave me, too. I rebelled because of it. I think that's why I was so close to my grandparents. I was sure of them. I knew they would never leave me."

The death of one of them, no matter how inevitable it might have been, came as a shock to Kelly at age twenty-one.

"I knew I might never see her again," Gruber says of that last visit with her before he left for Colombia. "I thought, I hoped, she might pull through until I could go and be with her one more time. All she wanted was a little more time with me, and I couldn't give it to her.

"She was the reason I was playing baseball. I was big on football. Loved the game. Loved the contact. Football in Texas, it's a religion. You play it well, you're a god. You're immortal. If it was just me I was pleasing, that's where I'd have been.

"When she died, a lot of the desire to play kids' games left me. For a while there, it was like maybe I ought to go on back to university, play football as a way to get an education, forget about this baseball deal. For a while, I really thought hard on it."

The fates, as they so often do, sent an important person

into Gruber's life at an important time. Gruber's shattered spirit was revived by Jose Martinez, who at the time was a coach with the Kansas City Royals of the American League, and spent his off-seasons managing clubs in Latin America.

Martinez, forty-one, had collected the reins of the Café Universale club after a long and tortuous route through the hinterlands of baseball. Born in Cárdenas, Cuba, during the Second World War, he learned early that the surest way to avoid a life in the cane fields was to become a ballplayer. About the time that Fidel Castro was telling the Yankee imperialist to go home, Martinez decided to follow his dream in the United States.

In baseball, as in life, nothing is so cruel as to get so close and fail.

"Had a cup of coffee," Martinez says as he tucks the striped jersey of his Chicago Cubs uniform into his pants one morning in the clubhouse at Wrigley Field. The term is ballplayer shorthand for saying his time in the major leagues was unmercifully brief.

As a utility infielder with the Pittsburgh Pirates of 1969, mostly as a sub in the late innings for second baseman Bill Mazeroski, he appeared in 77 games out of the season's 162 and batted .268 (45-for-168). His one claim to fifteen seconds of fame, his only home run in the majors, was struck off pitcher Claude Raymond of the Montreal Expos. It came with the bases loaded and was the first grand slam hit in Jarry Park, the original home of Canada's first team in the big leagues.

In 1970, under manager Danny Murtaugh, Martinez made all of twenty-one appearances at the plate and had one hit. "I was there for three months and I never played," he says, still hurt twenty years later. "That was the way. You got to take the sweet with the sour. Bad times. You never want to remember the bad times. So I try never to look back."

It had taken ten seasons in the Pirates' minor league system to get his shot and, after his "cup of coffee" with the parent club, Martinez spent three more at Omaha with the Royals' farm club before he turned to managing at the lowest levels of the minors.

"I got people here now who appreciate what I have done," he says. "I think they listen to me. I'm honest. That's all I can be. Maybe they don't want to hear the things I say, but I tell the truth that I feel is for their well-being."

It was this philosophy that he took with him when he sought out Gruber on the Café Universale team bus as it made a stop for gas and grub in the city of El Uruaeo by the Magdalena River. That was the midway point on the trip to play in Cartagena, a port city of 531,000 about a hundred miles southwest of Baranquilla.

"You could see he was down," says Martinez. "His grandmother was a big influence on him as a boy. The one thing I told him was that she would only be happy with him if he worked at his job and became the successful player he was talented enough to be. If you feel sorry for yourself, I told him, you're not going nowhere.

"I told him about my life. How I came over to the United States from Cuba. That my father and my mother died and I wasn't able to go to Cuba to see them buried. I explained to him, baseball, it's not an easy life. If you want to succeed, you got to pay the price.

"I told him that if he wanted to make his grandmother proud of him as a man, then God had given her the best seat in the house to watch him do it."

It was the second time in a week that Martinez had talked with him heart to heart. When Cleveland left Gruber off its forty-man roster, a fact Gruber learned from a two-day-old issue of the *Miami Herald* he bought in a hotel coffee shop in Baranquilla, Martinez prevailed upon the player not to pack his bags and head back home to Texas.

"I said, 'Lookit, that's the best thing that could happen to you. There's all kinds of scouts from the big clubs down here. Now somebody will see you who could use you. If you leave, you will be a quitter in their eyes.'

"Sometimes in baseball, you've got to be a father," Martinez explains now as the rest of the Cubs file out for their afternoon game against the Atlanta Braves. "Sometimes you've got to be a brother. Sometimes, not very often, you got to be the policeman."

As Gruber digested Martinez's advice at the back of the team bus a million miles from where he wanted to be, the memories of his grandmother came flooding back.

"She and my grandfather were at everything I played," he says now, back at his locker in the visitors' clubhouse at Comiskey Park. "Behind home plate, with their lawn chairs up against the screen in PeeWee, Little League and high school. I can remember the umpire blowing a call on a pitch. 'Oh popcorn!' she'd say. 'Oh, phooey.' She'd ride him. Really ride him. Was I crazy about them? I caused a fuss one game when I stopped in the middle of my wind-up to wave at my grandpa when he showed up."

He remembered being jarred awake on Sunday mornings as the sun spread across cattle country, his grandma struggling to dress him for the forty-five-minute drive to services at The Church of Christ in Pearland, Texas.

"I'd be there sitting in the pews, hugging my 'Maw-maw.' I'd get her to scratch on me, my back, during the service. Then I'd get her to rub my arms and it'd always make me fall asleep. 'Paw-paw,' my grandfather, he'd be sitting in the pew, falling asleep, a toothpick in his mouth. When he knelt to pray, I'd get down there with him, even though I was too small to see over the pews.

"Paw-paw, he was the quiet one. Laughed about everything, he did. My mom will tell you she never once saw him lose his temper, even raise his voice, in all her time with him. Now that is a feat. He used to call all of us little worry-warts. Every once in a while, when he was looking at the bank statement towards the end of the month, we'd call him a worry-wart."

All of his life, Archie Hunt had known what it was to work hard. After decades of driving a truck for a freight company, he drove a milk route in Corpus Christi for Borden's while his daughter went through high school. Later in life, he took home-study courses in refrigeration and worked until retirement as an air-conditioner installer and repairman.

"Maw-maw was more the voluble type. She would just chew Paw-paw up and down. And he'd say, 'Oh, Vita. Just hush.' To this day, I can see them, hear them. To this day."

If a quick bat is an inherited thing—all in the wrists, they say—then the genes just might have been passed on by his grandmother. The stricter of the two, she did not believe in sparing the rod. At times, when Kelly and his sister were making mayhem, she headed for the back yard and snapped off a switch from the willow tree.

"She could flick the hind legs off a blue-tail fly, she was that accurate," Gruber says with a straight face. "The trick was she had to catch us first. She was sort of cripply, so that gave us an edge. One day we were racing around the living room, making noise something awful, and Maw-maw was chasing us. Paw-paw, he was just sitting there, wouldn't raise a hand. 'Archie,' she said, 'if you don't catch them next time they come by, you'll be feeling this switch, too.'"

As it always does when we remember absent friends, one memory laid the foundations for another when Gruber thought back to that day on the bus at a pit-stop on a Colombian highway.

This one had to do with the service truck his grandfather drove for an electrical appliances company when the family lived in Houston. On his rounds, he allowed the boy to ride in the back of the pickup, playing fireman as he clung to the railings of the U-shaped tool compartment.

"Some of those rides," says Gruber, "they were the thrill of a lifetime. If we're talking about just getting pumped up, they were as exciting as hitting one into the seats to win the game in the bottom of the ninth."

While the death of his grandmother was a crushing blow, he was devastated by the death of his grandfather of heart disease a little more than a year later. As near as his grandmother had been to him, his grandfather might have been closer because he was Kelly's father figure during those infant years.

"Because he was male and I was male, he was a real leader to me," he says. "All my friends, through high school, after high school, they didn't call him Mr. Hunt, Archie, or whatever. They called him Paw-paw, too. He was that kind of man."

Physically, there was much in the grandparents' genes that found its way into the boy. Like his grandfather, Kelly had the legs of a ballet dancer and narrow hips, big hands and thick fingers. Like his grandmother, in her day an accomplished horsewoman and tennis player, he had broad forearms and lightning reflexes. Most important, it was from Vita Hunt, whose brother once played in the Philadelphia Athletics' farm system, that he inherited his love of baseball.

Baseball conspired to remove Gruber from the scene on January 27, 1985, when Archie Joe Hunt, seventy-four years old, joined his wife at Assumption Cemetery in Austin.

The boy and his grandfather's last moments together were in a hospital room in Austin where the old man, whose death might well have been hastened by having to care for his wife in her final eighteen months, was struggling to overcome the effects of a stroke, a weakened heart and clogged arteries. As Gruber took a break during the visit, his father approached him in the hallway outside the hospital room. He told him he might never see his grandfather again, that whatever needed saying had better be said now.

"It was one of the hardest things I've ever had to do. I spoke from the heart. 'Look,' I said, 'I'm going to play. I wish I could stay till you get better, but you are going to get better. For me. For us. For yourself.'"

It wasn't to be.

"I find myself talking to them often. Just driving down the road, all of a sudden, I see where they're buried. Assumption Cemetery in Austin. And, you know, I get to where, geez, I almost want to break down, wishing I could be with them again.

"It might sound as if I'm cold, but I don't stop to visit their graves. I can't. I'd just get angry and sad. They're not there. They're gone. I can talk to them anywhere, anytime, just as easy as I can in a graveyard.

"I think about how much I miss them, how much I'd like them to be around and what I could do for them now that I have the money. My wife Lynn, my baby boy Kody, they're the most important part of my life, and my grandparents never got to know them.

"My son, he'll never get to meet his Maw-maw, his Paw-paw. That hurts me. Geez, I wish they were here to see this little baby. They'd be so proud of him."

Outside the visitors' clubhouse, the evening breeze off Lake Michigan is blowing a welcome sigh of relief after a midsummer's day of high heat. The smell of freshly cut grass mixes with the buzz of the White Sox faithful scattered across a sea of emerald green seats.

It is time, for one of the last times, to play ball at Comiskey Park. Somewhere out there, Kelly Gruber is hoping, Archie and Vita Hunt are watching.

CHAPTER 2

 DIAMOND IN THE ROUGH

The Cincinnati Reds, a team that had finished second in the West Division of the National League the four previous seasons, had to figure its luck would change in 1989.

It did, too. It got worse.

Never mind that the Little Red Machine sputtered home in fifth place, 17 games behind the San Francisco Giants. It happens. You win some. You lose some. You wait for the tulips to bloom next spring.

What shamed this blue-collar town in Ohio was that Pete Rose, a native son who made good as the most prolific hitter in baseball history, a man whose very name is on the street that leads to Riverfront Stadium, had been given the bum's rush from the game of baseball for betting big money on sports.

The banishment for life of Charley Hustle from baseball was the last significant act of Commissioner A. Bartlett Giamatti, by all accounts a wonderful man. He died, of a massive heart attack, about a week after he rid the game of Rose.

The connection was an inviting one to make and Cincinnati, one of the founding franchises of the National

League in 1876, became a town in disgrace.

Which brings us to miracle worker Bob Quinn, one of the rare exceptions to that hoary maxim that says nice guys finish last. As general manager of the Reds, he persuaded old pal Lou Piniella of the New York Yankees—the manager the Toronto Blue Jays wanted before they gave the job to Cito Gaston, the right guy all along—to jump George Steinbrenner's ship, as Quinn had done, and become field boss of the Reds.

Then he swapped relievers with the New York Mets, John Franco for Randy Myers, and the Nasty Boys became a fact of life in the Reds' bullpen. When outfielder Eric Davis went down for the 26 games early in the season, Quinn had Billy Hatcher (.276, 28 doubles) there to fill a gaping hole. He also swapped with the Yankees for young Hal Morris, a splendid young hitter (.340, 22 doubles in 309 at-bats) and he got Glenn Braggs (.299) from Milwaukee. To add a soothing influence when throats, among other things, got tight in the September stretch run, he had veteran Billy Doran from Houston and his lively bat (.300, 29 doubles, 403 ABS).

The Reds led from wire to wire, coasting home five games in front of the L.A. Dodgers. Then they trimmed the Pittsburgh Pirates 4-2 in the play-offs. They then vinced the invincible Oakland Athletics four in a row to win the World Series. Quinn's a genius, right?

Which brings us, by a circuitous route, to Kelly Gruber.

If Quinn is so smart—and by the exacting standard that baseball sets, which is to win or else, he is—then why did he let a blue-chip prospect like Gruber, who belted 31 homers and drove in 118 runs in 1991, get away from the Cleveland Indians to the Toronto Blue Jays in 1983?

"The better he gets, the curiouser I guess it becomes," the Indians' former farm director admitted over the telephone one day from the GM's office of the best team in baseball.

"Ultimately, I suppose, I'd be a coward if I backed away from responsibility for the decision," he said in confirming that he, Indians GM Phil Seghi and assistant Danny Carnevale made the decision to expose Gruber to the major league draft in 1983. This was done by leaving Gruber's name off the club's protected list of forty players, to clear a space for pitcher Tom Waddell, a farmhand the Atlanta Braves would make available in the same draft where Gruber was scooped up by the Blue Jays.

"The judgement was that our most desperate and compelling need was pitching," said Quinn. "Gruber was a ways away and we thought Waddell could help us immediately. We were all right at third base [with veteran Toby Harrah, rookie Brook Jacoby] but we were hurting for pitching."

Drafting by inverse order of their finish the previous season, the Indians picked second. After Waddell was chosen, half a dozen other clubs passed on Gruber before the Blue Jays paid a mere $25,000 to stake their claim.

There are two hitches, one of them significant, in this method of redistributing talent aimed at improving competitive balance in the major leagues. If the new owners were dissatisfied, they could return the player for a $12,500 refund—peanuts, in the grand scheme of baseball things. To keep the player, however, the buyer had to make a place for him on its twenty-five-man team in the majors. As promising as the talent might be, therefore, a contender could be dissuaded from drafting a player who might not be quite ready to contribute much in prime time.

"It's not the proverbial crapshoot," Quinn said of the decision to put Gruber at risk, "but it is a calculated risk when you leave a young man out there. Sure, we hoped we could sneak him through. That was always in the back of our minds. It didn't look like a mistake then, when Toronto picked him, but it certainly looks like an error of gigantic proportions at this time."

Sneak him through?

"Who would they sneak him past?" asks Blue Jays vice-president Al LaMacchia, among the most trusted evaluators of talent with the Blue Jays. "Umpteen clubs had scouted him in high school. We missed him the first time around. We blew it. It wouldn't happen a second time."

When Blue Jays GM Pat Gillick called LaMacchia at his home in San Antonio, Texas, to tell him Gruber had been made available, the man on the other end of the line was "totally surprised."

"Jesus, I couldn't believe this," says LaMacchia. "Then Pat told me he had me on a flight down to Colombia and that Bobby Mattick [Blue Jays manager, 1980–81] would be going with me."

Security was uppermost in Blue Jays management's mind that day because any apparent interest might tip their hand to a competitor picking earlier in the draft. Keeping their intentions a secret would be no mean trick, since LaMacchia and Mattick have been known for years as two of the top scouts in the majors. Since no one would go to Colombia simply for the climate in early December, they concocted a story about the Blue Jays being in dire need of outfield help off the bench.

It did not fool Gruber, who twigged to what was up the minute they wandered onto the field of the Café Universale's home park in Barranquilla.

"Just taking a look at the other club's centre fielder," LaMacchia deadpanned.

"Sure," Gruber says with a grin years later, "the one with the white hair."

"Basically, the reason I told him I went out there," says LaMacchia, "is that I had known him from high school. I was like family. I was playing the long-lost uncle. I thought he was glad to see me just because I was another American. All I really wanted to do was to see if he had lost a leg.

"It stands to reason, if you were considering the kid for your top pick three years before, somebody who might cost you up to $100,000 to sign out of high school, why wouldn't you gamble $25,000 on him? Even if he bombed, you'd get half of it back."

"His raw ability was such that it made you think, 'What's wrong with this kid?'" says Mattick. "Why would they leave a guy like that open? I'm not saying it in retrospect. I'm saying, at the time, the guy's ability was so evident that it made you wonder if something was wrong with him."

As forthright as he is, there is reason to believe that Quinn was well aware of what might happen, that he desperately wanted to keep Gruber and was overruled on the matter.

"Easy to say now, I suppose, but Kelly was special in my own mind's eye," says Quinn. "Matter of fact, I met one of the old Cleveland scouts [Red Gaskill, who helped sign Gruber in 1980] on a road trip to Houston recently and he said he'd love to resurrect my reports on Gruber. I told everybody on the scouting staff he'd make it to the major leagues."

If there is a culprit—or scapegoat, perhaps, now that he is out of professional baseball—it just might be one Al Gallagher, who managed Gruber when he played in 1983 for the Buffalo Bisons of the Class AA Eastern League. Relations between the two were strained and the manager's reports on the player were less than flattering.

"There's a lot to be said for that," says Quinn, responding to suggestions that Gallagher was a major factor in the decision to try to bury Gruber on the roster of the Class AAA Charleston Charlies. "I don't want to put the finger on anyone. That wouldn't be fair, but certainly you lend a lot of credence to the field managers who are with the ballplayer throughout that current playing year."

Carnevale is a little more direct.

"The Buffalo manager didn't like Gruber," he said one

night prior to an Indians game in Toronto during the 1990 season. "Dirty Al said, 'Aaahhh, he'll never be a good ballplayer.' The way I see it, Gruber didn't get along too good with Gallagher."

Carnevale often attended Bisons' games when he returned home to Buffalo from scouting trips. The way he also saw it, Gruber was a decent prospect, but showed little of the superstar he would become one day.

"A .260 to .270 hitter is what I saw, maybe 10 to 15 home runs a season. Good defensive player, good speed. Steal you a base maybe when you needed it. A good journeyman player, but never a star. Somebody in the Toronto organization got hold of the kid and did a job. This kid who used to miss swings perpetually, he became a contact hitter with power. I don't know who did it, but the kid owes him his thanks." (This was Cito Gaston, of course, the Blue Jays swami of swat when Gruber came up—but that's the stuff of another chapter.)

Carnevale, who scouts opposing teams for Cleveland before the Indians come to town, also hints strongly that Quinn wanted to keep Gruber. He says the owner of the Cleveland franchise at the time, F.J. Steve O'Neill, participated in the decision but that it was made by "one person in authority who could not be convinced by anyone else he was wrong. It's as simple as that." This has to be general manager Phil Seghi, who died of cancer a couple of years back and cannot answer for himself.

Curiously, the Indians "failed to renew" Gallagher's managerial contract at the end of the season, according to Quinn, yet he admits the decision-makers still put much stock in his assessment of players.

The Indians' choice to opt for pitching help in the draft made sense at the time, as Quinn maintains, because Cleveland had finished the season in seventh in the AL East, a whopping 28 games behind the division champs from Baltimore. It is the kind of finish that puts an owner's finger on the panic button and executives' jobs on the line.

As the Oakland Athletics demonstrated so clearly in 1990, a line-up of booming bats sells lots of tickets, but what wins pennants, and this is a truism as old as the game itself, is defence and pitching. Put all three together, as Oakland has done the past few seasons, and visions of dynasties well up. The lack of pitching and defence, which afflicted them after the pennant was won, embarrassed the A's in the World Series.

For a couple of seasons, at least, the Seghi-Quinn-Carnevale triumvirate appeared to have made the right decision when they opted to shed Gruber in order to obtain sorely needed relief pitching in the form of young Waddell. Waddell, twenty-five, who had shown promise with the Braves' top farm clubs, became a workhorse in the Indians' beleaguered bullpen over the next two seasons while Gruber toiled with the Syracuse Chiefs of the International League. Waddell posted a 7-4 record (3.06 ERA) with six saves in 58 appearances in 1984. The next year, splitting his time between starts and the 'pen, he was 8-6 (4.87) with nine saves in 49 appearances.

The deal turned sour quickly for the Indians early in 1986 when Waddell, after blowing out his elbow, was forced to quit the game.

What might have prompted Quinn's moves in 1983 was a labyrinthian deal worked out by Seghi and Carnevale that sent the former Indians ace, Len Barker, who pitched a perfect game against the Blue Jays at Cleveland on May 15, 1981, to Atlanta for three unnamed players. They turned out to be a steal for Cleveland. In addition to a sorely needed $150,000 in cash—"The Cleveland club was always in a state of desperation and poverty," Carnevale says—they received outfielder Brett Butler, twenty-seven, third baseman Brook Jacoby, twenty-four, and pitcher Rick Behenna, twenty-four.

Barker, twenty-eight, made 29 starts for Atlanta in 1984 and 1985, finishing with 7-8 and 2-9 records before he shipped out to Milwaukee in 1987 and ended his four-club, eleven-year (74-76, 4.35 ERA) journey through the majors with a 2-1 record.

Jacoby, who spent five years in the Braves' farm system, entered the 1991 season with a career .276 batting average and surprising power reflected by his 112 career home runs and 176 doubles. In 1987, a career year, he hit 32 homers and batted an even .300. He has been a steady, if an unspectacular fielder, posting a .965 average at third base in that time. He entered the 1991 season, his eighth in Cleveland, on the heels of a year in which he hit .293 with 14 home runs and 75 RBIs.

Butler, who played a superior centre field for four seasons and averaged 41 stolen bases a year before fleeing to San Francisco as a free agent, twice led the American League in three-base hits (13 in 1983, 14 in 1986) and averaged .288 with 45 triples during his stay in Cleveland.

Considering the Indians' need for pitching, Behenna, a key player, was a bust. After making five starts in 1983, with two losses to show for it, he appeared but seven more times for the Tribe over the next four seasons before, as Quinn puts it, he "washed out of baseball." His career mark in the majors was 3-10 (6.12 ERA).

In spite of their machinations, the Indians continued doing what they have done best—losing—since the New York Giants wiped them out four straight to win the 1954 World Series to post one of the biggest upsets in baseball history. Ask any astute baseball executive and he will swear the Cleveland franchise is the "sleeping giant" of the major leagues. Put a winner in the city's new stadium, which will seat 55,000 at a site in downtown Cleveland, when and if it gets built, and the franchise could become a licence to print money.

Still, as former Indians farmhand Gruber says, "Has it

happened? Is it happening now? Will it happen? It remains to be seen. Everybody likes a winner. What tells me a lot about a place is if they'll come out when you're not going so good. Is that the way it is in Cleveland? C'mon."

If the Blue Jays brass was not snickering up its sleeve in the spring of 1984, even though they had landed a prize prospect for a mere $25,000, it was because they, too, once blew the call on Gruber. Almost four years before, they had every intention of signing him out of high school, but changed their minds on the eve of the 1980 amateur draft.

The Blue Jays might never have noticed Gruber in the first place had he not been a teammate of pitcher Calvin Schiraldi on the Chaparrals of Westlake High School. Schiraldi, who has pitched for four teams during his six years in the majors, was the ace of the Chaps' staff and his flame of a fastball began to attract the scouts to Austin a year before he would graduate and be available in the draft.

Among them was LaMacchia who, in thirty-five years of beating the bushes for prospects, found such roughs-in-the-diamond as Cito Gaston, Dale Murphy and George Bell. While LaMacchia was originally interested in Schiraldi, it was the Chaps' shortstop who caught his eye that day.

It would not be the first time LaMacchia had stumbled onto a huge talent while looking at another prospect. In much the same manner a couple of years before, he noticed a strong-armed outfielder during a college game in Charleston, Illinois. He told Dave Stieb that day he just might have the stuff to make it as a pitcher in the big leagues.

"Gruber just stood out," LaMacchia said of that first sighting. "You knew you were dealing with a tremendous athlete. The way he fielded. Nice soft hands. The arm. The way he hit. His stroke. It was all there and he was just a kid. First swing he took, I made a mental note to come back and see him the next year."

Gruber makes a valid point about the fortunes of

baseball when he wonders what turn his life might have taken had the scouting fraternity not been lured to Austin that day to catch Schiraldi's act.

"All the scouts were drooling over him," Gruber says. "Al's watching Cal, all of a sudden he sees me. If Cal hadn't been out there, who knows?"

LaMacchia did come back the following year and what he saw surprised him. Schiraldi seemed to have flattened out; "he just didn't develop the way people thought he would," says LaMacchia. But Gruber had made surprising strides during his senior year in high school. "Now everybody was looking at Gruber rather than Schiraldi."

The pity of it is that Schiraldi also might have been a Blue Jay had anyone taken seriously his explanations for the slippage of his fastball.

"Right before the baseball season started, I got strep throat for two weeks," he recalled one night in February of 1991 at an auction of sports memorabilia in Austin. "I lost, like, thirty pounds and I couldn't throw. Didn't have the velocity. That got the scouts down on me. In high school, it's not how you win, it's how hard you throw. That's a shame, but that's the way it is."

His 18-1 record and 0.96 earned run average drew a bite on the seventeenth round from the Chicago White Sox. Schiraldi opted instead for a university scholarship. After three seasons with the University of Texas, he became the first choice of the New York Mets in the 1983 draft.

LaMacchia, seventy, who pitched for three seasons in the mid-1940s for the St. Louis Browns and the Washington Senators, knows there is more than physical equipment that goes into making a major-leaguer out of a green-as-grass teenager. He needed to be convinced that Gruber had that intangible called character.

When LaMacchia and scouts John McLaren and Bob Zuk came to conduct a workout, Gruber had difficulty swinging the bat. Later, LaMacchia noticed the knuckles

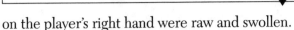

on the player's right hand were raw and swollen.

LaMacchia: "What happened?"

Gruber, sheepishly: "A little disagreement at school. Had to straighten things out."

LaMacchia: "Fight?"

Gruber: "I pulled a dollar from my pocket at the corner store near school and some change fell out. A guy from a construction gang was there and he put his foot over a quarter. 'My two bits,' I told him. He asks me if it's got my name on it. I ask him if it's got his on it. Then I told him I'd give him three to change his mind. The guy goes, '1, 2, 3.' That's when I popped him."

"I didn't need to see any more," said LaMacchia.

"We knew this was the type of guy we really liked," says McLaren, one of the club's original employees, who rose through the ranks to become the parent club's third base coach for five years before joining the Boston Red Sox staff prior to the 1991 season.

Gruber, as accommodating as he might have seemed on his rise to superstardom, has another side to him that was much in evidence during his formative years.

"I was forever getting in fights," he says. "I never started 'em, but I always seemed to get in 'em. School down the street, they'd say their mean, tough guy wants to see if he can whup this kid Gruber from your school. It's not that I love a scrap, but oddly enough I don't mind it if one comes along. I wasn't one to back down."

Howard Bushong, the Chaps' manager for the two years Gruber was a member of the team, agrees.

"He had that temper and every now and then it would come unglued," says Bushong, now a pitching coach with the University of Texas Longhorns. "Back him against a wall, he's not going to talk his way out of anything. He's gonna knock you on your ass."

As Calvin Schiraldi recalls, it was a quality Gruber also brought to the playing field in baseball and football.

"It was one of the best licks I've ever seen in a football game," says Schiraldi, setting up a story from their high school days. "A big guy from Del Valley came over the middle and Kelly, our defensive back, stuck him right in the chest in mid-air. Flattened him. As Kelly got up, he stepped on the guy's face mask. Turned out the guy was kicking and kneeing him as they landed. Not that Kelly was a dirty player, he didn't have to be, but he'd do whatever he thought he had to do to win.

"Football, baseball, in high school he was the most hated player in our district. We were young. We were good. We let people know. We've grown up a little since then, but not that much."

Bob Zuk, one of the Toronto scouts, had a qualm after the workout. Gruber, who had been wearing shorts, had a sprig of varicose veins on his right leg. Zuk was alarmed and, at his urging, Gillick had McLaren take Gruber for a medical check.

"The doctor said it might be a problem . . . if we were thinking of using him past his sixty-fifth birthday," said McLaren.

"In our eyes, they lost some credibility," said David Gruber, who oversaw negotiations for his son. "It was a laughing-stock. All the scouts were laughing at Toronto over that one."

The twist of fate that made Gruber an Indian, one that will gnaw at LaMacchia the rest of his days, was a workout he attended with McLaren to rate Garry Harris, a young infielder from San Diego.

"All our cross-checkers saw everybody, and right before the draft we took this kid and worked him out," says McLaren. "He was terrific. He just opened all kinds of eyes. Sometimes your last impression is your best impression."

"He was outstanding," said LaMacchia, "but the two times I went to see him play, the game was rained out. We based the decision to draft him solely on a workout. I'll never go again on what I see in a workout without seeing the guy in a game. We made a tremendous mistake."

As quick as LaMacchia might be to take the blame, the Blue Jays fairly crowed when they landed Harris, a .426 hitter who swiped 16 bases that season for Hoover High—the school that sent one Ted Williams to the major leagues more than 40 years before.

"He is the pick of the country," said Zuk, who had seen Harris play four games and, on that evidence, rated him above first choice Darryl Strawberry, who became a superstar with the New York Mets. "We have acquired a shortstop who hits for average and will steal some bases," said Zuk. "He is a very good-looking prospect."

"We had Strawberry on our list, but he wasn't on the top," agreed Blue Jays GM Pat Gillick, who rated Toronto picks Harris and outfielder Ken Kinnard as "the best athletes in the entire draft."

As much as Zuk and Gillick liked Harris, it was nothing close to the stamp of approval from coach Bob Warner of Hoover High. "I'd bet my wife and children that he'll make it to Toronto," said Warner.

Within three seasons, Harris was out of professional baseball.

"He played a little AA ball, then hung 'em up," says McLaren, who managed Harris with the Knoxville Blue Jays in the 1983 Southern League season. "Why? I just don't know. I think he just felt like he was going backwards. Just gave up his dream."

Harris was one of only seven selections in the first round that year who failed to make it to the majors. Among the 19 who did, an inordinately high number, were pitchers Jim Acker and Ken Dayley. Chosen by Atlanta, they would later become residents of the Blue Jays' bullpen. Among those who went in later rounds was Tom Henke, chosen by Texas, who went on to become the Blue Jays' top reliever.

Gruber spent the summer of 1980 in Batavia, New York, playing in the New York-Penn League, and the letdown of being passed over by the Blue Jays had something to do with the dreary season Gruber had at the plate and in the field. In 61 games there, he batted an anaemic .217, with a mere seven extra-base hits in 212 at-bats. In the field, he committed 21 errors on 263 chances for a .920 fielding average.

Batavia teammate Kevin Malone, now one of the Minnesota Twins' top scouts, supplies a clue to his feelings at the time.

"We were talking on the team bus one night, going I don't know where, and I think he was disappointed Cleveland had chosen him. The Indians at that time had a second-division stigma about them and it didn't look like they were going to improve in a hurry. 'Daggone it,' he said. 'Drafted by Cleveland. Toronto really liked me.'"

Considering that the New York Mets were waving a reported $200,000 at first choice Darryl Strawberry of Los Angeles, Gruber as a second choice likely would have started the bidding at $175,000. Keeping in mind Gruber's financial aspirations and the negotiation lever of a four-year scholarship at the University of Texas, there is some suspicion the Blue Jays opted for the far more conservative signing bonus accepted by Harris of San Diego. They were not the free spenders they would become later in the decade.

"Those seven, eight spots, they cost him at least $40,000," says Malone. "Plus he really liked Al LaMacchia. Deep down, he was a Texas boy, but deep down because of the way the Blue Jays treated him, he wanted to play in Toronto."

Although Gruber might never have guessed it, that's where the bus was headed that night. It would take a long time, the road would take many turns, but it would wind up in Toronto.

CHAPTER 3

 ## DREAMS DIE HARD

The dream is born on a baseball diamond just like the one around the corner. For years it takes shape—in the mud of early spring, through the dog days of summer, against the chill winds of autumn—until, one day, The Man comes to the house and tells Mom and Pop the boy just might make good at this kids' game he plays so well.

"Sign here, son, and you'll be on the bus to Visalia tomorrow. Why, in no time at all, a couple years at the outside, there'll be Caddies in the garage, T-bones in the fridge and enough Bud on ice to float a battleship."

In hundreds of homes across North America each June, including a few in the Great White North, the scenario is played out with precious few wrinkles in the telling. Right up there with running away to join the circus, where even the elephant gets paid peanuts, what red-blooded American boy wouldn't jump at the chance to follow in the footsteps of Willie, Mickey and The Duke?

Kelly Gruber, for one. Selected tenth in the first round of the amateur draft of June 3, 1980, neither the bright lights of Cleveland nor that city's doormat of a franchise in the American League held any allure for the star shortstop of the Westlake Chaparrals of Austin, Texas.

"I really didn't know how important it was," Gruber says of the procedure that would shape his every waking moment for years to come. "The Indians are going to throw more money at me than I've ever seen. So what? I'm a kid. Nothing is all that important. Geez, I'm immortal. Who says it isn't going to be like this forever?

"I was a high school star in everything I did, anything I did. Sports, girls, whatever. Anything I wanted, I went out and got.

"I always thought I would end up in uniform. Policeman, fireman, a Green Beret. Baseball player. Football player. Now a team in the majors is chasing me. What's the big deal?"

It would be stretching a point to say that Gruber was dragooned into the ranks of pro baseball, but his parents specifically had warned the Cleveland scouts not to fritter away so valuable a commodity as their first-round draft choice.

"In my mind, the Cleveland organization was beset with financial and structural problems," says Gruber's father David, who was overseeing the negotiations. "Its minor league system was considered weak, and because of it players didn't develop. They seemed to prefer trading one old man for another old man. They also had serious money problems and we couldn't see them offering much more than $50,000 to sign."

All other suitors, including the University of Texas and its offer of either a four-year baseball or football scholarship, were being warmly entertained.

Particularly impressive to the family was the Toronto Blue Jays, represented by vice-president Al LaMacchia and scout John McLaren. Not the least of their appeal was rooted in the fact the club was drafting second and could be expected to come close to the money the New York Mets would wave at top pick Darryl Strawberry of Los

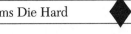

Angeles.

It did not happen. The Blue Jays opted instead for in-fielder Garry Harris of San Diego. The Indians selected Gruber tenth.

Gruber had more pressing matters on his mind that afternoon. As the selections were being made, by way of a telephone hook-up involving all twenty-six clubs in the major leagues, the Westlake Chaps were at Disch-Falk Field, home of the UT Longhorns, preparing for the tourney that would decide the high school champions of Texas.

Gruber, notorious for being late, had been benched once earlier that season by Chaps coach Howard Bushong, and now on the eve of the club's most important game he was a no-show. Assuming Gruber had been held up by matters connected with the draft, Bushong did not become upset until Gruber turned up at the Westlake field that afternoon a little worse for the wear of a car crash.

"He and his girlfriend were on the way to the morning practice," says Bushong. "They were arguing. Something goofy that kids do. The car spun off the road and hit a guard-rail. It was a legitimate excuse for missing practice, but I hate to think what could've happened."

The Blue Jays' rejection of Gruber, coupled with the Indians' insistence on selecting him, all but confirmed for Gruber that he would be spending at least the next three years with the Longhorns. With time to develop his skills in a university setting, he might well be even more attractive in the draft of 1983. Should he fail to develop, which is often the case, he would have the benefit of an education to pursue another career.

Such a choice can be critical for a teenager. The best and worst of what can happen is reflected in the paths three other careers took as they intersected with Gruber's on the way from his high school fields of dreams through the cow pastures of the minors to the cultivated greens of the major leagues.

Former Longhorns pitcher Kirk Killingsworth, twenty-eight, roomed with the same Roger Clemens who will earn $25 million from the Boston Red Sox by the end of the 1995 season. He never got to make one pitch in the majors despite six seasons labouring in the farm systems of the Texas Rangers and the Oakland Athletics. With a degree in organizational communications, earned while he played with the Longhorns, he is now sales manager for the four-star Stouffer Hotel in Austin.

"Unless you're drafted in the first or second round and they're throwing $150,000 to $250,000 at you, there's no choice but to take the scholarship," he said over French toast and orange juice at the hotel one day in February 1991. "The big reality is that you don't last long in the game and not everybody can become a coach when the good times are over for good. Long after that $150,000 is gone, a solid education will give a guy a way to put food on the table for his family."

Killingsworth quit the game before the 1989 season when Oakland refused to guarantee a one-year deal with their Triple A farm club, where salaries range from $1,700 to $4,500 a month. Attending spring training would have entailed him giving up the job he had just landed with an Austin computer firm.

"I'd seen guys who had wasted years at the Triple A level," he said, "and I decided I wouldn't be that type of player. I gave it my best shot and I knew I wouldn't get a chance to pitch even one inning in the majors. I had to get on with my life."

Spike Owen of the Montreal Expos, ignored by scouts when he graduated from high school in 1979, was scooped up by the Seattle Mariners in the first round of the 1982 draft after his tour of duty with the Longhorns. A little more than a year later, three seasons before Gruber would work his way through the three levels of the minors, Owen was in the majors to stay.

"I was lucky that a lot of teams were looking for short-stops," Owen says, trying to avoid comparisons with Gruber, "but college was the only route for me. Because of the work I got, the things I learned, I became a first-rounder. I'm not saying college is the only way to go. If the money is right, you've gotta take it coming out of high school. It might not be there three years later."

Geno Petralli, a catcher of some promise who spent six seasons in the Blue Jays' farm system, was dealt to the Indians in May of 1984. The Indians released Petralli the following spring and, equipped for nothing better, he was happy to land a job lugging crates of soft drinks at $6.75 an hour back home in California.

Petralli caught a break that summer when the Texas Rangers lost a receiver on their farm club at Oklahoma City. Before the season was over, he was with the Rangers. The difference between earning $270 a week, for break-ing his back stocking Dr. Pepper trucks in 1985, and $465,000, for picking Nolan Ryan's fastball out of thin air in the summer of 1990, was a fortuitous injury to some obscure receiver in Oklahoma City.

The most telling comment on the subject might be from the Chaps coach, Bushong, who doubled as Gruber's teacher for a couple of classes in high school. Diplomatically, he says Gruber was not "academically in-clined."

"I knew he'd make it in baseball," he says, "but I've of-ten wondered what would have happened if he hadn't. I had him in health class and he was getting Ds and Cs. Hell, I'd have done anything for him, but he just wouldn't do the work. He's smart enough to get a degree, but I don't know that he has the patience to read the books."

With their son having just turned eighteen a few

months before, Gruber's parents also were worried that he might be confronted with bleak career prospects should he falter in the minor leagues.

The selling of a pro career was a delicate task and, in this respect, the Indians were aided in no small measure when the Blue Jays sent the smooth Al LaMacchia and scout John McLaren to present the case for professional baseball to them.

"We told them we were a young organization on the move, that Kelly might get to the majors a little quicker with us than another club," said McLaren. "I think we opened their eyes a bit. We told them we were serious, that we weren't out for a quick fix. We told them we thought Kelly was mature enough, that he had a good enough head on his shoulders, to sign out of high school."

To help make the decision that would have a profound effect on the future of his eighteen-year-old son, David Gruber sought the advice of Rusty Staub, whose twenty-three-year career in the majors began with the Houston Colt .45s, and Austin native Don Baylor, who played for nineteen years in the big leagues. Gruber also gathered the impressions of a former member of the Indians' coaching staff, but declines to name him on the sound theory that baseball management tends to have long memories where blabbermouth coaches are concerned.

Considering the family's aversion to the Indians' way of doing things, David Gruber pegged the value of his son's signature at close to $100,000, including $15,000 compensation for the four-year "ride" he would be giving up at the University of Texas. If the deal were to be done, David Gruber decided, it would be done quickly and with a minimum of haggling.

Among the considerations was Cliff Gustafson, the legendary baseball coach of the UT Longhorns, who had offered Kelly Gruber a full scholarship. Since he was a family friend of long standing, the Grubers felt they owed Coach Gus a quick answer. Make him wait a couple of months, while the Indians beat around the bush, and it could hurt the Longhorns' chances on the field. A prompt answer, even if it were in the negative, would allow Gustafson to divvy the scholarship into halves or quarters and attract decent talent to his club. Make him wait and the pickings could be lean.

Just as eager to have Gruber, who doubled as a quarter-back and defensive back in high school, was coach Fred Akers of the football Longhorns. There was some thought that the football scholarship would allow Gruber to play baseball, improving Gustafson's hand, but it is doubtful Gruber would have been able to go the Bo Jackson route.

So intensive is the Longhorns' football program— "Around here when people are cut," says Gruber, "they bleed orange and white"—that spring-training sessions are considered a matter of course. For a couple of years at least, this would rule out serious commitment to baseball in the spring when the college season is in high gear.

Half-a-dozen defensive backs were graduating, so the Longhorns' football offer was tempting. It meant Gruber had a good shot at being a starter in his freshman year. To make the team, however, he would have been expected to bulk up by forty pounds. Since much of the muscle would have been added to his upper body, it likely would have "tied up" his baseball swing.

"Strictly on performance, he was a better football player than a baseball player at the time," says David Gruber. "Potentially, he could do more in baseball."

As David Gruber saw it, there were more important reasons to lean towards baseball.

"I was afraid that once he built himself up for football, once he became very macho, that he would take it into the bars," he says. "I was afraid he'd become very aggressive off the field, too. I also wanted him to become his own person. Nobody would ever say he played pro football because his dad played it."

By the time the prelims with Bob Quinn of the Indians were out of the way, the offer had been worked up to $55,000 as the final negotiating session began one Sunday morning at the La Quinta motor hotel off Interstate 35 in Austin.

Before it took place, however, David Gruber wanted one last talk with his son to confirm the course they were taking. They drove to a resort area overlooking Lake Travis on the outskirts of Austin, parked the family car and ordered breakfast at an outdoor restaurant. As the sun glittered across the water below, David Gruber talked about the things his son would have to sacrifice for a career in pro ball.

"There will be four or five years of not having much," he remembers saying, "and each winter when you come back, you'll be further apart from your friends. They will have taken another route. If you don't make it to the big leagues, your life will be a bust. You're going to have to go back to college and you might be thirty before you get something going. You're putting all your chips on the table."

At the age of eighteen, Kelly Gruber made the pivotal decision of his life. He would stake his future on the belief that he could play baseball in the major leagues. He had been told since childhood that "a Gruber never quits" and therefore "the thought that I might not make it never entered my mind."

It still might have come to nothing that Sunday morning had his father been unable to persuade Bob Quinn they were serious about taking one of the Longhorns' offers if the Indians balked at paying six figures for the signature.

"We seemed to stall at $65,000," says David Gruber, who was committed that afternoon to being on the site of a housing project in San Antonio. He told Quinn he would give the Longhorns their answer that afternoon, and having given his word, no amount of money would change it.

Quinn, speaking for a franchise in financial straits, doubted the Indians would set a club record for signing a kid who was at least three years from helping them in the major leagues.

"These negotiations can go on for months," David Gruber says. "I didn't want that for Kelly. I wanted him to get on with his life. They had all the information they needed. Finally they understood I was sincere."

Quinn put in a call to the Indians president, Gabe Paul. The Indians, Quinn said a few minutes later, would "give the kid what he wants."

Many times over the next few seasons "the kid" would wonder if he made the right decision when he told "Coach Gus" that night he would not be joining the Longhorns.

The family friend whose son Darren grew up playing baseball beside Kelly Gruber is a legend in U.S. college baseball. Among the things that make him unique is that he has been coach of the Longhorns for twenty-four years—the shortest time any man has held the job since the university started fielding baseball teams in 1910.

Billy Disch founded the program in 1910 and held the job until 1940. He turned it over to Bibb Falk, who graduated from the Longhorns to play 12 seasons (1920–31) in the majors with Chicago and Cleveland of the American League. Except for two years in the service during the Second World War, Falk coached the Longhorns for 25 seasons. In keeping with tradition, Falk handed the reins over to another former Longhorns player—Gustafson was their second baseman for three years in the early 1950s— but the current manager considers himself "nowhere near the legend these two were."

Some would argue. In the 23 seasons that he managed

the club prior to the 1991 campaign, Gustafson's teams have won 19 Southwest Conference championships and have been to the College World Series tournament 15 times; winning it all in 1975 and 1982, losing the final in 1986, 1987 and 1989. On those squads were 28 All-Americans (first team) and 100 players who signed pro contracts. In 1990, a dozen former Longhorns, including a winner of the Cy Young Award, Roger Clemens, found their names in major league box scores.

Gustafson came to the Longhorns after thirteen years as head coach at South San Antonio High, where he fashioned a 344-85-5 record that included seven state titles and twelve district championships. The year before he took the Longhorns job, South San went 39-0.

So good were the Longhorns in 1980 that winning the job at shortstop would have required Gruber to upset an eminently capable incumbent. Spike Owen had proved himself the previous season.

"Spike was the prototype player for Coach Gus," says David Gruber. "Disciplined at the plate. Good work habits. Everything. Kelly was the antithesis of what Gus wanted. For him to beat out Spike Owen would have been a real long shot."

"We could've worked something out," insists Owen. "Look at him now. You think he might have been able to play third or the outfield for us? We won it all in '82. I wonder how much closer we would have come if we had him in '80 and '81."

Indeed, the Longhorns of that era were stacked. In addition to Clemens, Schiraldi, Owen and Killingsworth, infielder Mike Brumley (Chicago Cubs, Detroit Tigers, Seattle Mariners) and catcher Jeff Hearron (Blue Jays, 1985–86) were members of the team.

Gustafson believes baseball at the college level is every bit as good a prep school for the majors as a four-year stint in the minors, aside from the instant cash that turning pro provides.

"Spike didn't have the tools Kelly had," he points out, "but he made it to the major leagues to stay [Seattle, 1983] three years before Kelly did. There's so many of them who were so close to being ready for the majors when they finished college."

Among famous Longhorns alumni who made it to The Show in quick time were pitchers Clemens, ace of the Boston Red Sox staff, Greg Swindell of the Indians, Schiraldi of the San Diego Padres and Jim Acker of the Blue Jays.

The Longhorns' season, like that of other schools governed by the regulations of the National Collegiate Athletic Association, is a rigorous sixty games. Toss in a dozen exhibition outings, play-offs and the opportunity to play sixty or so semi-pro games in the summer, and the schedule compares with any in the minor leagues.

"Our college players are involved in baseball about ten months of the year," says Gustafson. "They get a lot of attention."

A few days after all the wrinkles of the Indians' deal were ironed out, Kelly Gruber and his father went back to the La Quinta motel and quietly signed a sheaf of papers that tied his future to the Cleveland Indians.

"It was a weird moment in my life," says Gruber. "I wasn't sure of what I was doing in the first place. Now I gotta sign all these papers, telling me what I can and can't do. Silly stuff. No hunting in the winter. No snow-skiing. All the fun things in life. I can understand where they're coming from but, geez, to be so formal at such a young age . . ."

Gruber's secondary reactions suggested then and there that he already was thinking like a major leaguer.

"It made me wonder if we had set our price too low," he said, seriously, years later. "Could I have gotten $150,000 maybe? I've always wondered."

As young as he might have been, he showed a decided maturity in the way he handled the windfall. Not a dollar of the record $100,000 went on a teenager's splurge. On his father's advice, Kelly eased the tax bite by taking the sum in two annual instalments. Then he invested in condominiums, furthering his tax advantages.

"I liked to spend money and, like every kid, go on my little binges," Gruber agrees. "If I saw something I wanted, I bought it. No checking around town for a better price. At the same time, I was never in awe of money. 'Geez, I just got $100,000 handed to me. Ain't I somethin' because I've got a lot of money?' I didn't spend any of it. Not one little treat. Still, here I am eighteen years old and I'm a landlord. Weird feeling."

What truly impressed him in a financial way was the $600 a month he would earn for playing shortstop with the Batavia Trojans of the Class A New York–Penn League. "I thought I was stealing them blind," he says now. "First they give me all that money just to sign some papers, then they give me $600 a month to play baseball."

It was a feeling that did not survive a long plane trip to Buffalo, New York, and the short bus ride to Genesee County and Batavia, home of the Trojans for fifty-one seasons.

"Here I was, a Texan, going by free will to New York," Gruber remembered a decade later. "Here I was in another country. Another culture. Damn Yankees. The Civil War, it's like the Alamo, sacred to us in Texas. It might not be to them up there, but there are people down here who think the South will rise again. Seriously.

"I actually didn't know what to expect. At the time, I probably believed the Eskimos in Alaska still lived in igloos and hunted for their dinners."

As with most ill-formed conceptions, this one melted away when it collided with reality.

"Actually, any time you go to a small town, you can figure on meeting a lot of decent people. I don't care where you're at, small towns have good values. Not a lot of crime. There's no hustle and bustle, all that mess."

Social life, what little there was of it, revolved around a place called Big Daddy's that had made itself a reputation for volcanic chicken wings—a dietary staple of any watering hole within 100 miles of Buffalo—and good, cold beer to wash them down.

"Like a lot of little towns, they rolled up the sidewalks at night," he says. "Your existence was sleep, get up, eat, go to the ballpark. Eat some more and go to sleep. There wasn't a whole lot else to do. Maybe that's why the Indians picked the place for their team."

It is an assessment with which coach Luis Isaac agrees. He is a former catcher who spent ten seasons in AAA baseball and saw not one inning of action in the majors.

"All the kids, they came early to the park. The time to report was 3 PM, but mostly these kids were there a couple of hours by that time. It was a good place to learn. On the kids' minds there was nothing but baseball."

As far from home as Gruber might have been, the sense of isolation from all he knew and loved was somewhat eased by the camaraderie of the Trojans' clubhouse. Although he did not suspect it at the time, this sense of family would diminish as he progressed step by step up the ladder to the big leagues.

"The guys really seemed to get along, something you don't see all that much these days, especially in the major leagues," says Gruber. "A lot of times a guy will make it and he changes. He's a different person. You didn't see that there. We were young. Dead set on getting to the same place in the shortest possible time. We all thought we'd make it."

He and Jeff Moronko, a fellow Texan who would log seven seasons in the minors to win a month's stay with the 1984 Indians and 1987 Yankees, were sent by the Batavia club to room with a family. Together, they would take thirty minutes to make the fifteen-minute walk each afternoon to Dwyer Stadium, home of the Trojans.

"We'd talk baseball the whole time," says Gruber. "Every two steps, he'd pull his bat from his duffle bag, stop and show me his newest idea for a hitting stance. 'Maybe I should hit like this,' he'd say. 'Do this. Do that.' He was going on twenty-one years old, had gone to university for a couple of years and had a bit better handle on what he wanted to do with his life.

"I played short and he played third. There was no way in the world I thought he wouldn't make it. He was far more dedicated than I was at the time."

His first roomie in baseball, as Gruber recalls him, was the "spitting image" of Buddy Bell, the fine third baseman whose eighteen-year career in the majors included seven-year stretches with Cleveland and the Texas Rangers of the American League.

Curiously, and perhaps it was a subtle sign of things to come, Gruber's "patron saints" in the major leagues were not shortstops. Rather, as he played out the 1980 season at Batavia, he saw the shadows of Buddy Bell and another third baseman, George Brett, who at that moment was intent on becoming the first hitter since Ted Williams in 1941 to crash the .400 barrier.

"I couldn't find anybody else that I was like," says Gruber. "Whether I looked like them, played like them, whether I liked their speed or power, there just wasn't anybody at shortstop who struck me as a kindred spirit.

"I liked the way Brett and Bell played. Diving for balls. Scrapping. Getting their uniform dirty. I wore Number 5 in high school, football as well as baseball, because of George Brett, but he was a third baseman and I was a shortstop. What gives?"

In retrospect, considering the scattergun arm and limp bat he brought to pro baseball, there was any number of shortstops at the time whose examples Gruber ought to have been following. Just for openers in the American League, there were Alan Trammell of the Detroit Tigers, who hit .300, with 65 RBIs, and Rick Burleson of the Boston Red Sox, .278 with 51 RBIs. Over in the National League, there was Bill Russell of the L.A. Dodgers in the midst of a fine career and, beginning his fifth season with the St Louis Cardinals, Garry Templeton hit .319.

What shamed Gruber most that season, even more than his tepid .217 average at the plate, were the 21 errors he committed in 61 games at shortstop.

"I've always been blessed with quickness—not speed, but quickness," says Gruber. "In a sprint, I take two steps and I'm at full speed. A lot of guys, it's three, four, five steps. So I was always able to get to the ball. That wasn't my problem.

"There's a difference between a guy who has a great arm and one who has a live arm. One guy throws the ball straight. The other guy, which is me, throws and the ball moves. If I didn't grab the seams the right way, and this holds true today, it would sail, sink, rise, whatever.

"That year, someone in the stands had a Juggs gun, one of those things that measures how fast a ball moves, and he measured me at 92 to 94 miles an hour. And that was on plays where I didn't even have time to plant my feet. One step into the hole toward third, catch the ball, wheel and throw. When I could have taken a lot more off, gotten it there in plenty of time, I tried to throw the thing 100 miles an hour.

"I was raw. I had been taught well, I thought, but it turned out I still had a long way to go. Not a day goes by that you don't learn something in this game. The day you think you know it all . . ."

Coach Luis Isaac, since elevated to a similar post with the parent club, thought Gruber was "too quick" to be a shortstop, an assessment that requires some explanation in a game that worships fleetness of foot.

"As a third baseman, you have to be quick—make a step, take a dive, catch the ball, come up throwing—but at shortstop, you have a little more time to get to the ball," says Isaac. "The errors he was making, they were because he was too quick to the ball. Not fluid. In my reports to the big club, I would put that he was more suited to be at third."

Gruber's erratic arm was something the fans who populated the stands behind first base at Dwyer Stadium were quick to notice.

"Every game, I had such a live arm, I would set sail on that thing and it would go over the first baseman's head," Gruber remembers. "Pretty soon the people who had seats behind first base started coming to the game with the lids from their garbage cans. Every time a ball came to me, they would raise 'em up. Talk about an instinct for survival!"

As lightly as he treats it, the comedown from high school hero to these levels of mediocrity was a blow to his confidence.

"As decent as the rest of the guys were, part of the fun of playing baseball had always been doing it with friends," says Gruber. "Now I was playing with guys I didn't know. Kind of took the fun out of it. The little things began mounting up. Playing away from home. Using a wooden bat instead of the aluminum ones at school. The worse I did, the more pressure I felt. I began to wonder if I had done the right thing when I turned down Coach Gus.

"When I signed, I figured I was ready for the big leagues then. This summer in Batavia, it wasn't necessary as far as I was concerned. It was just to show the people in Cleveland there was no sense wasting time. Remember, I was immortal. I didn't know any better."

Reality took the form of pitching prospects, culled from the cream of the crop in cities and towns across the nation, who had been assigned to the Class A level to learn their craft. Though he had faced some pretty fair throwers in his time, there was no doubt the level of competition had been raised a notch and Gruber was pressed to live up to it.

Isaac, his manager at Batavia, could see the light at the end of the tunnel in which Gruber was trapped.

"He had a decent bat," he says. "Not the kind of power he has now, but I put in my reports that, a little later in his career, he would hit 20 home runs in the big leagues. Being eighteen years old, being away from home and stuff, he was sometimes lazy. Not because he was a lazy kid but because he was missing home. I would talk to him, try to get him to overcome being away. Sometime in your life, I tell him, you got to leave home."

The spirit of adventure inherent in travel evaporated early one morning when, after the players loaded up with a couple of quarter-pounders at McDonald's, the team bus refused to get off her haunches no matter how sweetly, or harshly, the players entreated her.

"There were a lot of cold mornings when we had to push that bus to the nearest hill," says Gruber. "The only way it'd start was for the driver to pop the clutch when it picked up a head of steam down the other side. Then we'd have to run to catch it. It might be funny if you saw it in the movies, but we weren't laughing.

"Getting your sleep was no joke either. You'd drop off for an hour, wake up for thirty minutes, then nod off again. This would go on all night until the sun came up and you just quit trying. You'd be a zombie the rest of the day. Then, just when your body was telling you to drop off for an afternoon nap, you're playing the local team and they're as fresh as daisies.

"It was afternoons like this when you wondered what your pals were doing on the beach back home. Everybody else is goofing off and here I am, playing baseball in another country. There wasn't a whole lot about it that I can think of as romantic."

Among his teammates who took note of his disenchantment was second baseman Kevin Malone, whose high tolerance for work, unfortunately for him, did not translate into talent on the field.

"I was a college senior, an older player, and I knew I didn't have a lot of time," says Malone, who was cut from the Trojans with a month left in that season. "I was focused, trying to be the best player I could be. I would show up early, eager to impress my coaches with my work habits. I'd take 150 to 200 ground balls at second base. Extra batting practice. Whatever it was, I was glad to do it."

How galling it must have been for him, now one of the Minnesota Twins' top scouts, to see his supremely talented teammate take the easy route through his first year of pro baseball.

"Kelly would be there when he had to be there, no earlier," says Malone. "He'd take 15 or 20 grounders, and if things weren't going right he might just walk right in and sit in the dugout.

"Here's the bonus baby, he comes in and does as little as possible to get by. Some of the older guys, college guys, were a little upset. I wouldn't talk to him directly, the way I'm talking now, but I'd say, 'C'mon, Kelly, let's take some more ground balls.' Or, 'Kelly, come on out early tomorrow. We'll do a little throwing.' He didn't go about his business like I hoped he would have done.

"The talent was obvious. Speed. Arm. Power. He had them all. He just wasn't into it. In a game, he was a little tentative. Couldn't hit. Made a lot of errors. Really didn't have a very good first year."

Although no one appointed him as such, Malone would like to think the Indians were smart enough to sign him out of college for their farm team so he could set an example for Gruber.

"I was the guy you draft, a guy you pay $650 a month, so the prospect has someone to play catch with him," he says. "Here's a young guy, a high school shortstop his first time away from home. Here I am, a college second base-man with marginal tools, a guy who has to bust his butt to figure out how to play the game. Maybe they thought some of that would rub off.

"Looking back on it now, being in scouting as I am, I see what was going on with Kelly. He really didn't know what he had to do to make it. There were some older guys on the club because Cleveland, basically, tended to draft college players because they were cheaper to sign, and they were resentful that it had been handed to Kelly on a platter. He had the ability, that was apparent, and he knew his chance of getting to the majors was a lot better than any of the rest of us."

It took a while, but Malone came to the conclusion that Gruber was not so much a prima donna as he was a unique spirit marching to the beat of his own distant drum.

"He was younger than most of us, a little confused, wondering. He was the big stud out of high school. I think he was wondering if he'd made a mistake in not going to the University of Texas and becoming Big Dawg on the campus."

The two are still friends.

"He's made it big, but he's still as down to earth as he was back then. Even then, I realized he wasn't cocky when he was coming out, even though his work habits might have tended to make you believe he was. A lot of times, I see now, first-round drafts out of high school, they think their poop don't stink. I got news for them.

"Kelly, he was a guy who could have fun. I'm around big leaguers and some of them just think they're above life. I see him talking to different people. Sometimes, enough is enough, but he's one guy who seems to take the time. On the field, he's one of the few who has fun and I think he plays hard in a disciplined sort of way. That first year out, he was a follower, a go-along, get-it-over-with sort of guy. Somewhere along the way, he changed."

CHAPTER 4

 WATERLOO

Of all the enemies the ballplayer faces on the long and winding road to the major leagues, the most implacable is the one who looks back at him each day from the club-house mirror.

Kelly Gruber, a couple of months out of his teens when he trotted from the Chattanooga Lookouts' dugout to take his place at shortstop for the Southern League home opener in 1982, was about to endure the most embarrassing nine innings of his career.

"We've got a nice little crowd on hand, maybe 6,500, and I'm thinking, damn, but this is a big change. I'm actually a little bit nervous out here."

Some of this was due, no doubt, to the calibre of baseball into which he had graduated after a promising 1981 campaign in Iowa with the Waterloo Diamonds of the Class A Midwest League. In 127 games there, he had batted .290 and demonstrated decent power: 43 of his 133 hits for extra bases. Even if he did lead league shortstops with 56 errors, this was buffered by the fact he made more put-outs at 180 and assists at 389 than any other at the position.

If Waterloo was a step up the ladder, his first real test as a professional after his baptismal season at Batavia, then Chattanooga and its Class AA brand of ball was bound to be that much tougher.

"I was a little too aware that making the jump from a place like Chattanooga to the big leagues was rare, but not impossible," says Gruber. "'Well, Kelly, is this the last stop?' I'm asking myself. 'Big leagues next year? Should have been there two years ago, right?'"

No sooner did that bullish thought make itself at home than a bearish interloper took its place. 'Maybe there is a bit more I can learn down here,' Gruber remembers saying to himself as he took his place at Engel Stadium before 6,381 spectators. 'Maybe I'm not ready.'

"As I'm standing out there, fielding warm-up tosses from first baseman Sal Rende, my confidence seems to dribble away. And if you don't have confidence, how can you succeed? If you don't believe in yourself, I've since found out, there's usually a good reason."

He made five errors that night, and in doing so proved he was nothing if not versatile. He dropped a ball thrown to him at second base. He misplayed grounders. He threw wildly, both to second and first.

"The last two I made, the last one for sure, they weren't actually errors," he says, still a little at a loss. "The scorer, I think he thought, 'Hey, we've got something going here. Nice little string. Maybe we'll make the record books.'" He did, too.

Most errors, game, by a shortstop, 5, Kelly Gruber, Chattanooga Lookouts vs. Birmingham Barons, April 15, 1982.

"I wanted to dig a hole at shortstop and crawl into it," says Gruber. "I was scared. 'Dear God, don't hit me another one. Not six errors. Not seven.' There are times when I still feel that way. Everybody does when they're having a bad night. They swear they don't, but there are times when they do.

"Dog me, but I embarrassed myself—even if I did go 2-for-4 with a triple—and it set the tone for that whole year. I never did get my feet back on the ground. Never really did get over it. I should've accepted what happened and put it behind me. Turn the page. That's what you do. Instead, I let it bother me the rest of the season."

His confidence was now in tatters.

"Here I am, thinking every step up the ladder, 'Do I belong? Am I good enough?' If you can answer that question early, know for sure you're not out of your depth, you can bet you'll have a good year. It was a question that dogged me that whole season in Chattanooga."

A year earlier, on opening day of the 1981 season in Waterloo, the positive frame of mind he brought to the park resulted in him swatting a couple of singles. 'Yeah, this is nothing. This is cake. Now I've got a good attitude for the rest of the year.'

"Mentally, Waterloo was a little tougher. It was supposed to be, had to be. At the same time, after that summer at Batavia, I knew a little bit better what to expect as a professional. Could be, too, that I knew I had to keep up with the company. 'Better get on it, Kelly. The big leagues are waiting.' That's what I'd tell myself."

The attitude, cultivated in Waterloo and nurtured through a winter of baseball in Venezuela, evaporated after the disastrous opener in Chattanooga.

The five errors that day—his mates committed three more in the 6-2 loss to Birmingham, making all the winners' runs unearned—contributed to 44 Gruber committed that season, the most by any shortstop in the league, and plunged his fielding average to a dismal .918 on 538 total chances. To complicate matters, he committed one of baseball's cardinal sins: he brought his problems in the field to the batter's box. His average plunged to a middling .243, with 13 home runs and 54 RBIs.

As badly as Gruber felt, sportswriter Dave Jenkins of the *Chattanooga Free Press* sheds a kinder light on that season.

"He looked shell-shocked after the opener, but he handled it about as well as anyone in that position could," says Jenkins. "It was a bad night, he told us, but it might be good enough to get him into the record books. It was a weak attempt at humour, but at least he faced up to it.

"To be honest, I thought most of the errors were bad hops. That infield was horrible, always had been. There really never was any money in the budget to fix up the field.

"It was a season where Kelly pretty much proved he wasn't cut out to be a shortstop and Cleveland got the message. In a funny, way, it might have turned his career around."

Among those who witnessed Gruber's early struggles to harness an insubordinate arm was Mike Gertz, who played first base in Waterloo and, at times, felt like a mosquito staring down the barrel of an elephant gun. He was spared a second season of target practice when an errant pitch broke two toes on his left foot during spring training as he, too, was preparing to ship out to Chattanooga.

"The joke is, and Kelly will admit it, that I saved him thirty errors that summer in Waterloo," he said one afternoon while visiting Chicago in the summer of 1990 with his family from Milwaukee. "I could pick 'em and he could throw 'em in the dirt, so I got a lot of practice," he said that day at Comiskey Park, a place he dearly would have loved to play. "The guy had a hose of an arm, but he didn't know where it was going.

"When they moved him to third, it was the move of his life. You can't think over there. It's bang-bang. Step and a dive. The kid, he could make the plays, but the ones he had time to think on, then he was in trouble."

The paths he and Gruber took, conveyed with the patter Gertz now employs to sell beer for one of America's biggest brewers, were mapped out as he watched Gruber suit up in the visitors' clubhouse.

"Look at the legs, like a ballet dancer's," Gertz says admiringly. "Rock arms. Solid chest. He takes his shirt off and, geez, he's still got the ribbed gut he had when we were kids." Pause. "So have I, but I got mine from guzzling beer . . . it's ribbed once over my belt."

Gertz got the call to first base at Waterloo through a caprice of fate. Had the manager not seen a first baseman's glove in Gertz's equipment bag one day, he probably would have reported a couple of weeks later to the Rookie League team to which the Indians had assigned him. Assuming the glove meant Gertz knew how to play first, the Waterloo manager put him there. He had no one else. Given the chance to impress at a higher level, Gertz did what any keen young kid would do. He told the manager he had found that glove in his cradle.

"Unfortunately, I was there for the rest of my time in baseball," he says regretfully. "The Indians already had Mike Hargrove, a seasoned vet, and he wasn't going anywhere. The Cleveland organization was notorious for screwing up players. I think I was one of them. Fortunately, Kelly got a break and he escaped."

Recovering from the injury to his toes, Gertz then damaged his knee. After another operation, he tried to become a pitcher. Another failure. After one last shot in Class A ball, this time in the Baltimore Orioles' system, he faded from the game. Five years later, it haunts him that he never will climb into a major league uniform.

"I could play with these guys. I was their 3-4-5 hitter. Kelly would hit fifth and they would flip-flop me depending on whether the other team threw a leftie at us. 'Geez,' I tell people, 'I played with him. We were down in the pits together and he floated to the top.' I'm happy for him."

Gruber understands Gertz's dismay.

"He had power. He could pick it. He had a good arm, knew the game and liked to play. Why he didn't make it, I'll never know. Every time we went up against Edwin Nunez, who had some of the nastiest stuff, Mike owned the guy." Nunez, who broke camp with the Milwaukee Brewers after spring training in 1991, had a 16-3 record, 2.47 ERA and 205 strike-outs in 1981 with the Wausau Timbers of the Midwest League.

Although the relationship began less than auspiciously, some of Gertz's most carefree remembrances are of the apartment he shared that summer with Gruber and two other roommates.

"First day in Waterloo, this guy comes up to me with this funny accent and says he's looking for a roomie to split the rent on a two-bedroom apartment on the university campus.

"I tell him it's a deal and I figure I'm pretty lucky, too, since it's only costing me a hundred bucks a month. When I walked in, I asked, 'Where's my bed?' Kelly points to a mattress on the floor and tells me to make myself comfortable.

"I called home to my mom. I was crying. 'Mom, I'm in an apartment with no furniture! My roommate doesn't speak English. My bed is on the floor. The couch is missing a leg. The kitchen table's a wreck and the toilet drip-drip-drips all night long.'"

To alleviate the interminable sense of waiting to be discovered in the backwaters of Middle America, Gruber and his roomies spent many a night in a game of make-believe.

"The four of us, we'd sit around that kitchen table and play 'Who's Gonna Be First to Make It to The Show?'" says Gertz. "Usually, fingers pointed to me. I'd say Kelly. 'Big Bird,' he'd answer back, because of my gangly legs. 'Big Bird, you should be there.' Looking back on it, it makes you feel good that it came from a guy who was on his way to becoming a superstar."

The high point of Gruber's life on the road to the top might have been hit at Chattanooga when he got to room with the relief pitcher, Nate Puryear, considered a man of means on the Lookouts' roster because he was working under the terms of a major league contract. When he opened the doors of his apartment to Gruber, there were all the comforts of home inside.

It also marked another sort of breakthrough for Gruber. Growing up in Austin, a city of 500,000 where visible minorities make up less than a fifth of the population, Gruber's exposure to blacks had been limited largely to athletic competition.

"I'd been raised to believe that all men are equal," says Gruber. "It's what being a free country is all about. For whatever reasons, social or economic or whatever, it happened that I grew up not knowing very many blacks.

"Some people say that and it's a cover for their true feelings. I'd like to think it's not that way with me. When I heard that Nate had room at his place, I didn't have to think twice about it. You couldn't help but like Nate. Good guy. Best of all, he could cook."

Although there were at least half-a-dozen Lookouts who one day would make it into major league boxscores, they finished both halves of the season well out of play-off contention at a combined 63-80.

Sportswriter Dave Jenkins furnishes the details.

"If that 1982 club is remembered for accomplishing anything," he says, "it might be that four of them married girls from Chattanooga.

"It was the last of five years the Indians had a farm club here and it was a season the players were in a rush to get through. Seattle was coming in the next year. At that point, to welcome the Mariners, you knew Cleveland had to be pretty bad."

As disastrous a season as it was for Gruber at Chattanooga, the best part of it just might have been the arrival of Joe Charboneau, a notoriously blithe spirit who had fallen from grace as American League rookie-of-the-year in 1980 with a .289 average and 23 home runs to AA ball a short couple of seasons later.

But he was not totally to blame for his precipitous fall from stardom in the majors. After wrenching his back while sliding into a base for the Indians, he made matters worse when he fell while painting the roof of his home that winter. The medics suggested spinal fusion to repair three dislocated discs in his lower back. Joltin' Joe, truly a bear for punishment, would have no part of any operation that almost certainly would have killed his career. It did not matter to him at all that he could well end up in a wheelchair.

"He was the type of guy, unless you amputated, he was going to play," says Gruber.

Charboneau was capable of all manner of outrageous acts. On a dare as a kid he once chewed the head off a live rat. How tough was he? Gruber tells a couple of not-so-tall tales to illustrate the point.

"He had a tattoo on his arm that, all of a sudden one day, started to bug him for some reason known only to Joe. So he took a razor-blade and scraped it off. He had a toothache one night. So he gets a pair of pliers and yanks it out. Some people say he could open a bottle with his eye sockets and drink beer through his nose. He told us he used to box bare-knuckles in the boxcars down by the tracks where he grew up. Put the money on the floor. Last guy standing picks up the cash. Nobody on the club doubted he was telling the truth.

"We'd be in a bar and he'd pick out the biggest bruiser in the house. 'It'll take me three punches to knock him out,' he'd say, and before the night was over, the money was on the table and he had asked that guy to go outside.

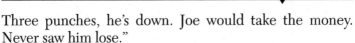
Three punches, he's down. Joe would take the money. Never saw him lose."

Charboneau came back to Chattanooga midway through the 1982 campaign, less than three years after he left the club following a spectacular 1979 season in which he led the Southern League with a .350 batting average. The next year, he was the sensation of the American League. He played in 48 games and hit .210 the next season. After 22 games with the Indians in 1982, batting a feeble .214, he was sent to Charleston of the AAA International League. His bat dead there, too, he dropped another notch to Chattanooga.

He was twenty-seven years old and this, for all intents and purposes, would be his last hurrah. In keeping with his station as the team's elder statesman, Charboneau liked to tell his fuzzy-cheeked comrades there would be only two situations in which he would force himself to take to drink. When he was alone or in company.

"Coming home from an out-of-town game one night," says Gruber, "Joe drank every drop of a fifth of whisky he had smuggled onto the team bus. Suddenly he gets the idea that everybody should have a souvenir of their summer with Joe. He wants everybody to cut off a hunk of his hair. No time at all, he was as bald as the American eagle."

The true test of Charboneau's courage, however, occurred one night later that summer at a bar called Images. As was his custom, Charboneau kept the waitress busy drawing steins of draught beer for his mates. No sooner would anyone sip once or twice than another round would be on the way. "You don't want another beer?" he would challenge. "So what if you've only had a couple sips out of each one. They're gettin' warm, aren't they?"

"The waitress, she's wearing open-toed sandals," Gruber recounts. "You know how when you wear shoes without any socks, how your feet get rank after a time? Well, this girl could use a ton of foot powder. Anyway, Joe bets he can get 'intimate' with her on a table in the bar before the night is done. The money's on the table. Know what he did? Stinky feet and all, she had a leg up on the table and in no time at all, he's sucking on her toes.

"Intimate? I guess it was. Joe wins. Again."

While Gruber was not in the same league as Charboneau, there were times when he was a disciplinary pain in the sliding pads for his superiors in the Cleveland hierarchy.

One such occasion followed the 1981 season at Waterloo, when his employers sent him to their Florida Instructional League team at Grant Field—coincidentally, the springtime home of the Blue Jays—for grooming by some of their ablest coaches. Heading up the operation was Danny Carnevale, assistant to the Indians general manager, Phil Seghi. Also on hand were Frank Lucchesi, who had managed three teams in the majors; Mel Queen, who played nine years in the big leagues and since has become the Blue Jays' director of minor league development; and one Jack (Scat) Cassini, an expert in the running game. (Cassini, by the way, is the subject of one of the oddest lines in *The Baseball Encyclopedia*, the statistical bible of the major leagues. Although he appeared in eight games for the 1949 Pittsburgh Pirates, he failed to record an official at-bat or make a play in the field. He did, however, score three runs, so he must have been hell on the basepaths.)

"All these people were veteran baseball people," says Carnevale, "who had been indoctrinated into the business, studied it thoroughly, gone through the ropes as players, as coaches, as managers and teachers."

They were, Gruber admits today, the last people in the world he wanted to see at the time. In addition to spending six weeks at spring training with the Indians in Arizona, he had played 127 games at short for Waterloo and now, he figured, he wanted time off to loaf around the house in Austin. Instead, he spent his afternoons in Florida battling ground balls "that would take your lips off on the worst infield I ever played."

Particularly galling was one drill in which the shortstop "circles" ground balls hit for him by a coach. The idea is to field the ball so that the body faces first base when the ball is fielded. This sets up a fluid toss to the base, instead of having to throw across the body and strain the arm. Good idea, too, except that the dirt on the infield apron had been pounded into the type of sand you find on a second-rate beach.

"As soon as the ball comes off the grass and hits the sand," says Gruber, his hands spread wide, "it sticks. Just sticks. Here I am, circling it, and I go fly by it by a couple of steps because it just died in the sand. What'm I doing down here? If you can't get a decent field for me to do my work, let me go home."

He had no problem communicating his feeling to his coaches. He understands now that it is not the type of ethic a newcomer ought to apply to his work.

"I'm like everybody else," says Gruber. "Every once in a while, you get bad thoughts. You're a little bitter. There's things you do that you wish you could take back."

Dealing with recalcitrant youth was nothing new for an old-timer like Carnevale, who had begun his fifty-year odyssey across the map of organized baseball in 1941 when he signed to play shortstop for a team from Cornwall, Ontario, in the Canadian–American League. He had managed minor league clubs in at least a dozen towns from the Atlantic to the Pacific after he hung up his shortstop's glove in the late 1940s.

He knows, too, what it is to fail. Carnevale hit .354 that summer he graduated from Canisius College in Buffalo and made his first dollar as a ballplayer in eastern Ontario. Then he fell prey to an inadequacy that has shattered many young men's dreams of playing beneath the big top.

"I could field the ball," he says. "I could throw the ball. It's sad, but some guys never learn to hit the curve ball if they play forty years. That's what happened to me. I couldn't hit a curve with a paddle."

There is no hint of rancour in his rumbling voice as he recalls the autumn he spent trying to pound his version of baseball sense into Gruber's head.

"He was more or less an individual at that time of his life," he begins. "It took him a little time to adjust to what was expected of him. He was going to play his game his way, without too much help from anybody who knew the game well.

"I've had players I loved because they would listen. I've had players I couldn't reach with a pool cue. If it was easy, I guess, everybody would be doing it. You get young people coming in, and all of a sudden they're not coachable. The best way to get a little humility is to fail for a while. That's when they come looking for help."

Gruber's reluctance was so deep-rooted that Carnevale had the Indians chief, Gabe Paul, who was in Dunedin to rate the club's top prospects, talk with Gruber about the making of a major league ballplayer.

"I told Gabe the kid had potential, but that he had a bit of a head problem. A good kid, a solid young man, no extracurricular activities that would hurt him. Gabe spoke to him in a nice way. Maybe it did some good. We did one thing for him at that camp. We made him play a shallower shortstop because he wasn't getting a good jump on the ball. I said, 'Maybe we should try him at third base.'"

CHAPTER 5

DIRTY AL

Dirty Al. Alan Mitchell Edward George Patrick Henry Gallagher came by his nickname honestly.

As a third baseman with the San Francisco Giants and the California Angels for four seasons in the early 1970s, both teams that played their home games outdoors and on God's own green turf, he made it a practice to mess up his uniform before the game's first pitch cut the heart of the plate.

Dirty Al, who outranks pitcher Calvin Coolidge Julius Caesar Tuskahoma McLish for the longest name in *The Baseball Encyclopedia*, continued to live up to his nickname even after he was promoted to the managerial ranks of the game.

Kelly Gruber, who also leans to the "lived-in" look in a uniform, came under Gallagher's influence in 1982 with the Chattanooga Lookouts of the Southern League and in 1983 with the Buffalo Bisons of the Eastern League.

He remembers him fondly. "He definitely was dirty. You'd look at his uniform twenty minutes after it had come out of the wash and there'd be flecks of tobacco juice all over the front. He couldn't spit without getting most of it on himself.

"And underwear? I swear the guy never wore it. You'd look at him, coaching at third base, and the first thing you'd see was his schwantz against his leg. Seriously. It was tough to keep a straight face and your mind on the signals he was supposed to be giving."

Gruber, however, stoutly denies that there was a move afoot among the hired hands to have "the schwantz" incorporated into the team's system of hitting signals. The appendage seemed to have a mind all its own and, as any right-thinking field marshal is aware, thinking can be dangerous in baseball.

On the road, Dirty Al also cut a dashing figure.

"You'd be getting off the team bus when it stopped for gas, there was Al sprawled across the front seat," Gruber recalls. "He'd be sound asleep, snoring. His mouth would be open, saliva drooling off his chin. He had a big chew of tobacco on one side of his mouth, a cigar sticking out the other. Dirty Al. Our leader."

According to management sources on the parent club, no love was lost between Gallagher and Gruber. At the same time, Gallagher was pivotal in two decisions that would make Gruber a multimillionaire superstar before he turned thirty years old.

Of prime importance to the Blue Jays, Gallagher advised his bosses in Cleveland that Gruber had bottomed out as a prospect (.243, 13 HRs, 54 RBIs in Chattanooga; .263, 15 HRs, and 54 RBIs in Buffalo). It was an assessment that played a part in Cleveland's decision to expose the player in the Major League Draft the following December. Of prime importance to Gruber's career, Gallagher yanked him as shortstop of the Bisons after five games that season and installed him at third base for the rest of the year.

It was a decision that discomforted Gruber because of its effect on a buddy.

"They flip-flopped us," says Gruber, "and I think it was the beginning of the end for Jeff [Moronko]. It messed up his mind and must have told him they thought he was expendable. He had been a third baseman all the way, a step-and-dive man, and they tried to make a shortstop of him. I was a first-rounder and they had serious money invested in me. They had drafted Jeff out of college. Cheaper that way.

"I told him, 'Jeff, man, I'm sorry. This isn't my decision. I don't know what they're doing.' I didn't like it any better than he did, but they made the choice real simple. Do it. Or go home. It's always that simple when you're looking at the candy from the wrong side of the counter. Jeff didn't complain to me. Not a word. I didn't complain to him. Texas boys, you know. We just don't do it."

Moronko did get his shot at the majors as a third baseman eventually. He played a total of nine games there, for Cleveland in 1984 and the New York Yankees in 1987, in addition to two at shortstop, two in the outfield and one as a designated hitter. In all, he went to the plate thirty times in the big leagues and got four hits, one of them a double.

The 1983 season was Gruber's fourth season in the minors and, ticketed as he was for Charleston of the International League (AAA) the following spring, the big paydays of the big leagues did not appear to be among his immediate prospects. So dismal did he consider his chances, in fact, that midway through the season he was on the verge of returning to his first love and casting his lot with the upstart United States Football League.

"Crazy idea," says Gruber, "but it sounded pretty good to me at the time. I don't think I've ever been more frustrated. Here I was, in my fourth season as a professional, and it looks like I'll be scuffling forever. I've been a shortstop since I was a kid, and now they tell me that if I'm ever going to make it I've got to learn a new position. My manager acts like I'm something the dog dragged home and I treat him like he's too stupid to bark. It was not a good situation."

It was at this point that David Gruber, the parent who played such a strong hand in his son's career choice of baseball, stepped into the picture. At the end of the season, he phoned Bob Quinn, the farm director who had signed Kelly Gruber three years before, and said the Indians were on the verge of losing a prospect they had once prized. The Grubers contended that Indians' management was unable to put a proper farm system in place. It had failed the boy. Didn't they feel they owed him something?

"A player can go so far on innate ability," says David Gruber. "Teach him the finer points and he'll blossom. Our experience was that they really didn't seem to work on the fundamentals. They also seemed to fail their players on an emotional level."

If nothing else, he pleaded with Quinn, could the club use its connections to spot Gruber on a winter league team so he could be better prepared the following season? Quinn's reply was less than enthusiastic. After a poor year at the Double A level, Kelly Gruber would expect little or no call for his services in winter baseball.

David Gruber tossed his trump card.

"If he didn't get him into winter ball, I told him, he's not coming back to the Indians next year. He'll be playing football, either in the pros or at the University of Texas. I could sense I had him squirming. As long as he kept playing, I felt, he would have a chance to get things turned around."

Kelly Gruber, after four seasons in the minor leagues, had come to many of the same discouraging conclusions that his father had done. "At the end of the '83 season, I began to have serious doubts about making it. I'm spinning my wheels here. Four years out of the way. It bothered me to think I might have been leaving the University of Texas about this time with a degree or close to it, maybe a Number One draft pick. I couldn't help but wonder if I had made the biggest mistake of my life when I was eighteen years old. I wondered where the time had gone."

Within six months, Gruber would be in the major leagues, even if the stay would be all too short. At least the light at the end of the tunnel would become far brighter than it was at the darkest moment of his career.

Toronto drafted him in December of 1983, a few days after he learned on the back of a Colombian bus that Cleveland had decided not to protect him, and he reported to the Blue Jays' camp in Dunedin, Florida, with some misgivings.

Among his concerns was the chilly reception he was sure he would be accorded by farmhands who had slaved for years in the Toronto system to earn their shot at a job in the majors. Under terms of the draft, the new kid is all but a lock to go north with the big club at the end of spring training. About the only way Toronto would have returned Gruber to Cleveland, for a $12,500 refund on their $25,000 draft fee, was if their "third baseman of the future" reported to them in the company of a seeing-eye dog.

"I knew going in that I had some enemies," says Gruber. "Any time anything is handed to somebody, any time somebody's been working two or three years for that very job, there's bound to be resentment.

"There were some guys at that camp who treated me like I was the little rich kid who came to the party in Daddy's limo. I wasn't. I had paid my dues in the minors, scuffling just like them. After four years, I understood their feelings, but what could I do?"

Little did he know at the time that he would have to spend another two years beating the bushes before he nailed down permanent work under the Big Top.

Also complicating matters that spring, management of the Blue Jays for the first time would have to be more careful about disturbing the chemistry of the club. In 1983, after seven seasons of losing, the Blue Jays posted an 89-73 record to finish fourth in their division, only nine games behind the Baltimore Orioles, who went on to win the World Series.

"I was trying to break into a tightly knit family," Gruber agrees. "Most of their everyday players—Lloyd Moseby, Willie Upshaw, Jesse Barfield, Ernie Whitt—had grown up with the team. I was afraid that Rance and Garth, who had been with the team since Day One, might look upon me as an intruder."

He refers to platoon partners Rance Mulliniks and Garth Iorg, who had combined to drive in eighty-eight runs the season before while providing stable and occasionally spectacular defence at third base. Veterans that they were, both of them knew that the club saw in Gruber the player who one day would make both of them expendable. Despite that knowledge they tried hard to make the newcomer feel a part of his new team.

"It was a relief," says Gruber. "And it was a surprise. They went out of their way to introduce me to people, called me over to take ground balls with them, showed me this, that and the other. Things I might be using to beat them out of a job one day. To be honest, I couldn't understand why they were doing it.

"When a young kid comes in and he's been touted to take your job, you're bound to be a little angry. Irate even. At least disappointed. The way I figured it, you've got to lose respect for your employers because you're thinking, 'Well, they've bled me dry and now they want to run me out of here for a punk who'll cost them half what they pay me.' Over the years, you learn that's not the way things work. You have to build for the future. You have to remember that you'll be there as long as you're valuable.

After all, nothing in this life is forever.

"Usually in spring training, when a guy's on the verge of making it, things can get a little edgy with the guy who might be on the way out. It's almost impossible not to think negative thoughts about the newcomer, even if it is the way it always happens.

"When my turn comes, and I can only hope it's ten years down the road, when some fresh-faced kid shows up to run me out of my job, I'll have to think back to the way Rance and Garth were with me and, I hope, act as appropriately. They might not know it, but they left a big mark on my life."

Like any rookie in his right mind, Gruber admits to having been "intimidated" by his first manager in the major leagues.

Bobby Cox had learned baseball the hard way, bouncing around a dozen clubs in the minors before he spent two all-too-brief seasons at third base for the New York Yankees in the late 1960s. With his knees a mess when he quit the field in 1970 at the age of twenty-nine, he spent the next six seasons managing in the minors before he took a coach's job with the Yankees in 1977.

For the next four years, he managed the Atlanta Braves, and when he had brought them to the verge of respectability in 1981 owner Ted Turner fired him because he thought a "name" manager, like Joe Torre, would mean better ratings when the Braves played on the boss's cable TV network.

With a year's pay left on Cox's contract with Atlanta, the Blue Jays GM Pat Gillick persuaded him to take over the five-year-old club after Bobby Mattick was reassigned following the 1981 season.

Cox had a temper. Once, during his playing days in the minors, a teammate hid his third baseman's glove. Cox put his fist through the window of the bus they were riding.

Early in his career as a manager in the majors, in times of extreme stress, he had been known to trash a washroom or two with a baseball bat. He had mellowed somewhat by the time he came to the Blue Jays but not all that much. When he thought Cliff Johnson's grumping might become a threat to team unity, he slammed the six-foot-five-inch 225-pounder against his office wall and threatened to punch his lights out if he didn't tone down the whining. During a closed-doors meeting with Joey McLaughlin, a reliever lacking sufficient courage, in Cox's opinion, he tore off a shoe and hurled it at the pitcher's head. "I was hoping he'd get off his butt and punch me in the mouth," Cox confided later. "I couldn't think of anything else to light a fire under him."

The secret to keeping on the right side of Cox, as any rookie with an IQ approaching room temperature soon learns, is not to get on the wrong side of him in the first place.

"He was very stern," said Gruber. "He commanded, not demanded, respect. And he could go the other way, too, if that's what it took. He had a way of getting your attention. Quick. He was personable, but never so that you felt you were close to him. Maybe it was because I was a rookie, maybe that I didn't feel a part of the puzzle, but I figured it would be better if he saw a lot more of me than he heard."

Cox has been arguably the most successful of the five men who have managed the Blue Jays since they joined the American League in 1977. What helped to make him so, says Gruber, is that he had two of the most astute minds in baseball at his disposal.

Gruber says that Jimy Williams and Cito Gaston, who would succeed Cox as manager of the team when he returned to Atlanta after the 1985 season, were the men most responsible for making him the superstar he has become.

"In those days, Jimy had a marvellous way of getting a point across to a young player," says Gruber. "I'd do something wrong and I'd know it. I figured I was sure to be chewed out the minute I got back to the dugout. Then, when nobody said anything, I'd get to wondering if maybe I really hadn't screwed up. That's when Jimy would come up and say, 'Now, what would you have done a little differently if that play happened again?' Eventually, without a hint of criticism, he'd get the answer out of you and make you feel like you solved the problem by yourself. Not once do I remember walking away feeling I had been brutal. I'm not saying it works on everybody every time—everybody needs a chewing-out every once in a while—but I think it worked real well with me."

Williams also had spent a decade drifting through the minors and wound up his playing career with a couple of seasons at Winnipeg when the world's coldest city outside Siberia had a franchise in the International League. For three years until 1974 he was out of baseball, working as a grocery store clerk and as a life insurance salesman, when the California Angels rescued him to manage their farm club in the Midwest League.

When Gruber met him, Williams had entered his fifth season as the Blue Jays' coach at third base. With Cox to play the heavy, Williams had a wonderful job and he became the most widely respected coach in the club.

The hitting instructor, Cito Gaston, unlike his two colleagues on the coaching staff, had had a long and relatively successful career in the major leagues. The highlight of his decade in the National League was the 1970 season in which he had a .318 batting average with 29 home runs and 93 RBIs. His farewell to the majors was the Atlanta Braves' 1979 spring camp. The man who cut him, even though Gaston had been hitting at a .300 clip, was Bobby Cox.

Two years later Gaston was tutoring young hitters in the

Braves' farm system. When Cox moved from the Braves to the Blue Jays, one of the first people he hired was Gaston.

In time, Gruber became a prime example of the philosophy Gaston hammered into the heads of his young hitters. As much as hitting is a physical act, he maintained, it is also a mental exercise.

"It would have surprised me to know it at the time, but looking back I can see I was short in both areas," says Gruber.

"One of the first things Cito taught me was to 'get something started,' as he called it. At some point during the pitcher's wind-up, he told me, I had to begin mine. For me, it was as little as tucking in the shoulder facing the pitcher. It's like coiling a spring. Keep your feet beneath you, of course, but you actually coil to uncoil. Like a boxer, if you don't cock that fist, there'll be nothing behind the punch. Hammering a nail, too. If you don't bring the hammer back before you strike, you'll be at it all day and won't make a dent."

The mental aspect is based on making an educated guess about the opponent's pitch selection.

"Go to the plate one time looking for a fastball, breaking ball the next time," Gruber says of the spring training exercise he maintained. "Just try to work out a swing on both pitches. Even though I had never hit the good breaking ball or slider, I started getting a piece of them. Geez, I thought, it can be a thinking man's game."

It also taught Gruber early in his career that spring training, even for a player who had the club made, is not the lark the sport pages make it out to be.

"Until you've got a club made, by necessity every at-bat is life and death. It could be the one to get you over the hump. When you've got the job nailed, spring training is the time to be a failure. What I mean is that you concentrate on your weaknesses, the things you don't do well.

Why waste a lot of time on the things you're doing right?

"I can't help but chuckle when I read in the sports section about the troubles last year's star is having at the plate this spring. Flash in the pan. Ain't hitting his weight. Going down for sure. Then, when the real fun begins in April, all of a sudden he's Public Enemy Number One for the pitchers. The most likely reason is he's been working on his weaknesses for six weeks, when batting averages really don't mean a thing, and letting his strengths take care of themselves. Sounds simple, I know, but you'd be surprised how many ballplayers spend the whole spring training trying to impress people."

He also learned a lesson in politics that first spring with the Blue Jays. It was delivered, unwittingly, by Jimy Williams in the lobby of a hotel in Vancouver where the team wound up its spring training schedule with a series against the Milwaukee Brewers. They would open the season the following week in Seattle.

"As I waited for the elevator, I got to thinking how good it felt to be in the major leagues, even if I'd only be playing once in a while. I was happy with myself in spring training, thought I'd shown them the talent they had paid their money to Cleveland to see.

"Jimy came up to me as the elevator door opened and stretched out his hand. 'Kelly,' he said, 'Congratulations. We've decided to take you with us.'

"It caught me off guard. Maybe I'm dreaming, but I thought Jimy looked back at me kind of funny when I didn't show that much emotion. I thought there was no question I would make the team. I'd come this far, hadn't I? I knew they could have got half their $25,000 back if I was returned to Cleveland, but why would they have gone to all the trouble in the first place?

"Finally, as I took it that Jimy was waiting for a response, I recovered my composure. 'Oh, great,' I said, trying to put some meaning into it. 'Happy to hear it. That's a load off my mind.' To this day, I don't know if he bought it. Here he was, a guy who might have died to hear those words when he was a player. Here I was, eyes wide open but still asleep when the boss calls 'round to give me what he thinks should be the best news of my life. Don't get me wrong, I was thrilled to my socks, but my thoughts were on that day in Colombia when they told me I was headed for the bigs. 'Great! Somebody really believes in me.' It reassured me that I had the talent."

As debuts go, his first time out in the major leagues— Friday, April 20, 1984, before what was left of a crowd of 37,241 at Exhibition Stadium—was less than auspicious.

Cox called upon him to replace Garth Iorg at third base in the twelfth frame of what became a 10-6 loss in 13 innings to the California Angels. Gruber, who fielded one ground ball cleanly, had Jesse Barfield to thank for the chance. Down 6-5 in the bottom of the eleventh, Barfield pinch-hit for Iorg, swatted a single into left field, advanced on a wild pitch and came home on a single by Ernie Whitt to tie the score.

"I'm happy to get the shot," Gruber told a certain newspaper reporter later. "I was a little nervous, but I guess anybody would be under the circumstances. It would have been nice to win the game, though."

Just as well, perhaps, he did not get a chance to pick up a bat that afternoon.

In a game during spring training, the specifics of which remain fuzzy to Gruber, he made a bid to impress his bosses by swiping a base. It proved costly.

"I don't remember if I started the game, don't remember if I even came to the plate, don't remember if I was sent in to run for someone," he says. "All I remember is the pain when I grabbed the base on a head-first slide."

Even though he was able to yank his right index finger back into its socket, it was too stiff the following day for him to consider anything but riding a bench for a while.

"'Oh, God, here we go,' I thought. 'I've finally made it and I'm not going to be able to play. Maybe they'll want their $12,500 back.'"

"I tried to make adjustments in my swing and my throw, but to no avail. I couldn't even swing the bat in the on-deck circle without feeling a sharp pain. With all that mental baggage weighing me down, wondering if I could stand the pace, now I was physically hampered."

Adding to his doubts would be one of the last plays he made before the Blue Jays sent him down to their farm club in Syracuse. He was at shortstop in Minneapolis, replacing Alfredo Griffin late in a game against the Minnesota Twins, when fireplug Kirby Puckett came to the plate. He hit a one-hop rocket towards Gruber that smacked into the wrong spot—the pocket of his glove—and dropped at his feet.

"Straight at me," says Gruber, still amazed by the sequence of events that night. "Hit me in the glove and just bounced out in front of me. One hop. I picked it up and threw it. Safe! My God, what kind of league am I playing in here? I was touted for having a strong arm, but how're you going to catch Superman?"

The next afternoon, Gruber watched the Blue Jays play from a seat in the upper reaches of the Metrodome.

There were no guarantees he would ever make it back to the bigs. Running through his mind were thoughts of having just finished his "cup of coffee" in the major leagues. When the two-game mini-series wrapped up and his teammates headed for Toronto and an eleven-day homestand, Gruber would catch the first of a series of flights to upstate New York late that night.

He had come to The Show to stay and he had lasted forty-three days.

Hindsight being what it is, it is easy to say now that a better decision could have been made.

It was worth giving up catcher Geno Petralli, now a member of the Texas Rangers, to get the Indians' permission to send Gruber back to the minor leagues for the seasoning he certainly needed. Six weeks earlier, in fact, the Blue Jays had balked when Cleveland asked for starter Jim Gott.

The immediate effect of Gruber's demotion—other than to halve the rookie's salary from the $62,500 major league minimum—was to make room on the roster for Willie Mays Aikens. The K.C. Royals had wanted to be rid of their twenty-nine-year-old first baseman after he and a couple of teammates were sentenced for cocaine possession to three months at a "country club" prison in Texas. Commissioner Bowie Kuhn raised the stakes in mid-December with one-year bans of Aikens, Willie Wilson and Jerry Martin. If they kept their noses clean, the suspensions would be reconsidered after six weeks of the regular season.

Four days later, while the three were doing time, the Blue Jays dealt a spare part, Jorge Orta, to the Royals for Aikens. It looked like a steal.

Aikens, who feasted regularly on Blue Jays pitching, was coming off a season in which his enviable .302 batting average had been backed by 23 home runs in a mere 410 appearances at the plate. Imagine, as doubtless the Blue Jays did, how well he might do if the only white lines in his life were the ones on a baseball field.

Knowledge of having done the "right" thing, it soon became apparent, would be the Jays' and Aikens's only reward. In batting practice with the club that first afternoon, which the sore-armed manager liked to pitch, Bobby Cox looked like the second coming of Sandy Koufax whenever Aikens stepped into the cage for his cuts.

In 93 games that season, he averaged .205 with 11

home runs and 26 RBIs. After 20 at-bats the following season, he bid goodbye to the major leagues forever.

Gruber, denied his chance, could have sulked away a season at Syracuse. It wouldn't be the first time a prized prospect, miffed by real or imagined slights by the parent club, let it all get away from him when he was sent back to the minor leagues. Gruber, better for the lessons he had learned under the tutelage of Williams and Gaston, batted .269 and swatted 21 homers for 55 RBIs in 97 games for the Chiefs.

"It's easy to pout, get down, angry, pissed," says Gruber, "but it does no good even if the bosses aren't always right. What you do is accept it. Turn the page. The sooner you start doing things to change their minds, the sooner you'll be back up there. Just do your job better than it's ever been done. The rest takes care of itself."

Still, as September and the end of his fifth season as a professional drew near, it weighed upon him that he had yet to hit so much as a single in the major leagues.

The long wait was about to come to an end, and in a spectacular fashion, at the greatest little ballpark in the big leagues. A snippet of history was waiting to be made at Fenway Park.

CHAPTER 6

 GWOO–BAH!

It has been fifty years since Ted Williams of the Boston Red Sox, known as The Splendid Splinter during the nineteen summers he played the outfield at Fenway Park, became the last man to finish a season in the major leagues with a batting average above .400.

When he says that hitting a baseball is the single most difficult act in all of sport, Kelly Gruber is among the first to take his word for it.

The trick is to arrange a head-on crash between a round ball and a round bat after maximum force has been applied to each by competing agencies with diametrically opposite objectives.

To do it requires nailing the epicentre of a ball a shade less than three inches wide with a "sweet spot" on the upper part of the bat about the size of a nickel.

Make a hit three times in ten, which reflects a failure rate of 70 percent, and breweries from Quebec to California will line up to drop bales of $1,000 bills (U.S. funds, too) at your feet in homage.

What makes the proposition particularly tough is that the ball usually approaches the hitter at speeds of more than 90 miles an hour; is likely to veer, dart or drop at the last millisecond; and, according to the rule book, passes through a hitting zone about eighteen inches wide from the hitter's knees to his armpits.

Parameters aside, the hardest part of the job well might be convincing oneself it can be done. Gruber had been going through the tortures of the damned, battling the customary swarm of self-doubts, that September night of 1984 when he came to the plate late in a game at fabled Fenway Park. He was in search of his first hit in the major leagues.

"I was feeling kind of not sure again," he recalled one afternoon years later in the Blue Jays' dugout at Fenway Park. "Why am I here? Am I good enough? Was I good enough to get my shot, but not good enough to stay? That would have been the cruellest cut of all.

"Sure, I'd had a great summer in Syracuse, leading the International League hitters with a .500 slugging average, but that was then and this was now. I was a mess."

With the club hopelessly out of the game that night in Boston, the Detroit Tigers having made a runaway of the American League East that year, Blue Jays' manager Bobby Cox sent his hitting instructor, Cito Gaston, over to tell Gruber he would pinch-hit against reliever Al Nipper of the Red Sox.

"As soon as you get the call, the mental process starts. 'What do I have to do to help the club out?' In this case, being down a touchdown and a field goal, the answer was pretty easy. 'No need to be fancy. Take a few pitches. Get on base and don't be too daring when you get there.'

"The next set of thoughts are the ones that had bedevilled me my whole career. 'Geez. Hope I don't screw up. Geez, if I have to strike out, I hope it's swinging. Geez, how 'bout a hard-hit grounder? Never know, it might squeeze through.' It happens to everybody, I guess, even if nobody admits it.

"First, I should have been thinking about what pitch was working best for Nipper that night. 'What pitch does he throw when he's ahead, even or behind in the count?' Second, I should have decided which one of these pitches I wanted to hit, and if you want to get real fine about battle plans, at what place in the count I was likely to see it.

"Then, after I've got all this mapped out, I should have been flooding myself with positive thoughts. 'Sure, I belong. Why the heck else am I here? What's so special about his guy that I can't hit him?' And in that situation, with his team ahead by a bunch, you could bet he wouldn't be getting too cute about his pitches."

Gruber's real concern that night was making sure he had the right end of the bat in his hands when he went up to the plate.

"I wasn't sure what I was doing," he says. "I was just kind of there."

What made matters worse was the chant rising from the seats behind the Blue Jays' dugout: "Gwoo-bah! Gwoo-bah! Gwoo-bah!"

"I'm up there thinking, 'Oh, great! Now I got people riding me. Making fun of me.' And they were all over me. Every pitch. 'Gwoo-bah. Gwoo-bah. Gwoo-bah.' Well, as anybody knows who's spent an hour at the ballpark, the best way to cool out the other team's fans is to hurt them on the scoreboard."

Al Nipper hung a slider and Gruber hit it into the net behind the Green Monster.

"The ends of my hair felt like they were standing on end. Unbelievable! When that ball cleared the wall in left-centre field . . . well, it's like a pal telling you what it's like to be a dad. You nod your head and think you know what he's talking about. Until you've had one, though, you don't know what it's really like. Same with that home run."

What he had misconstrued was the response of the "cheering section" of Boston fans behind the Blue Jays' dugout as he took his place in the batter's box.

Coach Jimy Williams told him later the 'Gwoo-bah Serenade,' still popular in Boston, was all in good fun that night, particularly since the game was out of reach. What the droll fans of Fenway dearly wanted to see was a piece of baseball history played out for them. The clue that such might be the case was there for all to see when Gruber's 0-for-12 predicament flashed on the scoreboard in centre field as he came to the plate.

Gruber knew the cheering section in his own dugout was sincere.

"We were down quite a few runs, so it wasn't quite as lively as if I had just won the game," he says. "I can still hear them cheering me outside and, for the life of me, couldn't figure out why they're still going nuts. 'Gwoo-bah. Gwoo-bah. Gwoo-bah.' Finally, Jesse Barfield came over to me and said, 'Hey, they want you out there.' I figured he was putting me on, so I tried to ignore him. Then Lloyd Moseby came over and he told me to go out and take my bows.

"What the heck. Even if they greeted me with a chorus of boos, which is what I expected, it would be good for a chuckle later on. So I popped my head out over the roof, expecting a pie in the face, and the crowd went bananas.

"Later on, one of the guys who works the scoreboard out there brought the ball to me. I've heard of it happening that three or four people might show up at the clubhouse door with *the* ball. Fenway, with its Green Monster rising thirty-seven feet and a net on top of it, makes it one of the few parks where you can retrieve souvenirs.

"That ball is on the mantel at home in Texas. On it is written 'First hit, Home run, Al Nipper 9-25-84.'"

His first slump in the major leagues had come to an end.

There would be more, of course. Many more.

"Like a cold," says Gruber, "they creep up on you.

You're a little stuffed up. Your eyes water. Your nose begins to run. Next thing you know, someone's stuffed a towel down your throat and dropped a ton of bricks on your chest."

The first indication of a slump, says Gruber, is that a hitter does not "see" a ball as well as when he does on a hot streak. While it is one of the most common complaints in baseball, there never has been a truly satisfactory solution to what causes the phenomenon.

"When you're going good," Gruber explains, "it looks the size of a beachball. It doesn't matter if you're two strikes in the hole, you could put wood on it wearing a blindfold. You're that confident. I know it sounds crazy, but it's true. When you're not going good, you might as well be swinging at something the size of an Aspirin. You don't pick up the ball as quickly as you did before and your concentration tends to blur more quickly.

"And you're afraid to let a strike get past you, so you swing at everything coming your way. You go up there saying, 'OK, I'm not really seeing the ball all that well, I'll take a pitch.' Then what do I do? I swing at the first thing I see. Now you've had a horrible at-bat. Mentally, that might be all it needs to put you into the slump. You think, 'Gee, I stunk out there. It was like I never played this game before. What the heck am I doing out there?' Now you're thinking negatives."

The temptation is to suggest this amounts to a hill of the stuff that makes the grass grow green, but a lesson in elementary math provides some insight into the dilemma. All hitters, great and small, must confront it dozens of times throughout the course of a season.

A ball travelling at 90 miles an hour covers 132 feet a second. Since the strip of rubber on the mound where the pitcher stands is sixty feet six inches from the plate where the hitter stands, that means it arrives in the hitting zone about half a second after it leaves a pitcher's hand.

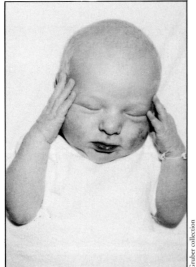

Gruber collection

Gruber collection

Mama's Boy   *It's not the thing people call him today but there was a time when the term fit. At top, newborn Kelly and a little later, visiting Santa. Below, Gloria Gruber as Miss Texas in the late fifties.*

Albert Kelch/Gruber collection

Gruber collection

First Love   *Although Kelly made baseball his career choice a few short years after this picture was taken on the gridiron, football played a major role in the formative years of his life as an athlete.*

Two of a Kind   *Sister Claudia, who led the cheers when brother Kelly played, leans on a sturdy shoulder while she struts her stuff.*

Gruber collection

Gruber collection

Grand People   *Archie and Vita Hunt, shown at a family celebration, played a pivotal role in raising grandson Kelly after his mom's first marriage ended.*

Gruber collection

All in the Family   *Kelly, older sister Claudia and younger brother David pose for the "official" family portrait. Unofficially, Kelly (above) was the class comedian at Westlake High in Austin, Texas.*

Gruber collection

Prized Prospect *Scouts from the major leagues started to flock to games at Westlake High in 1980 to rate Kelly Gruber's work at shortstop. Cleveland signed him for $100,000, a franchise record at the time.*

Jon R. Fory

Gruber collection

All Dressed Up... *and a couple of places to go. When Kelly graduated from Westlake High in 1980, he had a hard choice to make: to turn pro as a baseball player or to be a student athlete at the University of Texas.*

Gruber collection

In the Beginning... *Coach Howard Bushong of the Westlake Caps and high school star Kelly Gruber. Within a year, Kelly (below) would be at Waterloo, Iowa, in his second season as a pro. He batted .290 with 14 HRs for the Diamonds.*

Gruber collection

Chattanooga News-Free Press

Look Out Chattanooga! The Chattanooga Lookouts may not have taken the Southern League by storm in 1982, but they were true champions at having a ball off the field — as this "unofficial" team photo suggests. Finding Kelly should take about five (hint, hint) seconds.

Going, Going, Gone *Kelly Gruber watches one of the 42 home runs he hit for the Syracuse Chiefs disappear from MacArthur Stadium. After two seasons there, he joined the Blue Jays to stay in 1986.*

Jim Commentucci

"That half-second is all the time you have to make up your mind what kind of a pitch it is and if you're going to swing at it. Does the rotation of the seams form that whirling red dot in the middle, telling you it's a slider that will break sharply and sink? Is it a curve and how much will it break? Is it a fastball? A forkball? A screwball?

"Next question is whether it's a strike. Then, will you be swinging?

"People think it's a bunch of bull when you tell them all the decisions you have to make in such a short time. I've surprised myself at times by the number of things that have gone through my mind while a pitch is on the way. 'It's a slider. It's hanging. It's not the pitch I was looking for, but it's sorta asking to be hit. Now it's out of the strike zone, but still hittable. Nah, I'm gonna lay off it. The heck with it, I'm gonna take a cut.' Just as surprising, to my way of thinking, is when you draw a total blank as the pitch comes down the pipe.

"Whatever the thought process, when you're going good, you park it a foot inside the line in right for a double. When you're going bad, its second-short-first for a double play. Either way, back on the bench someone's asking you why your bat was so slow. When you tell them, they look at you as if you sailed through the hole in SkyDome on a flying saucer."

When concentration fails, Gruber says, all too often other bad habits resurface.

"When your concentration is not there, you tend to yank your head away as the ball comes through the strike zone. Now you're seeing the ball with only one eye. You might tend to jump at the ball. It doesn't take a genius to figure that if you're moving toward something that's coming at you, the time frame narrows. We might be talking about a thousandth of a second here, but when you consider that the "sweet spot" in the centre of the bat where you hit home runs is about the size of a nickel, you need all the time you can get. When you're quick, when you're seeing the ball really well, it seems like you have all day."

Another factor is even more mundane. No one goes to work feeling on top of the world every day.

"Your intensity level isn't up to par. Your concentration is faltering. Maybe you're tired. A little sick. Hurting a little bit. Maybe you should ease up for a couple of days until everything is back in sync. You go through two or three days like that, you can jump off the right track. Now it's tough to get back on it. You've lost that edge. It's tough and now you're making it tougher. I don't know how many times my coaches have told me that you can't turn this game off and on, but everybody is guilty of it at one time or another.

"You might be on a little streak. 'Geez, I'm going to turn it down a little bit, coast a while.' The biggest sin is when you're up about ten runs with three or four innings and a couple of at-bats to go. It's tough for me to go out there when the game's out of hand. When the game's on the line, there's this mountain to climb. Up ten runs, I tend to become a little lax. You just turn it off because it's not that important any more.

"That's when the other team scores six runs and then you try to turn it back on. A lot of guys fall into that trap. You lose the edge. You've got to remember you're only as good as your last at-bat. You have to keep telling yourself that every second you're out there it's the last pitch you might ever see. Otherwise, it's a good way to get into a slump."

There were other tests of his resolve that he would have to endure in his rookie season. One of them involved his teammate Damaso Garcia.

During the infield warm-up before a game at Exhibition Stadium one night in September, Gruber and Garth Iorg were fielding grounders and practising the pivot on the double play.

Gruber gripped the ball incorrectly after fielding one of the grounders and the throw to second dipped at the last moment, handcuffing the temperamental Garcia.

"By this time, there were quite a few people in the stands, so when he yelled at me, I took it as him trying to show me up. Then he stood there, hands on his hips, and stared at me. I was out there scuffling to be just a part of the puzzle, and he treats me like a bush leaguer. I was embarrassed."

Gruber, the steam seeping out from beneath his collar, returned to his station beside Iorg and decided to give Garcia something to complain about.

"'Hey, Garth,' I said. 'Watch this. I'm going to throw the nastiest sinker you ever saw. And hard.' Man, did I let it go. And after it some kind of handcuffed him, it bit him.

"After I threw it, I didn't even look his way. Like I was supposed to do, I went over to the base to take the throw after it came around to the catcher. As I planted my feet, my eyes on home plate, I saw the ball wing by me at about hip level. I knew who had thrown it.

"My back's to him and he throws the ball at me. If it had hit me, it might have caused damage. I turned and stared at him. Just stared. Had he as much as dropped his hat, I would have been at second base duking it out with my own teammate in front of thousands of fans. I don't care what it would have cost me."

Gruber completed his work in silence, but knew that his teammates, manager and coaches all had seen the incident. Without a doubt, they were more eager to see how Gruber would react and they would measure his manhood in the process.

The rookie waited inside the hallway that led to the back door of the Blue Jays clubhouse. When Garcia arrived, Gruber suggested a few other ways for Garcia to act. Gruber was ready, even eager, for something to settle it in a far more inflammatory way.

"Don't you ever do that to me again!" he said. "Never!"

If looks could have killed, the Blue Jays would have lost a very good infielder and a prime prospect simultaneously. Fortunately for both of them, there was a team on the other side of the diamond that would require all of their energies.

Gruber had met the challenge. On and off the field.

CHAPTER 7

 LIFE IN THE SLOW LANE

The wreck of many a promising career litters the slow lane to the big leagues, the slippery path that all but a favoured few are forced to travel, and the most treacherous part of the trip is saved for the final mile.

It is called Triple A baseball.

Take the word of seasoned traveller Mitch Webster when he says that life one step from the top is the stuff of which heartache is made.

"Sometimes it seems like it's an endurance test, survival of the fittest, the guy who lasts the longest makes it," the Cleveland Indians centre fielder was saying one afternoon in the summer of 1990 in the visitors' dugout at the SkyDome. "Sometimes there's no way you can see the light at the end of the tunnel. I've seen some unbelievable moves made. As players, you learn there's no way to figure the system, so you just go out and do your job. Or you go nuts."

Across the diamond, sitting with a stack of fan mail in his lap and his feet crossed against the beam of his locker, Kelly Gruber of the Blue Jays agrees with his former teammate's assessment of life in Triple A as he remembers his own days with the Syracuse Chiefs of the International League.

"Dog-eat-dog," he says, shifting in his deck chair. "Look out for Number One. Everybody's that one tiny jump away from The Show and they don't care who they step on to get there."

On the other side of the room, beyond a clutch of players engaged in a rowdy game of hearts, the erudite John Cerutti agrees.

"I always looked at Triple A ball as a place where half the guys were on the way up and half were on the way out," he says, putting aside a book entitled *The Physics of Baseball.* "In that regard, it's difficult getting a close team chemistry. I had more fun at Single A and Double A ball. Everyone was in the same boat, starting out, trying to get to the big leagues. At Triple A, it became a business. Guys were playing for a reason and it wasn't quite as much fun. It was baseball. I don't mean to say it was all work, but it just wasn't the game you played when you were a kid."

Webster was in his ninth season in the minors, his fifth in Syracuse, when the Blue Jays did him a huge favour. They dealt him to the Montreal Expos in June of 1985 for pitcher Cliff Young, who made seventeen appearances in relief for the California Angels in 1990, his first season in the big leagues. Webster, traded to the Pittsburgh Pirates early in the 1991 season, has been in the majors ever since 1985. He is a capable switch-hitter, with a .270 career average, who plays all three outfield positions and has swiped upward of thirty bases a season.

One might wonder, as Webster did, why Toronto seemed so unwilling to employ him at least as a fourth outfielder, an item that seemed to have been high on the Blue Jays' Christmas list for years after he was shipped out.

When he speaks of the "unbelievable moves" he has seen, he might well be thinking of what happened to him and his career in the spring of 1983. After leading the

Blue Jays with a "hard" .464 batting average (13-for-28) with five doubles and two triples in 16 games during spring training, manager Bobby Cox opted to take Mickey Klutts north when the club broke camp.

Klutts, so plagued by a variety of knee injuries that he appeared in only 199 games during eight seasons in the majors, had been 0-for-2 in his one spring outing. He played in 22 games for the Blue Jays that year, batting .256 (11-for-43) before he, too, was dispatched to Syracuse.

Insult was added to injury for Webster that June when a relative newcomer, George Bell, was called up to Toronto from Syracuse. In the light of subsequent events—most notably Bell's MVP season of 1987, in which he clubbed 47 home runs—it is difficult to argue with the move, but at the time it cut Webster to the quick.

"I thought, 'Where in the world is there any loyalty in this game?' It told me they don't care much about you as a person. It didn't matter how long you busted a gut for them. 'What were your stats this week?'"

Five years later, as he looked out across an empty field beneath the splendid SkyDome, the bitterness has faded. Still, as he takes a pull from a paper cup of clubhouse coffee, he wonders what might have been had he done what legions of others did when their dreams turned to dust.

"A lot of guys get buried," he says. "I put up decent numbers. Had some pretty good years, but I've seen better who didn't make it. There were no knocks about my total game. They just thought I was a little shy all the way around. I felt like an insurance policy. If someone got hurt, I was down on the farm, ready to go. That always gripes you. Nobody likes to play second fiddle."

His first impressions of Gruber were less than enthusiastic. "First while there, he seemed like an airhead. He was just young, I guess. You didn't know if he hardly understood the game, or if that was his way to relax. He came off like he was breezing along."

Webster, to give him his due, was never one to cling to first impressions.

"Every once in a while, he'd jolt one about 420 feet," he says, surprised the kid could generate such power. "Then he'd go 15 feet in the hole behind third, field a ball and toss the runner out by 10 feet. He surprised a few people, me included. Far as being a white guy, he was super-quick laterally. Powerful, too. Shoot, he hit 21 home runs that year in no time at all. If the guy ever learned to hit the breaking ball, you knew he was going to be some kind of player."

What left Webster truly in awe, however, was a spur-of-the-moment prank Gruber pulled during practice one afternoon when his concentration wandered after he had fielded his fiftieth ground ball.

"Only guy I've ever seen standing flat-foot who could do a backflip," said Webster. "Wouldn't believe it if I hadn't seen it. You could get on the TV late at night with that trick!"

It is easy to watch Gruber beneath the SkyDome these summer nights and see the stuff that has taken him up the ladder to superstardom since that fateful 1988 home opener when he came off the bench to replace the injured Rance Mulliniks and go 4-for-6 with two home runs and five RBIs against the New York Yankees.

Long before that day, while they waited their turn in Syracuse and on the bench in Toronto, pitcher John Cerutti saw good things in store for Gruber.

"I always thought there was a year like 1990 in his future," said Cerutti one September night as the Blue Jays stoked the coals of that year's faltering pennant drive. "The question always was whether he would put it together. Our first couple of years, we lockered together at Exhibition Stadium and he went through some rough

times when his performance didn't match his expectations. I saw the frustrating side of it. I used to talk to him
quite a bit.

"All of a sudden, Rance Mulliniks goes down and he
has to be in there every day. First, you need opportunity.
That's what the game is, preparation mixed with opportu-
nity. All of a sudden, he's the third baseman. 'I'm there, so
I better produce.' And he did. That builds confidence.
Now he does it every day, every year."

If heart alone were the decisive factor, Cerutti saw
enough of it in Gruber when they were in Syracuse.

"I remember him vividly, climbing the tarp on foul balls
that were in the stands. There were times when he didn't
have a prayer, but that's just his effort. And, of course, always getting hurt. Always nagging little injuries that would
knock him out a week or two. He could always run. He
could always throw. Always hit with power. The question
was whether he was going to put it all together at the
plate."

A view from the other side of the field comes from
Johnny Hart, now the Indians' director of baseball operations, but who was managing in Triple A when Gruber
was with the Chiefs.

"He was an up-and-down kind of guy, certainly no polished player when I saw him in Triple A a couple of years
after the Blue Jays got him," Hart said during one of his
clubs' visits to Toronto in the summer of 1990. "The question was always whether the guy was going to hit a breaking ball. The thing you liked about him was he had a
strong make-up. He was a balls-out kind of player."

He also feels that Cleveland did the Blue Jays a huge
favour by allowing them to send Gruber back to Triple A.
Had Gruber been left to deteriorate on the bench the rest
of the 1984 season, there is no telling how his progress
would have been impeded. Manager Bobby Cox pre-
dicted less than 100 at-bats for him that year. Considering

Gruber's inability to hit the breaking ball, a failing that kills many careers, he needed to see live pitching every day to learn to combat that crucial weakness.

"To learn to hit the breaking ball," said Hart, "he has to see it every day. Lefties or righties, I don't care, they like everything in so they can get wood on the ball and drive it somewhere. You're a big swinger, they throw that breaking ball away until you show you can hit it. You got to show you can go the other way on the ball. Some guys can adjust. Some guys never learn.

"All of a sudden, Gruber started going to right-centre."

Gruber, blinded by his ambition at the time, looked upon life in Triple A as another year tacked on his sentence to the galley ships of baseball. Conditions there were better than they were at other stops along the way, granted, but what taunted him was the taste he had had of life at the top.

"From the parks, to the players, to the hotels, to the money you make, everything is different, a lot different," he says. "That's why they call it the majors and minors. The hotels where you stay, the ones that always have a set of rails right behind them and freights to wake you up all hours of the night. And cockroaches, some of 'em were so big they should have come with a leash!

"It starts out fun—'Heck, they're paying me to play'— but it wears off quick and it becomes a rough life. My first year, I remember pals swiping packs of peanut butter and jelly off café tables to make sandwiches at home. If you have wheels, it's usually a piece of junk, or you can't afford gas. To have a decent meal in a good restaurant, you save up all week.

"Then, the night you've stunk out the stadium and you're trying to get comfortable on the piece of foam you call a mattress, you're thinking about all the kids back home and wondering what beach they went to that day.

"Looking back, I can laugh at it, sort of. That's because

I made it. For a lot of guys who didn't, there won't be many fond memories. They might talk like there is, but I'll bet it breaks their hearts.

"It's not like the best man wins. I've seen lots of players who should play in the big leagues and won't. It's politics. It's numbers. It's who likes you. Everybody gets the one opportunity, I guess, but if you're liked, if things don't fall your way, they might give you more than an opportunity. A lot of times it's the first impression you put in the bigwig's mind. It always seems to stick with you.

"From what I understand, the brass in Toronto liked me from the time they saw me in high school. Cleveland left the door open and they snapped me up. I think the talent would have shown up sometime with Cleveland, but it's anybody's guess where I'd be if Toronto hadn't remembered that impression I made in high school."

If nothing else, his "fling" with the Blue Jays in the spring of 1984 wiped out any doubts he had harboured about belonging in the select company of the world's best baseball players. Believing has always been half the battle for Gruber.

"I came down from the majors to the Triple A level, saw the big difference, and even though I'm back in the minors there's no doubt I'm going to make it. Before I even step into the box, I believe. It was the kick in the butt I needed."

If it took a final two seasons for him to cover the final lap, Gruber admits much of the blame rests on his own shoulders.

"I could have learned a lot more, done a lot more to develop my skills. I didn't take in all the things people tried to teach me. A lot of it went in one ear and out the other. I knew where I was going, but I didn't work at it like I should have. I always gave everything on the field, the only way I know how, but I cheated myself on the little things.

"I could have talked a lot more baseball, picked people's minds for that one little tip that might win a game five years down the road. I should have asked for that little extra bit of help from the coach. I should have come out early for extra hitting. 'Put me in, Coach, I'm ready to play,' that was me, but I didn't want to work for it. 'Geez, how long do I have to suffer down here, take these lousy bus rides, wear these sloppy uniforms, sleep in ratty hotels?' My attitude could have been better."

The gaping hole in the system becomes apparent each time a rookie right fielder misplays a single into a run-scoring double, and using the rifle arm that helped get him to the majors, wings the return throw over the catcher's head, allowing all aboard to take an extra base.

"It's getting so nobody really knows how to play the game when they get up here," says Gruber. "And it's not because their coaches aren't doing their job. The minors are so dog-eat-dog, they're not interested in learning the game. They're interested in putting up numbers, moving themselves along, getting to The Show. It's the only thing on their minds. Unfortunately, it works."

What makes it particularly frustrating for the elders in the executive suites is that most of them grew up in a time when a graduate of the minor leagues was a finished ballplayer in all respects. What made them so capable is that they often were forced to apprentice at the lower levels until their late twenties before they were given their turn. They knew the fundamentals of the game, the evidence of which is the numbers of "career" Triple A players who became managers in the major leagues in the last generation.

All this changed when the major leagues, once a matched set of eight-team circuits employing a total of 400 players at the upper reaches, expanded over the years to the 26 teams that today have places for 650 players. Complicating matters is the simple economic truth that it is far cheaper to employ young prospects than seasoned vets. The theory is that the green-as-grass rookie will make up with reflexes and enthusiasm for the experience and coolness an old-timer brings to the team. As was obvious in the 1990 season or any other in recent memory, such has not been the case.

The fault, according to Gruber, lies in the philosophy with which the major leagues view their feeder systems.

"When do you start saying, 'I'm bringing this guy up because he gets runners over, hits the cut-off man, doesn't make mistakes in the field'? Take two kids in Triple A. One hits .280, 25 homers and drives in 90 runs. The other hits .265, but he can bunt, gives himself up to move the runner along, throws to the right base, always has a good presence on the field. Who's going to tell the kid with 25 homers and 90 RBIs that he's not going up? First, you don't want somebody else picking him up, so you do everything to protect him. Ready or not, if the guy puts up numbers, he's going up. Bottom line."

For all of his disenchantment with the vagabond's life he lived travelling the backwaters of baseball, Gruber thinks there is no college quite like it for learning to cope with life's hard knocks.

"I'd come home every winter, meet up with the old crowd and know I was a little more aware of what was out there," he says. "I had grown up a little bit quicker. I'd been through more. It sounds corny, but hard times build character."

Although he had precious little financial capital to show for it at the time, the economics of life in the minors also taught him lessons he applies today in dealing with the $10 million he will draw from the Blue Jays for his work in 1991, 1992 and 1993. It is a money management course denied college grads who hit the jackpot after being drafted by the National Football League.

"You take one of these football players, signs out of college for $2 million a year," says Gruber. "Ten years later, the newspapers say he's flat broke. What it tells me is he never learned to handle money. All through college, he lived in a dorm, knew when and where every meal was being served. 'Be there on time for practice.' 'Don't miss the bus on game day.' No mess. No stress. Miss a school assignment, the coach gets a whiz kid to do it for you. Nowhere did he have to learn to budget his money.

"Here I was, living in the real world on $600 a month. You learn real quick to count every dollar. One day you're broke and it's a week until payday. X amount for rent. X for food. X for gas. X for fun. Hey, what happened? You learn that if you want to go to the movies on the weekend, think twice about those couple of beers earlier in the week. You want steak and trimmings on Sunday? Pay for it on Wednesday night."

After receiving close to $100,000 to sign with Cleveland out of high school, an eighteen-year-old tycoon's first trip would be to a used-car lot, one would think. With the family sedan tucked safely in the garage back in Austin, Gruber did need a set of wheels to get around Batavia.

Coupe de Ville? Continental? Imperial?

A bicycle. Used.

"Cost him $15," says his father. "He never touched the signing money and we never sent him a penny. He lived on what he made. By his third year, at Chattanooga, he was putting money away. I had to make him understand he had to live within his means."

CHAPTER 8

 ## THE HARDER THEY FALL

As Goliath found out the day he dug in at the plate against Little David, bigger does not always mean better. The same goes for the Oakland Athletics.

It was a lesson they learned in 1988, when the Los Angeles Dodgers shocked them by winning the World Series in five games. It was a lesson underscored in 1990, when the Cincinnati Reds shamed them by winning The Fall Classic four in a row. Not the Toronto Blue Jays, not the San Francisco Giants, not even an earthquake could stop The Mighty A's in 1989.

And, for at least one very obvious reason, that bothers Kelly Gruber.

"As long as everybody did their part, they were there to be had," he said one day early in the 1991 season, recalling the way the Blue Jays had assessed their chances in the 1989 American League play-off.

"To beat them, you have to do the small things. The same way I think pitchers have to pitch inside to win. It doesn't have to be fancy, but get on base. Move the runner along. Make the right play in the field. Every time there's a crack, jump right in there.

"Sure, Jose Canseco and Mark McGwire are big sticks and big sticks make big noises. No matter how loud it is, no matter how big the dent is they put in that bleacher seat, it's only one run if there's no one on base when they do it. Good pitching eventually will beat good hitting."

As the Dodgers and Reds have proved, that philosophy is flawless. The problem in 1989, during the American League Championship Series between Toronto and Oakland, was that the Blue Jays left their battle plans on the chalk board.

"You can't count on the big inning. What about the little guys in the line-up? What are they supposed to do? Why couldn't we get a guy on, steal a base, take third on a grounder and come home on a sacrifice fly?

"Instead we tried to play their game. And it's power. And we lost. You can't go toe-to-toe with them. They can put a beating on you in an awful hurry."

Five games, to be exact. After losing the first two in Oakland by scores of 7-3 and 6-3, the Blue Jays came home to win 7-3 in the first play-off game ever at the SkyDome. Within two days, it was all over and the scores, 6-5 and 4-3, made it seem a lot closer than it really was.

Although the Oakland attack had been devastating, out-gunning the Blue Jays in virtually every category, the Blue Jays did hold leads in the first two games, won the third in a walk and lost the final two by a run apiece.

As Gruber suggests, the Blue Jays failed because they were unable to put together their "little game" in the face of so many howitzers. Oakland, led by Jose Canseco's missle shot into the top deck of the SkyDome in Game 4, out-homered Toronto 7-3.

One need check no further than the infrequency of the big inning to see the folly in refusing to chip away at the Athletics. Only twice during the series did the Blue Jays score more than two runs in one inning, when they counted four and three runs in the third game for a 7-3 victory.

It was disturbing to watch seven months of baseball go down the drain in less than a week. However, what embarrassed the Blue Jays was the humiliating way in which Oakland accomplished its mission.

Principal victim was Ernie Whitt, the last physical reminder of that first crew of Blue Jays to show up at Dunedin at the inaugural spring camp in 1977. What made it especially painful was that the series was to be his farewell performance in Toronto.

Series MVP Rickey Henderson, who early in 1991 surpassed Lou Brock of the St Louis Cardinals as the most prolific base thief in history, spoiled Whitt's farewell bash by setting a play-off record with eight stolen bases. Of absolutely no help to their catcher and his failing reflexes, his battery-mates walked Henderson no fewer than seven times and allowed him six hits in fifteen other plate appearances.

The truth is that Henderson was showing off.

"I don't think Ernie Whitt can throw me out," he told the world after the second game in Oakland. "If they want to win, maybe they should put some other catcher back there."

That was the insult. The injury, as a miffed Whitt saw it, was inflicted when Henderson swiped a base late in the second game with the Athletics ahead by three runs. Henderson got such a jump on Whitt that a throw to second would have been an exercise in futility. Aware that there was no challenge, Henderson came up short on his slide and performed a dainty little jig before he stepped on the bag to make the theft official.

"Hot-dog!" Whitt howled, among other epithets.

Gruber, while admiring the numbers written beneath Henderson's name in the record books, does not admire the style with which they were put there.

"I'll be honest," he says. "I don't know Rickey well

enough to like or dislike him as a person, but I've seen enough to offer an opinion on his style of play. I don't like it. Losing the way we did bothers me, but the incident with Ernie upset me because it was intended to show up a teammate. You're talking about a guy who goes back to Day One with this franchise. A guy who would never go out of his way to make a guy look bad. So when somebody does it to him, he does it to all of us."

If Gruber was miffed at Henderson, he was livid with slugger Dave Parker and his drawn-out stroll around the bases after hitting a home run in the same game. The press was waiting when Gruber stepped, still steaming, out of the shower.

"They asked me what I thought about Parker's style of play. I knew I was being set up, and at first I tried to play Mr Diplomat. They were watching the same game, weren't they? What did they think? They wouldn't let me off the hook. It was time to chase the rabbit.

"Yes, I called him a hot-dog. I wasn't misquoted. What I said next, though, people didn't read in the papers the next day. I said that a lot of teams have to play that way to win. Intimidation. If that's the way the A's have to play, then they should stick to it. Just don't expect to win any popularity contests.

"They can beat me, and like any athlete worth his sweat I hate to lose. Nobody said I have to make like a welcome mat at third base so someone can wipe his feet on me. Treat my teammates that way, like Rickey did to Ernie, and you're doing it to me, too."

Parker responded in kind: "Who's Kelly Gruber to tell me how I'm going to trot? I've got kids his age. You know how long I've been using that trot? My whole career. Is there some kind of school of baseball etiquette or is Kelly Gruber starting one? And if there is one, have there been any graduates?"

What infuriated Gruber, who was all of eleven years old

when Parker broke into the majors with the 1973 Pittsburgh Pirates, was that the old guy's theatrics on the basepaths would not have been tolerated two decades ago. What with the price of talent being so exorbitant today, there is far less emphasis on the "chin music" pitchers play today, but this was not the case when Parker began his climb. One would think, then, that Parker had been schooled in the etiquette a hitter follows after he has planted a pitch beyond the outfield fence.

"Self-preservation," Gruber explains. "When I hit a homer, and I've hit a few, I want to get around those bases in fairly quick time. Not a sprint, maybe, but an efficient trot. The way I figure it, the less a pitcher sees of me, the less he's going to be sore about next time I pick up a bat.

"I'm not out there to show up anybody. It's embarrassing enough for a pitcher when you light him up. Why stuff it up his nose too?"

Parker, completing his seventeenth season in the majors as he entered the play-off against Toronto, had been educated in the "old ways" of country hardball by the time he came to the National League at the age of twenty-two.

"If the game was like it was back then," said Gruber, "he'd get drilled the next time up. Bottom line. To tell you the truth, he's lucky I'm not a pitcher. I'd send him a message. Up and in. Know what I mean? Beat me, that's OK. But walk on me and, no matter how big—or old—I won't accommodate."

Both these breaches of baseball etiquette might well have been put to rest before the first pitch of the following spring had it not been for relief pitcher Dennis Eckersley delivering the coup de grâce in the series-long war of insults.

It began with the discovery late in the series that Eckersley was not playing by the rules. "We had proof, beyond a shadow of a doubt," Gruber swears.

A part-time clubhouse boy working the visitors' dressing room spotted a piece of sandpaper in Eckersley's glove. Eckersley responded to the allegation by saying the glove in question was one he no longer used in official play.

By using sandpaper to rough up a ball and gripping it where it has been scuffed, a pitcher can impart more spin on his pitches and when the aerodynamics go to work on that rough spot the ball moves better as it speeds towards the batter. Such sleight of hand has been employed by pitchers since Abner Doubleday, said to have invented the game 150 years back, was in short pants.

Rarely, however, is the evidence of chicanery so compelling as it was when the Athletics were putting the finishing touches to the Blue Jays in the fall of 1989.

After fourteen seasons in the major leagues, not to mention closing a few nightspots in the early hours, Eckersley's arm has become a delicate thing. Although his fastball retains some of its zip, in latter years he has had to put movement on it and his off-speed pitches to make him more effective.

Manager Cito Gaston decided to raise the "scuffing" issue as the Blue Jays prepared to take their last swings of the season, down 4-1 heading into the bottom of the ninth against the ace reliever.

Gruber was sitting by the bat rack with outfielder George Bell nearby when Gaston came over and told them to watch Eckersley as he completed his eight warm-up pitches before the inning would get under way.

"Cito tells us, 'I think this guy is cheating. Keep your eye on him. I'm going out there.' You could see Eckersley looking over at Cito as he went out to the umpire. Then he goes to his glove and tugs at something. Then he kind of tugs at it again. The whole time he keeps glancing over at Cito and the ump jawing. He throws a couple of pitches, then tugs at his glove again. This time, something falls out. He bends to pick it up off the ground, but misses the mark. He goes down again, grabs a whole handful of dirt this time, then reaches for the belt. He yanks on it, tucks the hand in his pants and starts to throw again.

"I'm not going to sit here and say I know exactly what fell on the ground. I'm sure he'll say it was all show, just messing with our minds. Or maybe even that he performs better with a handful of sand in his jock. I'd like to give him the benefit of the doubt, but that would be a big benefit and an even bigger doubt.

"Credit where credit is due, Eck's a fine pitcher. I'd hate to take anything away from him, but it looked as if he was cheating. If you cheat you have to live with it. If you can live with it, fine. If you have to cheat, though, how can you feel good about beating me?"

As thoroughly frustrated as the Blue Jays were when Eckersley sent them home for the winter a few minutes later—home runs by George Bell and Lloyd Moseby, making his last appearance in a Toronto uniform, made it close at 4-3—all still might have been forgotten had it not been for one unseemly act by Eckersley.

"I never saw it, but all the guys say he shot us the finger," says Gruber. "Gave us the bird. International language for 'Up yours, Jack.' He throws the last pitch, then he throws the bird up to the dugout."

Gruber is too big a boy to have gone into his dressing room, buried his head in his glove and cried. "Obviously, I was down, but I didn't get frantic. It was the chance of a lifetime, and in less than a week we let it get away from us.

"What I did think about was all the guys who started out with me who never got to play in the major leagues. I thought about all the guys who make it but never get a sniff of the playoff experience. I couldn't help but wonder, too, if I'd be one of those guys who never get to the World Series."

It was the second time he had come close.

It was no single play, or misplay, for that matter, that turned the tide against the Toronto Blue Jays in the autumn of 1985.

What buried them in that championship series against the Kansas City Royals, in which they held a commanding 3-to-1 lead at one point, was something as seemingly trivial as a change of attitude. Like a cancer, it spread before Gruber's eyes.

He was privileged to be in a position to watch the spectacle that gripped Toronto that fall from the best seat in the house, the dugout, but he knew well it was not a rookie's place to tell the "real players" they had lost faith in themselves. He had been called up to the Blue Jays after the post-season rosters had been set on the final day of August and would play only if it could be proved that a regular was seriously injured.

Like the mist of cheap champagne that permeated the clubhouse after the East Division was clinched with a day left in the regular season, there was an aura of confidence about the Blue Jays as they trained their sights on the Royals.

"Everybody knew we were going to win it," says Gruber. "Not cockiness, but supreme confidence. 'I'm gonna do my job, buddy. The question is, are you gonna do yours?' Usually, it's two or three guys who have it and the rest catch it. Not this time. Everybody had the feeling. To a man, we knew we were going to the World Series.

"Listen to me using 'us' and 'we'! I wanted to be a part of it so badly."

For a while, as Toronto revelled in the glory about to befall it as a city of champions, the Blue Jays lived up to every one of their expectations.

After Prime Minister Brian Mulroney tossed the "ceremonial first pitch" for the opening game, ace Dave Stieb of the Blue Jays staff trimmed the Royals on three hits over eight innings to underwrite a 6-1 victory. After blowing a 4-3 lead in the ninth inning of Game 2 and allowing the Royals to go ahead 5-4 in the tenth, the Blue Jays clawed their way back to win it 6-5.

Back in Kansas City a couple of nights later, the Blue Jays frittered away a 5-2 lead to lose the third game 6-5, but with Stieb back on the mound and reliever Tom Henke on form Toronto took a commanding lead in the series with a 3-1 victory. All their runs came in the ninth inning.

Outfielder George Bell is among those who will swear that the turning point in the series occurred in the sixth game on a play involving him at third base. Behind 2-0 and stalling as each opportunity presented itself, he tried to go from first base to third on an ordinary single to left fielder Lonnie Smith. It was not a thoughtless move on his part, considering Smith's notoriously weak arm and the need for an explosive play to wake the Blue Jays from their lethargy.

Gruber, on the bench directly in front of the play, was shocked at the call umpire Dale Ford made.

"George is sliding," he says, his mind's eye recalling the play frame by slo-mo frame. "His outstretched toe touches the bag. The bag crawls up his calf to his knee, to his hamstring muscle. He's sitting on the bag when the tag from George Brett comes down. The umpire calls him out.

"I remember, as clearly as if it happened last night, because everyone was so upset. I can still see guys running back into the clubhouse to watch the replays, as if somehow the figure on the screen would make the right call this time.

"Unbelievable. I mean it's like, 'Welcome to the Twilight Zone.' Wow! Ask anybody who was there, and most likely they'll tell you it all started going downhill at that point. The problem is that it shouldn't have. 'These things happen,' you have to tell yourself, but we let it affect us."

Gruber, having had five years to reflect upon the inequities committed by the umpiring crew in that series, sees things in a different light today.

"I don't remember the exact point when the force field went down," he says, "but something strange happened in the middle of the series. Coming out of Kansas City, I remember a lot of people saying things like, 'That's OK, guys. All we got to do is win one more.' It was the first time I had heard that kind of talk. 'All right, all we have to do is win one of the next two.' There was something about it that didn't sit well with me.

"The first four games, we went into each one thinking this was the one we had to win, like each game was the only one we'd ever get to play. Win the opener, we weren't thinking about playing .500 over the next six games to make it to the big one. Win the second game, it wasn't, 'Hey, all we gotta do is go two-for-five.' Every game was do-or-die.

"Now, all of a sudden, we leave Kansas City ahead 3-2 and we're talking about having to win one of the next two. 'If we don't do it tonight, we've got another one for insurance.' One guy even kept saying the Royals deserved to win if they could take two in Toronto.

"It seemed like the attitude changed from how we had to win this one and win it now, to how we had to win the one tomorrow or the next night. Then, all of a sudden, there were no tomorrows, no more next nights."

The Royals won the sixth game 5-3 and on a blustery night at Exhibition Stadium catcher Jim Sundberg broke Toronto's heart. In the sixth inning of the final game his wind-blown pop bounced off the top rung of the fence in right field. His three-base hit, with the bases loaded, put the game and play-offs in the bag.

As low as his teammates were in the dressing room afterward, Gruber failed to plumb their depths because he had been such an outsider throughout the series.

"The only pressure on me was taking infield, batting practice and trying to look involved as I sat on the bench," says Gruber. "I was worried that I might find a way to screw it up."

A joke, of course. Although he also serves who stands and waits, as the saying goes, the process touched off that old tug-of-war in Gruber's mind.

"I wanted to be part of it. You feel like a fifth wheel. It's like, 'I really don't belong here. Maybe I'm not good enough.' You're not there, are you? That's got to tell you something. You can also be optimistic. 'I'm not ready yet, but I will be soon.' Eventually, it builds a hunger in you."

What he fails to remember is that he had been named the International League's top third baseman that year, leading the circuit with 309 chances and 217 assists, and also proving he was putting his hitting game together with 21 home runs.

"It's also an experience you can use later. Well, I've seen a real, live one. It's not fantasy. Now I know how intense it has to be for a winner."

He remembers taking his place at his locker in the dressing room, and like many of his teammates, turning his back on the horde of newspaper stiffs pouring through the clubhouse door.

"I was going to mind my own business," Gruber remembers thinking. "I was not going to be looking into too many eyes or gawking around the room. Not only did I think I was out of place being there, but now I felt like I might be intruding on their grief."

If he took home anything that 1985 season, it was the bit he did for the cause in a game against the Milwaukee Brewers one long Saturday afternoon at Exhibition Stadium.

In typical fashion for Bobby Cox, a National League manager at heart, he had used twenty-one players that day—including George Bell at third base—by the time Gruber put away a 2-1 victory in the bottom of the fourteenth inning.

Gruber, who came on to play third base in the ninth inning of the four-hour fourteen-minute marathon, was hitless in his first two at-bats before he came to the plate. The bases were loaded with one out in the fourteenth. On an 0-2 pitch from Danny Darwin, he dumped a single in right field to score Bell and send the faithful home to a late dinner.

It would be Gruber's only RBI of the season, the third of his career in the majors, but it was a winner in a game the Blue Jays were desperate to win. He liked the feeling. He wanted more.

CHAPTER 9

 THE BRASS RINGS

And then there were two.

Garth Iorg, one of three Blue Jays remaining from the motley crew of ballplayers who showed up for work the first day of that first spring camp in 1977, was gone.

And Kelly Gruber thinks it was something he said that sent him on his way. He really had no choice.

It went back to one day early in 1988 when, out of the baseball blue, executive V-P Pat Gillick and field manager Jimy Williams telephoned Gruber at his home in Austin.

"We're coming down to see you," said Williams. "We need to have a talk."

No doubt.

In their second campaign under Williams' guidance, the Blue Jays had finished a dismaying second, two games behind the Detroit Tigers, in a division race that looked to all the world to have been locked up with a week left in the season.

There was not a soul in Toronto who parked his frozen buns in Exhibition Stadium that year who does not know the details by heart. Ahead by 3½ games after winning three of four from Detroit on the last stand at Toronto, they were ahead going into the ninth inning of the fourth game when a home run by Kirk Gibson stoked the dwindling fires in the Tigers' eyes. Sound familiar?

They won in extra innings.

Still, the Blue Jays could have put it away on a three-game home stand against Milwaukee. They lost each of them by a single run. Despite marvellous pitching performances by Jimmy Key and Mike Flanagan, acquired late in the season from Baltimore for the pennant drive, they also managed to lose three more in Tiger Stadium. All by a single run.

There were excuses. There always are.

A hard block at second base by Bill Madlock of the Tigers dumped shortstop Tony Fernandez out of the line-up during the series at Toronto. Catcher Ernie Whitt, his cracked ribs swaddled in surgical tape, could not lift a bat for the final charge.

As alibis go, they were not good enough. When the going gets tough, the old saw goes, the tough get going. The Blue Jays folded in the crunch.

For all of the disappointments, the Blue Jays had reason to believe the future was theirs. The pitching, anchored by Key who finished second in Cy Young balloting with a 17-6 (2.67 ERA), was sound. Dave Stieb, rebounding from a woeful 1986 season, showed signs of his former dominating self with a 13-9 (4.09) mark, and reliever Dave Wells came up late in the season to set up a one-two punch with Tom Henke in the bullpen.

MVP George Bell would be coming off a career year of 47 home runs and 134 RBIs and the club's tall thinkers thought they could eliminate the defensive liabilities in left field by selling him on a career as a designated hitter. Centre fielder Lloyd Moseby had swatted 26 home runs (96 RBIs) and right fielder Jesse Barfield had clubbed 28 (84 RBIs). Together they had contributed mightily to the 215 homers the Blue Jays had hit, the sixth highest team total in the game's history.

At first base, part-timer Fred McGriff had hit 20 home runs and was ready to replace the revered Willie Upshaw. Fernandez, a .322 hitter, would be back at short to anchor the infield and keep platooning second baseman Manuel Lee and Nelson Liriano in line. With Ernie Whitt, the catching was ancient, but could hold out for another season while his heir apparent, Pat Borders, learned his trade.

Now if only they could get the situation at third base straightened out. It does not require a degree in advanced mathematics to figure that in Gruber, Iorg and Rance Mulliniks, the Blue Jays had one too many third basemen. While Mulliniks held up his end in 1987, batting .310 with 11 home runs in limited action, Iorg was a bust at .210 in a utility role while Gruber showed little of his heralded promise with a .235 batting average and a dozen homers. It was only a minor improvement over 1986 when he hit a dismal .196 with five home runs and 15 RBIs.

If there was anything remarkable about Gruber's first full year in the majors—and it was to become an acute source of embarrassment to him—it was the home run he hit at Exhibition Stadium one fog-bound night in the middle of June off left-hander Dick Scherrer of the Detroit Tigers.

"I had two strikes on me, so I was protecting the plate. Anything close and I would be swinging. He threw me a slider, and since I didn't take a healthy cut I didn't hit it as well as I'd like.

"Up it went. Kirk Gibson started loping toward the infield and then, all of a sudden, he throws up his hands. You could tell he'd lost it in the fog. It landed about thirty feet to his right and started rolling to the wall in centre field.

"Cliff Johnson, one of the runners on base, was there to meet me at the plate. All that night, all that year, Johnson wouldn't let me forget the thundering home run I had hit in the fog.

"'Foggie,' he called me. And CJ's voice carries. 'Foggie.' It became a nickname I couldn't shake. Because it fit in with the thoughts of a number of teammates, no need to mention names, it became a millstone around my neck. 'Foggie.'"

For Gruber, it was just one more boulder to go around on the hill he was climbing.

"Just staying up a full year was an experience," he says. "It was a test. Exciting, nerve-wracking, the kind of stuff that sets a nest of butterflies in your stomach at times. As much as I sat on the bench, there wasn't a whole lot of control I could exert in the situation.

"For whatever the reason, some of it being my fault, I wasn't given much opportunity. I had to keep telling myself things would get better, that I could prove I was every bit the ballplayer I thought I was. I didn't hammer on the manager's door, run my mouth and tell him what a fool he was for not putting me out there every day.

"Sure, there were times when I was afraid it might not happen at all. Everybody has doubts. Fear of failure. Negative thoughts. The key is to drown the negatives out with the positives. I've got to be optimistic, constantly turning the pages. 'One day's over. One game's out of the way. Turn the page. Sink or swim.'

"Hitting .196 was nothing I looked forward to happening, but that's life in the big city. I kept thinking the opportunity would come, that I'd take advantage of it and make a home here."

It was this very question that had brought Gillick and Williams to Austin a couple of months before the 1988 spring camp opened. For Gruber, it would prove to be a particularly stomach-churning day.

Things started going wrong about the time the plane carrying Gruber's bosses touched down at the Robert

Mueller Civic Airport in Austin.

Gruber, cutting his sense of punctuality on the fine side, left himself fifteen minutes to make the ten-minute drive to the airport and, somewhere along the way, pump five dollars worth of gas into the pickup truck that would carry the party to a downtown hotel.

"Just my luck," says Gruber, "I run into traffic. It's sweatin' time. My God, not only am I not going to get there on time, but I might not even get there at all!

"If I do make it, am I as good as telling them what a dope I am because I have to stop for gas on the way to the hotel where we're having this meeting? Do I take a chance of running out on the way there and look like twice the fool? It's stress enough that they're coming down to see me, now I'm even more nervous because I might not be there to meet them.

"'Oops, sorry, boss. Was that ten o'clock Toronto time or ten o'clock Texas time?'

"I finally get there and Pat Gillick is tapping his cowboy boots waiting for me. Jimy's face is a mask, which it usually is, but his eyes are giving him away. Or maybe it's all in my imagination.

"Anyway, I pick 'em up, Pat in the front and Jimy in the back, and I can tell right away they're not too cheery. All morning I've been feeling my ears burning and I'm betting right about now, as I'm praying for a gas station to jump up and bite me, that they've been talking about me. I fake something about the needle on the fuel gauge acting up and, better safe than sorry, we'd better pop into this here service station to fuel up."

After checking into their hotel room, the three men repaired to the restaurant to eat lunch and discuss issues. Gruber ordered chicken fajitas, one of his favourite Tex-Mex dishes. Accompanying it was a molcajete salad with guacamole, sour cream and pico de gallo. There was also a stack of flour tortillas. All of it, Gruber was thinking, quite tasty. Maybe it wouldn't be such a bad morning after all. Before the food arrived, though, he had lost his appetite.

"They begin to say things like, 'Do you love the game of baseball, like it, or can you take it or leave it?' 'Where are your priorities?' 'The success we've been looking for, you haven't shown it.'"

All Gruber's doubts, nourished over the seasons, bubbled to the surface.

"With some players, and I'm referring to myself here, their mind is their worst enemy," he says. "Not so much that you'd stop believing in yourself, but you get these vague notions that you might be sitting in this hotel, staring at an untouched dish of fajitas for a very good reason. After all that time of trying to tell yourself you belong, little notions begin to creep in that maybe you're not good enough. It's a mind game and sometimes it can play dirty tricks on you.

"All this time that I'm fumbling for answers, there are thoughts running through my head. 'If I got a chance to play more than once every three days, maybe I could show you people something. Shining the bench, I didn't even feel like I was part of the puzzle, much less want to come out and get in some extra work. I just didn't feel right. I'm not the type who can sit and wait and think up all kinds of scary thoughts. I have to be in the heat of the battle.'

"I guess you'd call me a creature of reaction. Hit a ball at me, show me a hole in the line, I know what to do. Give me a couple of seconds to think about things and odds are I'll come up with an answer when the ball's in left field or I'm under a pile of tacklers.

"Do I care about the game of baseball? Do I love it? Just like it? Take it or leave it alone?"

Gruber, thinking discretion the better part of valour, kept his mouth shut. The fajitas grew cold.

"Frankly, I thought they were asking some pretty stupid

questions," Gruber says now. "I knew what my priorities were. I hope I'm not insulting them when I say so, but I felt their questions were an insult. Hell, I was no party animal. I might not show up at noon for a game at 7:35 that night, but that didn't mean I didn't want to play as badly as the next guy.

"'You gotta be kidding me. I don't like this game? If I didn't like it, I wouldn't be in it. How could you even think that? Man, are you serious? I picked it over football and, like I said earlier, football ranks right up there with going to church in Texas.' I wanted to puke."

It occurs to him now that Gillick and Williams, no strangers to psychological strategies, were trying to light a fire under him.

"They could see I was getting a little better. It's going to take this guy a little more time, but who's to say it wouldn't have happened earlier if I'd been in there right away? Instead of putting me in and then letting me think about what I'd done for a week before I played again. It's something they'd done with a whole lot of other guys."

As Lloyd Moseby once pointed out, only somewhat in jest, the makeup of those early Blue Jays teams was decided largely on the basis of "the first twenty-five guys who smiled." The results were such, too, that such a selection method might not have been all that amiss.

All that changed in the era of BobbyBall. When Bobby Cox took over the Blue Jays in 1982 and guided them out of last place in the AL East for the first time, he did so by relying heavily on a platoon system. Success being the narcotic that it is, platoon became a familiar word for Blue Jays' followers until the 1990 season when, with some exceptions, Cito Gaston tended to a set line-up.

Among those whose playing time was particularly affected by the strategy back then were Mulliniks, Iorg and Gruber.

"What I did tell Pat and Jimy that day was that I didn't

think I could be the kind of player they expected me to be if I got to play once a week. I'm saying it now. I've said it before. I can't do it. I have to play every day or as damned near it as possible.

"I went home and really started to think, 'Where'm I going? What'm I doing? Why am I here?'"

As Gruber recalls, it was not long afterward that Iorg became a closed chapter in the history of the Blue Jays. Now, from that first band of upstarts who gathered at Dunedin in the spring of 1977, only battery-mates Jim Clancy and Ernie Whitt were left.

"I remember how open and encouraging Rance and Garth had been with me in those shaky days of my first spring camp. I felt badly that it was over for Garth, worse still because it soon became clear that no other team was going to pick him up.

"I think Garth was released because of that little talk. For him, it was over. For me, it was beginning. I'd be getting more playing time. It might be a platoon, but at least it wouldn't be a three-man platoon. It's a start. It's the right direction."

The brass, having made the move, sent one of their most trusted emissaries to ensure that Gruber reported to camp with, as the old-timers say, "his mind right."

Al LaMacchia, who had scouted Gruber during his high school days at Austin, arranged to meet him at a family outing in San Marcos, which is about halfway between Austin and LaMacchia's home in San Antonio. Gruber, accompanied by his wife of eighteen months, his parents and sister Claudia, was there to attend a Southwest Texas State University game involving Gruber's younger brother, David.

"The club had told me the year before that they were a little upset with some things," says LaMacchia. "They asked me to talk with him about a couple of things."

Examples?

"For example, I say to him, 'You're asked to come out at three o'clock for batting practice. You show up with five minutes to go, get into your clothes and make it out there with a second to spare. What does that say about your attitude? It tells them you're there because you have to be there.'

"I told him he should be there at 2:30, in uniform, on the field, waiting for them. 'If you're asked to take 50 ground balls, ask for 75. If you're asked to take 50 swings, tell 'em you want 75.'"

"I said, 'If that guy you decked back in high school was to swipe your money today, I don't know how you'd react. Back then, you dropped him. I don't know what you'd do today.' I told him I wondered if he'd lost that edge."

LaMacchia's trump card was sitting nearby.

"The only way you're going to make a living for that young lady there," said LaMacchia, nodding to Gruber's wife, "is to go out on the field and perform. Play up to your capabilities.

"Baseball is drive. Without it, no matter how talented, how else are you going to succeed?"

With ten days left in spring training, as is the custom with the Blue Jays, the top scouts and executives gathered in Dunedin to discuss the shape the team should take to begin the season.

"I asked how he was doing," said LaMacchia. "They said he was working his tail off."

Often they don't, but this time the figures said it all.

After that dismal 1987 campaign in which he hit .235 with 12 home runs and 36 RBIs in 341 at-bats, he wound up the 1988 drive with a .278 average, 16 home runs, 81 RBIs and, most important, took part in 158 of the club's 162 games.

At last, he had become an everyday player.

CHAPTER 10

 FIELDER'S CHOICE

See ball. Catch ball. Throw ball. Sounds simple enough.

Even George Bell, whose hands of stone twice made him the American League's most errant left fielder, had these three golden rules of defence down pat after a couple of seasons of slamming into the fences at Exhibition Stadium.

The problem with Bell, not to mention dozens of other offenders afield on whom the Blue Jays have dumped tons of money through the years, was that he knew precious little about the fourth step in the process. Far too few in the major leagues know what to do with the ball once they pluck it from the pockets of their gloves.

And all it requires, says Kelly Gruber, is a little thinking.

"It's not done enough," he said one afternoon in August 1990 after a failed cut-off throw cost the Blue Jays a victory they would sorely need in the first week of October. "'Where the heck'm I going with the ball?' It doesn't take a rocket scientist to figure it out."

The play to which Gruber refers occurred with two out in the late innings of a game against the Milwaukee

Brewers. Off with the crack of the bat that bounced a single through the infield, the runner on second base could have trotted home before any throw from the outfield reached the plate. Even in such situations, there is no harm in making such a throw, so long as it remains low enough that the cut-off man—in this case, second baseman Manuel Lee—is able to "cut it off" and guard second base from the advancing hitter.

The throw, a bullet, sailed over Lee's head and was fielded on the fly by catcher Pat Borders about ten feet up the third base line.

"Instead of holding the guy to a single and the RBI," Gruber groused, "now there's a run in and another at second waiting to come home on another single."

You can guess what happened next.

"Physical mistakes are going to happen; there's nothing that can be done about it until they teach a machine to play the game," says Gruber, who led the club with nineteen errors last season. League managers and coaches voted him a Gold Glove for fielding excellence anyway. "Mental errors? Ridiculous. They're going to happen, sure, but there'd be far fewer if players did a little more thinking."

To a large extent, a player can put his brain into neutral when the opposing team has no runners on base. "My, what a lovely pair of earrings on that young lady in the second row behind the enemy's dugout . . . The hitter's a righty, Stieb's slider is on the money, I'll give him a little more of the line. Who's that loudmouth in Section 8? I can smell his bad breath from here! Oops, Stieb's going to change up . . . Geez, in the gap, a double for sure. Go to the bag. Wait for the throw."

Simple enough. Where it gets complicated—still, not the stuff to make Werner von Braun break out in a sweat—is when runners are already on base.

"One out, men on first and third, the guy at the plate's a

flier," Gruber says, setting up a situation that begets a series of responses. "Hard grounder, that's simple. Around the horn, 5-4-3 on your scorecard, for the double play. Line drive, I'm looking to double off the runner at first because the guy on third freezes on anything in the air until it gets through the infield. Soft grounder or hit-and-run, I know I'm not going to get two. Look the guy at third back to the base if I can. Make the force at second if I can. At the very least, get one. At the worst, there's two out and two runs in scoring position, but it's better than bases full and one out because I miscalculated at second and the hitter beat the relay to first. A grounder in the hole takes me away from the plate, so I have to go to second and hope for the double play. Smash down the line, I take what I can get, which just might be the guy at first.

"Once you've programmed all these possibilities—it's called successful visualization—the play becomes a matter of doing it. Who's got time to think after you've just made a three-point landing and you're trying to find a ball in the bushel of dirt you just scooped up with your glove? It has to be automatic or it doesn't get done."

As well as these reactions, which mutate into an entirely different set of defensive responsibilities in the event of a fly ball or a hit to the outfield, Gruber also might shade a player close to the line or more towards the shortstop, depending on the pitcher and how well he might be performing that given night.

In fact, one of the primary rules of defence is to key it to the pivotal point of the action—the man on the mound.

"Since they know what they've got and where they intend to throw it, I always ask the pitcher where he wants me to play each hitter. I take up my position, look at him and, if he wants me to move, he gives me a look. If I'm a little doubtful, I'll go over and ask him before the guy comes to the plate.

"Some want you closer to the line. Some want you in

the hole. Some change their minds on a given pitch or count.

"With the count 2-and-1, for instance, odds are heavy he'll see a strike—a fat one, if the pitcher makes the slightest mistake—so he's got his mind on ramming it down your throat. Most guys, they get a pitcher in the hole, they're looking for a fastball inside. If they're right-handers, which most are, a third baseman whose family isn't complete would be wise to make sure his cup is sitting right.

"Now, with the count 1-and-2, a hitter wants to stay 'on' the ball. At the very least he wants to get a piece of it, even if it's only a foul ball to avoid the strike-out. If he hits it, even if it isn't as hard as he'd like, it might sneak through somewhere for a hit. Knowing a hitter will be holding back that split second, to make sure he isn't fooled on a pitch, means I'll play a little more toward shortstop.

"What you have to watch for, and it happens often enough, are the pure pull-hitters. Mostly young guys, too. Pitch 'em any way you want, they're aiming for the fences. They have one swing. Pull, pull, pull. There are smart hitters, too, who shoot for whatever you leave."

There are tall thinkers in the game today who would scoff at the notion of a hitter being so precise that he could find such holes in an opponent's defence, but the roots of such a tradition are buried at least a century back. Wee Willie Keeler, all of 140 pounds, had a lifetime batting average of .343 when he retired in 1910 after nineteen seasons with New York teams in either major league. Amazingly, more than 2,500 of the 2,947 hits he struck in 8,585 at-bats were singles. The secret of his success, in an era when defence was king, has been made immortal in a line he uttered to explain it: "Hit 'em where they ain't."

For all the foregoing, Gruber will admit that the most difficult play to master is knowing when not to make a play. Over the years, he thinks, it would have saved him many debits in the fielding columns.

Most of his errors, as those who brought along the lids of their garbage cans to games in Batavia and Waterloo well knew, have been of the throwing variety. An overpowering and recalcitrant arm was his chief problem in the early going, and it was compounded by haste to put things right when they went wrong.

"I have what they call a 'live' arm," he says. "At times, the ball would plain get away on me. Whether it would be a different release point or gripping the seams of the ball a different way, the effect would be the same: Sink. Ride. Take off. 'Get those garbage lids up, folks. Here it comes.'

"A lot of times, it happened after I got up out of the dirt, after I'd taken a shot off the body, and hurried the throw. What I should have done was eaten the ball, but being young I never knew when to concede. Or a bunt play, when I didn't have a prayer to get the guy, I'd come up throwing anyway. I never assumed anything.

"Sometimes the hardest part of your education would be knowing when to pull the plug. It goes against everything you've learned, everything they tell you about never giving up, but it's one time you've got to do it. I still haven't mastered it."

The foundations of modern-day defence are laid before each new series when the team's coaches go over the charts: every hit and where it landed, every out and where it was made in previous games against that opponent. During the game, particularly when a pinch-hitter comes up, one of the coaches in the dugout might be shifting the defence according to the charts kept within arm's length on the bench.

One of the more debatable tenets of defence is the one that insists the lines at third and first be protected late in the game against the hit for extra bases, but conceding the single. While it prevents the big knock, its detractors argue, it allows easier access to the bases in the late going.

Gruber, while reserving the right to make exceptions, generally agrees with the philosophy of preventing the extra-base hits in the early and late going. He is not alone; so does the greatest third baseman in the history of the game.

"One of these days I'm going to get my courage up and ask him to give me a couple of hours of his time, just to jaw about the game, but Brooks Robinson tended to guard the line in the first three and last three innings of a game."

Robinson, whose 2,870 games over twenty-three seasons with the Baltimore Orioles are at least 450 more than any other man who played at third, figured the extra-base hit during these innings played a more pivotal role in the outcome of a game than if it happened in the fourth, fifth or sixth inning. Since no statistics are kept to do justice to the view, Robinson's ideas about giving up a big hit in the early going obviously are rooted in the psychological effects of drawing first blood. Later in the game, when time is short, the imperative to guard a lead or keep the advantage to a minimum is equally obvious.

The Blue Jays' record in this area, arguably the best in the major leagues last season, is borne out by their success rate when leading the game after seven innings of play. They retained the lead on all but two of 77 such occasions, compared with the 65-7 record of the division-winning Boston Red Sox. On the other hand, the difference between winning and losing the race also can be traced to the team's success rate in games decided by a single run. Boston was 31-22, Toronto 23-27.

"I agree with guarding the line late in the game," says Gruber, although he describes the strategy as frustrating in that it allows a hitter a certain intrinsic advantage— "more space to the shortstop side, while cutting down the likelihood of something going down the line."

Shading towards the line is also a tactic he will employ with two outs and a runner on first base.

"There's no way I'd want to give up a two-out double down the line," says Gruber. "A guy with any kind of speed, he could make it home easy. The math is simple. That double scores the run that beats us. Otherwise it takes two singles. Since team batting averages range from about .240 to .270, you figure the hitter has a 1-in-4 chance of getting a hit. Facing those odds twice, obviously, is better than doing it once.

"There are a lot of times with a guy on first, especially if a pitcher wants me to shade toward shortstop, that I'll go over and warn him that this guy is likely to take us down the line. 'Like, pal, you've got this guy at first, two outs. Make 'em get two hits, maybe even three, to beat us.' Unless he's got a very good reason, he'll generally agree with what you have to say. Which proves that pitchers aren't as slow as they sometimes look."

Having covered the forgotten rule of fielding—what to do with a ball once one has gained possession of it—it is perhaps in order to cover the basic tenets of this athletic art.

According to Gruber, the first rule of fielding is balance.

"Basically, you can compare it to guarding a man in basketball. You have to be balanced. Have your feet far enough apart so that you can go in either direction to field a ball.

"Second, as much as possible, stay in front of it so that if you box up the play it will bounce off your body and you can make up for the mistake.

"Third, follow it all the way into your glove. The temptation is to pull your head off it, something you'll see kids do in the school yard, because you're afraid it will take a bad hop and take your lips off. The truth is, if you keep your eye on it, you'll have a split second to deflect it with the glove or at least move your head out of the way. If you're not looking, how are you going to stop a bad bounce from breaking the cheek or jawbone?

"Fourth, when you're catching a grounder, treat it as if it's an egg. Coddle it. That's what they mean when they say a fielder's got soft hands. He's afraid that if he stabs at that ball, he's gonna break it. Time it so that as soon as the ball hits leather, whether it's a lazy bounder or a one-hop shot down the line, your hand gives just that little bit to make sure nothing bounces out of the glove."

As it is in anything that involves movement, from playing baseball to ballroom dancing, footwork is vital. And, as it is with the sweeter of these two sciences, the key to success is in observation, first, and then practice.

"There are all kinds of theories on footwork," says Gruber, "just like there is in what stance you should use at the plate. There's a crow-hop some guys use to get themselves in motion as soon as the ball is pitched. Some guys use a crossover step on their first move toward a ball, rather than starting with a half-step of the foot on the same side as the ball. The theory is that the crossover not only gains a few inches on that first step but also generates more thrust at the start of the chase. You can also take 'routes' to get to the ball, so that you're facing the target base the instant you gather up a grounder.

"The trick is to find what's most comfortable. It might not be a textbook example of the way things are done, but what you've got to remember is that they don't allow textbooks on the field. All they give you to protect yourself is a glove."

Like most major leaguers, Gruber is as close to his glove—and as fussy about it—as The Lone Ranger was to his saddle.

"Your bat and your glove, they're the tools of the trade. They're just as important to you as a wrench and a pair of rubber boots are to a plumber. Even though the bat makes the big money, a ballplayer tends to cherish his glove more. On a rough afternoon, you can go through a couple of bats, so what's the point of getting close?

"A glove, that's different. Every day, seven months out of the year, it's a part of your life. Put it this way. Try to think of something else you wear more often, even more than your favourite pair of cowboy boots. You can't, right?"

Great pains are taken in the choosing and maintenance of the glove. Gruber's own "best friend," a four-finger Easton model, has an open web that enables him to track pop flies while using his glove to shade his eyes from the sun or stadium lights. In the interests of saving time on the double play, shortstops and second basemen place a premium on being able to get a quick grip on the ball and a smaller glove makes that easier. Since the batted ball gets to Gruber quickly, he can afford a bigger glove to flag it down.

"Working it in" begins with a preliminary pounding of the glove with a baseball bat, in much the same fashion that a fencepost is rammed into a hole. There are few sights more curious to the casual observer than a player lovingly lathering his mitt with shaving cream after he has pounded the bejammers out of it with a Louisville Slugger.

"Shave cream is the best because it's light," says Gruber, "and it's got the kind of lotion in it that keeps your face soft after you've run a razor-blade over it. One of the things I won't use on it is oil. It tends to make a glove heavy."

It can take upward of a season of working in a glove during afternoon fielding practice to prepare it for use in a game. Inevitably, there is a steady rotation of them throughout a player's career: one in waiting, one for practice, one for the real thing.

There are always exceptions, one of the most extreme cases involving the former Blue Jays manager, Bobby Cox. Cox, who played third base with the New York Yankees for two seasons in the late 1960s, forever fought the battle of the bulge that afflicts most former athletes in their later years. As a consequence, he regularly pitched batting practice to his troops in Toronto, and after undergoing surgery on both knees over the winter of 1990–91 he was at it again with the Atlanta Braves. Close by was the glove he had brought to the pros with him thirty seasons ago. During his time in Toronto it had become a rag. A cobbler acquaintance of his completed a surgical overhaul on it in one off-season. With that life-saving miracle, the shoemaker became Cox's friend for life.

In somewhat the same vein, Gruber will consign a glove to the trash heap only when it is in tatters—although a different fate awaits the one he used in his Gold Glove season of 1990. It will be bronzed.

The price of gold being what it is, what did you expect?

CHAPTER 11

 TO HAVE AND HAVE NOT

The big myth about spring training, the one that flowers each March with sports page photos of yawning ballplayers doing their morning stretches on the outfield grass of tiny, perfect, sun-drenched ballparks, is that it is a time free of care.

Like all myths, there is much in this that is true. Like all myths, there is much in it that is false.

For the established player in the middle years of a contract that guarantees he need never work a day in his baseball after-life, it is indeed the best of times. All the others, from the fuzzy-cheeked rookie chasing the visions of boyhood to the old vet kidding himself that one more season can be wrung from his aching joints, are going through their own very private hells.

Kelly Gruber, who became a member of baseball's rich and famous in the spring of 1991 when he signed a three-year contract for $11 million, knows well what it means to be a have-not.

For a rookie in such circumstances, even if he is privileged to have been a top draft pick, the penalty is often paid in social terms.

"You saw three types of big leaguer," Gruber says of his first trip to camp at Hy Corbett Field in Tucson, Arizona, with the Cleveland Indians.

"The first doesn't want any part of you. Wouldn't give you the time of day that you break for lunch. You're a rookie. Don't forget it. He might say two sentences to you all spring and never look you in the eye when he does it. They even might be for your benefit, but they're said in such a way that anybody who happens to be nearby—and there always is—knows you've been put in your place.

"Then there are the middle-of-the-roaders. As time goes by, they might get a little more personable with you, but it doesn't amount to much more than saying 'How ya doin'?' 'Nice catch today.' 'See ya later.' From Day One till you break camp, you'd never learn the guy's home town if you didn't have a program.

"The third guy is your straight-shooter. You say hello. You kid around. You feel okay going up to them, no matter where they stand in terms of their success, your success."

A guy like Rick Manning.

"A good kid, a hard worker," Manning, a broadcaster now, recalls before the Blue Jays take the field for a game at Municipal Stadium in Cleveland. "We tried to corrupt him and we were making headway, too. We would have done it for sure, but we just didn't have the time. First thing you knew, he was off to Toronto. Did his career a lot of good, but he sure missed a lot of fun with us."

He chuckles. It is a line of patter he used often while working games for his old club and Gruber was in the process of overhauling Wade Boggs of Boston as the premier third baseman in the American League.

"Gruber was a top draft pick," says Manning, slightly more serious now. "You knew he had the potential. That's not what gets you from there to here to stay, though. Lots of Number Ones, they never make it. They have to get the chance to play every day. Then they have to jump on it. Hard. Believing in yourself is a big part of it. If you don't, and there are lots who don't, you're buried.

"You could tell the way this kid carried himself, the way he walked around, that he had that confidence in himself."

It would not have raised an eyebrow had Manning, entering his eighth season as an outfielder with the Indians when the Tribe opened its 1982 camp in Tucson, brushed Gruber aside at their first meetings.

Another veteran who was not too big to welcome youth to the fold was first baseman Mike Hargrove, now a coach with the club.

Hargrove, thirty-two years old and entering his ninth term in the majors, had reason to fear the up-and-comers. Although he had hit .317 in 94 games during the strike-shortened 1981 season, leading the league in on-base percentage at .432, any pretense of power was long gone.

Since baseball wisdom dictates big guns be stationed at the corners of the infield and considering the penurious ways of the Cleveland club at the time, Hargrove's future was cloudy at best. He lasted another four seasons, fooling the experts and the Indians' perennial youth movement, and retired at the ripe old age of thirty-six.

"I remember him calling me Little Tex," Gruber says. "To be as far from home as I was and find someone who had the time of day for me, that gave me a sense of security, a little blanket for comfort when things were going wrong."

And going wrong they were. Gruber, in his third year as a pro, had yet to find himself. Hell, he was deep in the woods and didn't know north from south.

Youth being as arrogant as it is, it stunned Gruber that he had not burned a vapour trail through the minors and nailed down at least a part-time job in the majors two years after he signed for that $100,000 with the Indians.

"Once you get involved, once you start to put the pieces of the puzzle together, you start to learn there's more to it than getting your laces tied right, trotting out to third base and waiting for the ump to yell 'Play ball.' I was starting to learn there was a whole other game within the game, so to speak. Call me a dunce, if you like, but it was something that had never even dawned on me.

"In the beginning, at the bottom of the ladder, the first question you ask is if you belong. That's when you have to convince yourself you're good enough. 'Don't get infatuated with th is game. Don't be awestruck. I belong.'

"You see the same thing at every step of the way. I see it now in kids who come up here and get their first at-bat in the majors. They're in awe. It's tough enough to dig in at the plate, wait for Roger Clemens to air-mail his fastball and then try to put that tree trunk across your shoulder on it. If you're out there watching a legend, if you're fascinated by him, you'll have a shady seat in the dugout in no time at all.

"To my mind, there are two reasons for it when some young phenom takes the quick route to the majors. First, he's got talent. But we all have the talent, don't we? More important, he can apply it to the task at hand. Now that's something not all of us can do right off the bat. Me among them.

"Looking back on that first spring camp, I realize I had a lot of physical tools, and until that time they made up for whatever else I might have been lacking. Wherever I had been, I had been a standout. I can't say, looking back on it now, that I was quick to make the most of those tools. I often wonder today how much quicker I would have arrived if I had applied myself a little harder.

"At the time, I figured I'd passed the other tests. Yes, I belong here. Yes, I'm capable of staying here. The question I was only beginning to ask had to do with my 'game plan.' 'How will this guy try to get me out? What pitch will he use in this situation, in that situation? Fastball? Off-speed? In or away?' Then it turns into making adjustments. 'They're going to pound me inside because last time I tore 'em up outside.' As soon as I catch a couple of hints that they're changing their approach, then I have to change mine. Adjust and attack, that's all this game is."

Among those who remember him vividly from those early days is the Indians' clubhouse chief, Cy Buynak, who has been keeping the tepee tidy since 1965.

"He's a young kid, first time in the big leagues, wondering what's happening," Buynak recalled during the Blue Jays' last visit to Cleveland in 1990. "He was just happy to be there, happy to have a uniform. You could tell he was lost. It was written all over him. A lot of our drafts, they come out of college, so they've been away from home for a while. You could tell it was his first time. He was awful quiet, worked awful hard. Real polite. That's why I liked him.

"He was a baby when we lost him to Toronto. It's a shame. The front office, they just tried to sneak him through that draft. You can only guess where we'd be today if we kept him."

Buynak has evidently refused to snip the ties. Gruber reported for work that day, a customary five minutes before he had to be dressed and on the field for batting practice. Since he found his socks, sanitary hose and uniform pants in knots, Gruber punched the clock five minutes late—good for $25 in Kangaroo Court fines, Chief Justice Dave Stieb presiding.

"Lucky he didn't bring his shower shoes," said Buynak. "I was going to nail them to the floor."

For all of the foregoing, perhaps the best piece of advice that ever came Gruber's way came from the veteran Bake McBride, at the time playing out the string with the Indians. Certainly the timing was crucial.

Traded by the Philadelphia Phillies for pitcher Sid Monge six weeks before the 1982 camp opened, McBride was leaving one of the best teams in the majors for one of the worst. The Phillies, who had won the 1980 World Series, lost a play-off for the National League East title to the Montreal Expos the next season and were picked to be contenders again in 1982. As ever, the Indians were looking for a way out of the swamp.

Gruber first met McBride at the batting cage, where the younger player was trying to impress his bosses by ramming every slo-mo fastball over the fences in left and centre fields. The problem was that most of them were travelling no further than five feet—into the netting above his head.

Suddenly, a voice from the side of the cage . . .

"Quiet as can be, so nobody but you and him could hear it," Gruber recalls, "McBride said, 'You can't hit what you can't see.' Obviously I'd been pulling my head up a fraction of a second before I made contact with the ball. It was the simplest piece of advice ever given to me, and the one that has stuck with me the longest. To this day, I re- mind myself—and a lot of rookies, too—that you can't hit what you can't see.

"Now I'm not saying a lot of guys won't help you out in baseball, but a lot of them do it in a way so that everybody knows they're doing it. 'Yeah, I'm going to help you. Yeah, I want to help you. But, yeah, I'm going to show you up, too, so everybody knows what a smart guy I am.'

"You eat it. You might not like it, but you eat it."

McBride's decency also spilled into the clubhouse. In the spring of 1983, the Indians management and Cleveland press were making much of shortstop Julio Franco—rightly so, as his first full season in the major leagues turned out—who had been a key figure in the five-for-one trade the previous December that sent out- fielder Von Hayes to Philadelphia. Franco, at twenty-two, six months older than Gruber, had made his way smartly up the ladder, never batting less than .300 during five preparatory seasons in the Phillies' farm system.

"Nobody was talking to me," says Gruber, who was ticketed to spend the 1983 season at Buffalo in the Eastern League. "Who was Kelly Gruber? A guy who hit .243 at Chattanooga, made 44 errors and was about to be switched from shortstop to third base."

The player on the fringe notices one result of his performance in a particularly tangible way. Freebies.

Naturally, manufacturers of baseball equipment are keen to see players using their wares. With brand names plastered all over bats, gloves and helmets, the television cameras provide free advertising every time they home in on a player.

In order to keep promotion costs at a minimum, the equipment firms adopt a blanket policy of signing up all the warm bodies early in their pro careers. While the money might be viewed as a pittance ten years down the line when a survivor of the climb strikes it rich, it might amount to a much-needed month's salary when the kid cuts the deal in the minors. Thereafter, depending on a player's success, the manufacturer supplies their walking billboard with all the tools of his trade. First draft or otherwise, failure to impress the bosses in the minors means the freebies are kept to a minimum.

"Julio was getting all kinds of gloves tossed at him," says Gruber. "People fairly drooled when they talked to him. The shoes were stacked, pair upon pair, in his locker. Really, I wasn't jealous. What I was, though, was in need. I had a couple pair of spikes, one extra glove and three or four pair of batting gloves. I'm not saying a kid should be pampered, but I know of guys who had to put out their own money to get the equipment to play. Now that's ridiculous.

"I didn't get my shoes, my gloves, my freebies. I'd have

to ask for anything I got. Cy Buynak, the clubbie over there, he was great. Anything I needed, he'd help me out. If he couldn't get 'em, he'd try to direct me to someone who might be able to help."

It might surprise the civilian to see the stacks of equipment a rising star acquires over a short period, his locker crammed to overflowing, and find that he refuses to part with any of it. It is *his* stuff. He worked to earn it; nobody gave him anything. Why should he give it away to some snot-nosed punk who, when it comes down to it, would be happy to swipe his job from him?

McBride was different.

"When I got sent down, Bake came over to me and gave me a whole box of Brooks spikes to take with me. Top of the line. A whole box. There wasn't a pal in Buffalo that season who didn't have a decent pair of spikes to wear.

"There was just one condition: he had to be a size ten. Or close to it."

McBride, battling an assortment of injuries, was given his walking papers by the Indians following the 1983 season. The impression he left on Gruber, who has not seen him since that day he left the camp in Arizona, is evident whenever he looks into the keen eyes of a rookie at spring training.

"Sure, your first thoughts are selfish ones," Gruber admits. "I see him coming in the door, especially one who might be after my job one day, and there is a little bit of resentment right off the bat. You might not be as nice, as outgoing, as you would be to someone who posed no threat to you. You owe it to people, as a human being, to try to get over those feelings.

"That's when I think of guys like Manning, Hargrove, McBride and a lot of people like them. It's something you never forget. They set an example for me that I promised I'd follow when, and if, I was in their shoes and some young kid looked up to me for help."

As tall as his assignments might have been at those first spring camps, Gruber was confronted in March of 1991 with the onerous task of "breaking in" an infield entirely different from the one to which he bid his goodbyes five months before in Baltimore.

Gone was Fred McGriff, the large target across the diamond who had been scooping Gruber's miscues out of the dirt at first base for the past four seasons. In his place was John Olerud, whose rookie year had set the table for the blockbuster trade with the San Diego Padres the following December. Gone was the supremely gifted but insular Tony Fernandez, to be replaced at shortstop by Manuel Lee, and that meant adapting to the double-play pivot of Roberto Alomar at second base.

Although George Bell, his lively bat and his hands of stone were lost to the Chicago Cubs when the Jays' bosses cold-cocked him on the contract front, there were eminently adequate replacements at hand in Joe Carter, late of San Diego and Cleveland; Devon White, acquired from the California Angels in trade for problem child Junior Felix; and veteran hitter Pat Tabler, formerly of the New York Mets and the Kansas City Royals.

There were great regrets about losing McGriff at first base. Even so, Gruber felt strongly that it was time for Fernandez and Bell to get out of Toronto. The Blue Jays would miss Bell's bat and would have "waltzed" into the 1991 World Series with it in the line-up, Gruber agreed, but Bell's power stats had been slipping since 1987—the MVP campaign in which he batted .308 and hit 47 home runs for 134 RBIs—and would have continued to do so. At the same time, Gruber is well aware that bats with 85 to 90 RBIs in them have a way of busting into any line-up.

"If only we could have talked him into staying off the field," Gruber mused, "but George didn't want any part of it. He also wasn't interested in practice and it hurt his performance out there."

Gruber blames Bell's fielding, or what passed for it during his nine-season hitch with the Blue Jays, on his practice of "only coming out for game time." It is a complaint Gruber says he and others aired in Bell's presence. It caused "problems in the locker room."

"I wanted to see Bell play the way he could," says Gruber. "He did enough to get by. It was all he needed to do because he was so good. If he had just put out a little more, he had a chance to be one of the best players of his time.

"The reason he blew out his arm is because he never worked at getting it in shape. I have to give him A-plus for courage, though, for just going out there and playing left field. The shape he was in, there was no reason in the world he should have been out there."

The team's mercurial shortstop, Tony Fernandez, walked out of a game during the 1989 pennant drive after being struck out three times by Bret Saberhagen of the K.C. Royals. Despite the quitter's rep that was hung on Fernandez by the Toronto newspapers, Gruber refuses to question his former teammate's character.

"He loved the city. He loved the Blue Jays uniform. I can say honestly that he gave it his all. Sure, he took a walk a couple of times, but look at the records. He was out there 150 games or more a season, playing through all kinds of hurts. How can you call him a quitter?

"Baseball looks on what he did as a mortal sin. It's called not having your mind right. Believe me, there's more than enough reason to get pissed off with a player who does it. What you have to know is if it's bullshit or not. C'mon, at least 150 games a season. Anybody who says he didn't come to play is full of it.

"Maybe a time or two he wasn't treated as fairly as he thought he ought to have been. Maybe it hurt him. Maybe he started changing his attitude toward the way he approached the game.

"The fans were beginning to take him the wrong way. 'C'mon, Tony. Smile. Look like you're having a good time out there.' It started weighing on him. Tony wanted nothing more than to play baseball and preach the gospel. More than a few times, he thought about quitting the game and going back to his homeland, taking the knowledge that he had, the relationship he had with God, and relaying that to his people.

"As a Christian on this ball club, he was lost. All the people close to him had gone: Ron Shepherd, Lloyd Moseby, Jesse Barfield, Roy Lee Jackson. I was about the only one left for him. That might have been another piece of the puzzle as to why it was time for him to go."

During their last talk as teammates, a telephone call from Fernandez the night he and McGriff were traded to San Diego, Gruber wondered how well second baseman Manuel Lee would adapt to playing shortstop.

"I wanted to know if I would have to 'cheat' toward my left because I wondered if Manuel would show the range that Tony had over the years," Gruber recalled. "Tony told me I'd be surprised at how far Manuel could go into the hole. I bought it, since he and Manuel grew up in the same place, but what surprised me was Tony's insistence that Manuel had as good an arm as he did from the hole."

The key to the deal was John Olerud, the "veteran rookie" whose play at the plate and in the field in 1990 suggested he could take over first base and make McGriff available for the blockbuster trade with San Diego.

"We gave up a lot," says Gruber. "We got a lot. You're asking Olerud to fill an all-star's shoes. Any other kid of twenty-two, and I'd have said, 'Don't do it.' Olerud has his priorities in line. He knows where he's going, what he wants to do and how to go about it.

"One thing's for sure. The noise level at first base isn't likely to go up any. John, Fred, they were the same day in, day out. Every day you come to the park, they're there, even if you might not know it until you trip over them at their lockers. Neither one of them wore out their jaws talking nonsense. It's not something you could say about a lot of us in that room."

Gruber has been around long enough to know that only a fool guarantees he will improve upon his numbers of the previous season, especially when they have been of all-star calibre. Who needs that kind of pressure?

"I've never been a numbers guy when it comes to setting goals in the spring," he says. "What you did, you did. Turn the page. Then do your job day by day.

"I'm what the everyday Joe Blow would call a company man. No one guy gets us where we want to go. Team goals, they're the ones you set. Win the division. Win the play-offs. Win the World Series. Get that done, do all you can do, and the personal stats fall into place."

What Gruber thought he might be able to give the New Jays, now that he has matured to all-star status on and off the field, was some of the leadership they so sorely lacked over the years.

"If it happens, it happens," he said, "but it's not an election and I'm not hustling votes. I'm not going to go in there and say, 'OK, guys, I'm your leader. Follow me through this brick wall.' A true leader has to prove himself. Has to be worthy. He can't do it with talk. I could see myself rising to the occasion. Otherwise, I'm not going to force myself into the position."

Whatever role he plays, Gruber says he will not button his lip as he did in 1990 when and if transgressions on the field become as flagrant.

"If I'm out there and something happens that I don't feel should happen, I won't have any qualms about expressing myself to that person. Who hears, who listens in on it, that's secondary to me. If guys are out there busting guts, spilling sweat, and somebody's loafing, you can bet I'll say my piece."

In the spring of 1991 there were more pressing matters to deal with. The upshot of the busiest winter in franchise history—save for 1976–77, when the Toronto ship was about to be launched—was to shake up the team as it had not been since it became a contender midway through the 1980s. As Gruber points out, confirming an opinion that had permeated the club's executive suite, the moves had to be made because the club was not winning with what it had.

"For the first time since I've been there," said Gruber, "I think we're going to have nine guys on the field who give 100 percent. Unlike a lot of other springs I've seen, it's one I wish were a little longer. Just to get the kinks worked out with all those new guys."

As consuming as the process might have been, it was a joy compared to the tumultuous camp over which manager Jimy Williams presided in 1988.

George Bell, coming off his MVP season of 1987 and the ink barely dry on a three-year deal worth more than $6 million, rejected the eminently logical conclusion at which management had arrived. A swell hitter Bell might be—in seven full seasons with the Blue Jays he cracked 195 home runs and totalled 711 RBIs—but he played the outfield like a bull let loose in a souvenir shop.

Although the decision to make Bell a pure hitter had been thrashed out at the upper levels of management, Bell took it as a personal affront when Williams delivered the verdict. Bell refused one day soon after to report for duty as a designated hitter, a breach of baseball etiquette akin to mutiny at sea, and vowed in the subsequent commotion that Williams would leave Toronto long before he did.

He was right, of course. Williams, a career minor-leaguer who played out the string as a weak-hitting middle infielder with the 1971 Winnipeg Goldeyes of the International League, could not break down the fences

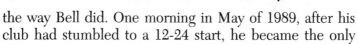

the way Bell did. One morning in May of 1989, after his club had stumbled to a 12-24 start, he became the only Blue Jays manager to be fired in mid-term.

He had taken the job on a moment's notice in the winter of 1985, after the revered Bobby Cox jumped ship to become general manager of the Atlanta Braves. Ironically the same club had canned Cox as manager four years previously. When the Blue Jays named their popular third base coach as field general, the move was greeted with widespread approval from the players.

"His knowledge of the game, the kind of person he was, the rapport he had with us," says Gruber, "there wasn't anyone on the club who didn't think he was going to be a great manager. Until he took the job. I started noticing right away that he didn't command a lot of respect from the older guys. Maybe they had problems with Jimy that I knew nothing about, but there's no reason in the world not to show respect for somebody or, at the very least, the position they hold.

"Maybe he changed some of the things he did, in a way that was consistent with him having a little more authority as the manager, but it didn't alter the person behind the desk. A lot of guys will read this and say, 'Kelly, are you nuts? Are you blind? Where the hump were you when all that stuff was hitting the fan?' I really can't say I saw Jimy change all that much.

"I heard the bickering. People didn't want to hit here. People didn't want to play there. People didn't want to play on Tuesday, Thursday and Sundays. Then or now, I don't think those things are a player's decisions. As much of a union man as I am, I still believe we're employees."

Among those who soured on Williams was centre fielder Lloyd Moseby, whose 1,400 games with the Blue Jays stands as a club record. The roots of his disaffection lie in Williams' first camp as manager, when he ticketed Moseby for Bell's job in left field. The situation turned poisonous midway through the 1988 season in a game at Toronto.

"Two out, Moseby's on second, Fred McGriff's on first," says Gruber, picking up the threads of the story. "Someone hits a line drive right at the left fielder. Lloyd makes the turn at third, looks over his shoulder and sees there won't be a play at the plate. He slows up and, about twenty feet from home, goes into his Moseby stutter-step. Any slower and he'd be down to a brisk walk.

"Meanwhile, here comes Freddie. Steaming into third. Just a bonehead play. He gets thrown out, a second before Moseby crosses the plate. No run.

"Well, Jimy is pissed off. Raging mad. He confronts Moseby. Lloyd, who knows he has embarrassed himself, doesn't need Jimy all over his back. So he blows up, too. Ask him today, and I'd bet that Lloyd would admit he screwed up. He just wasn't going to take any guff that night from Jimy.

"The point is, Jimy couldn't tell anybody anything without them getting back in his face. You don't have to agree with everything he does. There were times when I didn't. What you do is go into a room and take care of it. The door was always open."

It may be of little solace to Williams, who returned to baseball as one of Bobby Cox's coaches with the Atlanta Braves, but Moseby offers his regrets for the way Williams was treated.

"I always felt bad that he was blamed for some of the things that happened. I think it was a tough transition for Jimy to go from being such an unbelievable coach, and probably the jokemaster of the club, to having to handle the players he had known for so long. I don't think the guys took him as serious as we should have taken him. He knew his baseball backwards and forwards, but we took him for granted. We just never responded to him. At the end there, the response to him was zero. It wasn't Jimy's fault. It was our fault because we didn't hike it in gear. I would have liked to say this to his face, but when he got the axe he was gone. I've never seen him since that day."

His beneficiary, if that's the word, was Cito Gaston.

"When he took over, it was like turning on the lights," says Moseby. "It's sad. The same players were there. Only now we had something to prove. 'Oh-oh, fellas, if we don't do it now, we got no one to blame. It's our fault.'"

"It's still a mystery to me why the job didn't work out for him," says Gruber. "I don't know what happened, but there's only so much blame you can attach to somebody else for losing before you start looking at yourself.

"What makes a good manager? The players, of course. Win and he's a genius. Lose, he's a bum. It's not always right."

Gruber isn't blowing smoke when he says he often found fault with some of Williams' strategies. One of the most glaring examples has to do with a classic Blue Jays swoon at the end of the 1987 season that allowed Detroit to win the East Division. With 10 dates left on the schedule, the Jays swept the first 3 of a 4-game series at home against the Tigers to pull 3½ games in front. Leading the fourth game with 3 outs to record, Kirk Gibson of the Tigers homered in the ninth to set up a Detroit victory in extra innings. The Jays promptly lost 3 in a row to Milwaukee, all by a single run, to set up the crucial, season-ending 3 games in Detroit. They lost each of them by a single run and finished in second place, two games behind the Tigers.

What miffs Gruber, who hit 12 home runs in 340 at-bats that season, is that he saw each of those one-run losses from the bench while Rance Mulliniks and Garth Iorg did all the playing. Mulliniks had 11 HRs (330 ABs) and Iorg had 4 HRs (310 ABs).

"I'm not saying I should have been in there instead of them, but I can't help but think that one home run, in any of those games, would have made the difference. He never even gave me a look. Sure, I was upset with him, but I kept it to myself.

"The problems he had, they just got over Jimy's head. There was no way of stopping the snowball. Dissension is always that way. A bad call here, a bad call there, that's part of it. I don't pay a lot of attention to these sort of things. I have trouble enough doing my own job.

"It could be, too, that Jimy was paying for Bobby's success. Cox took us to within a game of the World Series in 1985, so there was only one way Jimy would escape his shadow. When Bobby slipped up, nobody said much. Jimy Williams didn't get as much forgiving. Maybe people developed their nerve when he took over."

Cito Gaston, the current manager, might have caught a break when he became manager on a "temporary basis" in May of 1989 while the club courted Lou Piniella of the New York Yankees. Under the "interim manager," the Blue Jays pulled out of their early funk to play like the pennant contenders they were touted to be in spring training. When Yankees owner George Steinbrenner refused to let Piniella leave his broadcast booth, it was left to Gaston to decide who would lead the club. Already well-respected by the players for his work around the batting cage, he now brought a healing influence to a disturbed clubhouse. For once, though it had been dictated by a most curious set of circumstances in New York, the dog was wagging the tail.

Still, Gruber had to wonder.

"I thought Jimy would make a good manager, and he got fired. I thought Cito would make just as good a manager, but could I be that far off-base again? The brass was saying that the players took advantage of a guy who had been a friend and were worried that we might do it again. It's like saying the axe-murderer who killed ten people last month had blond hair and blue eyes. Therefore anybody with blond hair and blue eyes is an axe-murderer. Which, now that I mention it, puts me in a tight spot. The point is that just because the policy failed one time doesn't mean it's going to fail again.

"The last thing we needed was to adjust to somebody new at that point of the season. We needed stability and he gave it to us. The right man in the right job at the right time.

"Now it was up to us."

CHAPTER 12

 ## GOOD OL' BOYS

Memories. A good ten years after it happened, they still talk about The Play as if it had been made the afternoon before. Two out, first inning of the final game in the 1980 Texas state high school championship series and the Westlake Chaparrals are in trouble. Deep trouble.

Calvin Schiraldi, looking nothing like the ace who had fashioned an 18-1 record with a microscopic 0.91 earned-run average that season, had walked six batters from DeSoto High. Five runs had scored, the bases were still loaded and the Chaps coach, Howard Bushong, was on his way to the mound with the hook in his hand.

"Somehow Schiraldi talks me out of it," Bushong says a decade later from behind the desk in a cubbyhole of an office at the University of Texas, where he is now employed as pitching coach of the Longhorns. "On the way back from the mound, I'm telling myself, 'Heck, we've got two outs. Only need one more. Hey, he's the guy who got us here, isn't he? No time to abandon him now.'"

He almost came close to believing himself.

The delusion lasted as long as it took the next hitter to drill a ground ball into the hole between shortstop and third base. With the runners off at the crack of the bat, the sixth run of the inning scored and the seventh was on its way to the plate.

"All of a sudden, I see this blur on the outfield grass behind third," says Bushong. "Kelly backhands the ball, which could have been the play of the game itself. Then he leaves the ground, and in mid-air he throws a bullet to home plate to catch the second runner.

"I have seen ten years of baseball since that day, maybe a thousand games at the high school and the college level, but I've never seen a play to match it. Every now and then, I'll pull out the film and watch it all over again. I still don't know how he did it."

Schiraldi, cut by the San Diego Padres in the spring of 1991 as he was about to embark upon his eighth season in the majors, has an even more vivid recollection of the play.

"I don't know how he got to it, but it saved my butt," he said at a charity sports auction in Austin a few weeks before he reported to the Padres' camp. "If he hadn't, I was off to the showers. It was one of those plays that lights up one team, blows out the candle for the other.

"It's a funny thing to say about a team leading you 6-2 after an inning, but that's the way it was. We scored three runs in the top of the second and it was a game again. I was able to settle down and our offence took over."

After Schiraldi delivered 188 pitches that day, Gruber clinched the victory for the Chaps and Schiraldi with the game-winning hit in extra innings.

It is the type of story that good ol' boys, their high school days long gone, remember around pitchers of beer during a long lunch at a place called Chuy's on the outskirts of Austin on a grey afternoon in the dead of a Texas winter.

The place is a direct steal from the late 1950s, complete with a mini-shrine to Elvis at the entrance. There are two sprawling rooms with private booths on the side and kitchen tables by the windows at the back. The bar looks like a stand-up, but for the weary or the suddenly infirm there are soda-fountain stools. The music is loud but not abrasive, and the colours garish but not overbearing. The Tex-Mex grub is good, there is lots of it and it is cheap. Best of all, the beer is cold.

Around one of the tables at the back is a group of faces that have been familiar to Kelly Gruber for a long time; in some cases, since he was a boy.

Terry Peschka, for instance. He was on school patrol duty the day Gloria Gruber, young Kelly in tow, reported to the business office to sign up Westlake's newest student-athlete. At his desk a short while later, Peschka remembers the teacher, a Mrs Gerhard, introducing Gruber to his new Grade 5 classmates.

"I remember our teacher telling Kelly they would put him next to the athlete of the class, which happened to be me," says Peschka, who these days is a consultant on corporate retirement plans. "Athlete of the class . . . it was a title I wasn't long in giving up."

If there was a passing of the torch, perhaps it happened in gym class when the kids played a game called Bombardment.

"Two teams of kids line up and, at a count of three, someone tosses out a basketball," says Peschka. "Pick up the ball and hit somebody, he's out of the game. He catches it, you're out.

"To make a long story short, we banned Kelly within a couple of weeks because he was laying too many people out. He was a terror. Twelve years old and already he was a machine!"

Peschka, built short and wide and powerful, was the perfect foil for the lighter, quicker Gruber on the Westlake High football teams he quarterbacked on autumn Friday nights in the late 1970s.

It is time, the audience willing and the beers on the table disappearing swiftly, for Peschka to play a little Texas Crude.

"There were a lot of girls at the time who envied me," says the former centre, setting up a line he has been using for years. "Every Friday night, for a couple of hours, Kelly would be wiggling his hands between my legs."

Big laugh.

"Like every other football team that ever suited up, we had a play called the quarterback sneak. Unlike every other football team, we had our own name for it: QB Sneak-on-Goose. Very effective, too.

"Kelly didn't even have to call out the signal at the scrimmage line. First, he'd 'read' the other team's middle linebacker or noseguard and simply touch me on the side where he wanted to take the ball. That's the guy I'd push out of the way. Then, when he wanted me to snap the ball, there'd be the goose. Trouble is, the little S.O.B. took advantage, especially in practice. There were a lot of gooses, clamps and squeezes. It was all you could to not to jump offside. It took a while to get used to it."

Among those who can attest to what a cut-up Gruber was on and off the field is Terry Kearns, who moved from Grand Rapids, Michigan, to Austin when he was eleven years old. He became a classmate and close friend of Gruber in Grade 6.

"The class comedian, of course, but he never did master the art of how not to get caught. Always in trouble with the teachers. Always had to have the last word."

The definitive story might be Gruber's first and only brush with firearms and the law a couple of years later. He and his younger brother David, about eight years old at the time, were given pellet rifles by their father, with strict provisos that they be used only for shooting at targets under supervision.

Kelly Gruber, ever the ringleader, interpreted the

definition of targets to include the windows of a house being renovated near the Grubers' home on the outskirts of Austin.

After "target practice," the brothers ventured inside the house to inspect their marksmanship. Paint cans and brushes were waiting for them, so it seemed only natural for Gruber to paint his initials on some of the walls.

"It didn't take too much to figure out who KWG was," says the father of the perpetrators. "I took Kelly's air rifle and paddled him with it until the plastic stock broke. Not a peep out of him until it shattered. *That's* what broke his heart. God, he was a tough kid."

There were girls, too. Plenty of them.

"Kelly and I, we had all the prettiest ones," says Kearns. "We'd go back behind the school and neck with them at recess. Kids' stuff back then, but we were learning. We were too scared to do anything too much.

"We were such good friends that we'd also share the girls. One week, I'd go around with Peggy Sue Whatsername. The next week it'd be Kelly. The girls didn't seem to mind. Not at all."

The harem era ended when the young ladies left the young studs after discovering the charms of "older men."

"When they started going out with guys in Grade 8, we started calling them names," says Kearns. "Trod, for one."

Trod?

"Yeah, T-R-O-D. Trader, Raider, Obstinate Dork. It didn't take long before we had a lot of them in tears."

The "chicks" came home to roost in a way a few years ago when Gruber and Kearns were out at an Austin bar one night.

"We were talking about old times, having a couple of beers," says Kearns, "when this girl came up to us. We knew her from school. Then, after a few words, she started breaking out in tears. Then she started hitting us. With her fists. She told us how upset she was at how mean we had been back then.

"Geez, we were getting a lot of bad looks from other people in the place! I apologized to her. Then Kelly apologized. We told her we really didn't know what we were doing back then. After a while, she calmed down a bit. It sort of took the edge off the night, though."

Now it's Mike Konderla's turn. He met Gruber in the summer of 1980 when both were playing for American Family Life in a semi-pro league that operated in the Austin area. Even though Gruber turned pro and Konderla chose the University of Texas and the Longhorns, they continued to work out together during the winters.

Konderla, a pitcher whose shot at the big leagues was scuttled by three knee operations over five years in the minor leagues, set out with Gruber one Sunday in December 1980 to hunt deer at a 300-acre estate near Brownwood, about sixty miles west of Austin.

"Kelly's driving his pickup and I'm doing lookout on the hood," says Konderla, "when we both spot a beautiful buck on a cliff across a river and about 200 yards to our left. Kelly hits the brakes and I go flying into the bush. By the time I get back on my feet, Kelly's over the hood and he's gotten off his first shot. Miss. I fire. Another miss. Shoot again. Miss again.

"The buck's gone to cover, but we're not quitting. We get back in and look for a crossing. Next thing we know, the truck is up to its axles in the mud of a creek bed. We push. We pull. Pretty soon, we're muck from our boots to ears. Finally we realize there's no way we're going anywhere without a tow truck."

With only the trees and forest critters for company, Konderla and Gruber began the trek back to civilization. They trudged a mile north. A mile east. A mile south. A mile west. Finally, in the distance, a farmhouse.

In no time at all, the tow truck responded to their frantic phone call.

"The guy shows up and we tell him—we'd been real careful about noting all the landmarks on the way to the farmhouse—how to get back to the riverbed," says Konderla. "'Must be four or five miles,' we told the guy."

"'Are you nuts?' he says. 'Unless they've moved the creek you guys're talking about, it's just over that hill.' We'd walked four, maybe five miles to make 250 yards!"

They made it back to Gruber's house in time for Sunday dinner: "A little muddy, maybe, but what the hell, we were on time. And for Kelly, that's something of a miracle. You've heard that saying about time waiting for no man? Well, Kelly waits for no time."

Did someone mention punctuality?

"He was such a polite kid but, goshamighty, he could drive you crazy," coach Bushong had said earlier that day. "He had a tendency to sleep in. He had a tendency to be late. He had a tendency to forget. I just can't think of Kelly being on time. Just when he's got you steaming mad, he'll pop up all smiles, apologize all over the place. Pretty soon he's got you laughing. He's his own piece of work."

Oddly enough, Gruber is right on the button that night for a charity sports auction at one of Austin's swankier hotels. After signing autographs dutifully for forty-five minutes, he will grab a sandwich and a beer with a couple of pals from the old days who also were on hand to do their bit for a good cause.

Shortstop Spike Owen of the Montreal Expos, a member of the high school team from Cleburne that proved such an implacable foe for Gruber and the Westlake Chaps, says they were at the centre of a war of comparisons when they were teenagers.

"It was like one top gun coming into town to go up against another," he says. "Back then, it was fun. Kelly was a good ballplayer, but at the time I think he was a lot better athlete. He'd make mistakes, if you know what I mean, but he'd make up for them. What I mean is, he might not be strong in a certain area, but because he had such ability he could overcome something wrong he might have just done."

Owen, who will launch his tenth season in the majors in 1992, swears he was not surprised by Gruber's emergence as an all-star in the 1990 season.

"First, he's a great athlete. The rest comes with hard work, learning from experience and having the confidence to put it all together. Offensively, you knew he was made of the right stuff. What surprised me was the way his defence came around. He's always had that cannon of an arm, but the plays he made—I'd see them on the TV highlights after our games—some of them were unbelievable. I'd be as proud of that part of my game if I were him as anything else he's done."

This is particularly high praise from a man who made a mark of his own as a fielder in 1990. Owen did not commit an error until June 23, a National League record streak of sixty-three games, and led the circuit in fielding average (.989) for the second year in a row.

As might be expected, the praise for Gruber's talents is even more effusive from the other top gun on the Westlake Chaps.

"Kelly could play baseball, football, basketball and run track," says Schiraldi, "and he could do all of 'em well. You just shouldn't be able to find all these qualities in one person. You can imagine, with all that talent in four sports, what he could bring to any one of them if he put ten years of work into it."

Even though Schiraldi was considered the leader of the team there is no trace of rancour in him that the scouts who flocked to Austin to see him throw his fastball in 1979 snubbed him the following year when he became eligible for the draft.

Gruber got rich quick, with his $100,000 signing fee from the Cleveland Indians, and Schiraldi took the university route to the major leagues after being drafted by the Chicago White Sox in the seventeenth round.

What the scouts ignored, in spite of Schiraldi's 18-1 record and 0.96 earned-run average, was the reason behind the dip in velocity of the fastball that radar guns once tracked at ninety-plus miles an hour.

"Hell," says coach Bushong, "he wasn't even throwing eighty miles an hour."

Two weeks before the beginning of that final high school season, Schiraldi developed a case of strep throat and lost thirty-five of the 205 pounds he considered his normal playing weight.

"I just didn't have the firepower," he says, "and that got the scouts down on me. In high school, it's not how you win; it's how hard you throw. If you don't have the tail on the fastball, they're not going to come knocking on the door."

Once his fastball regained its pop and with three years of college baseball on his résumé, Schiraldi was a first-round choice of the New York Mets in the 1983 draft.

Another who was there at the outset of Gruber's climb to the majors was Kirk Killingsworth, now sales manager of the hotel where the auction was held. He often pitched batting practice to Gruber in those days.

"He'd just signed the big contract, but it hadn't gone to his head," says Killingsworth, who used to pitch for the University of Texas Longhorns at the same time. "He wasn't the big-headed kid, first choice out of high school, who knew it all. As far as talent goes, he had a real quick bat with a lot of pop. For a guy his size, a guy his age, he already had developed a skill a lot of hitters never acquire.

"When he made it, he was like a lot of Texas boys. Roger Clemens, my roomie at UT, Calvin Schiraldi, Spike Owen, everyone kept that even keel no matter how well they did. Not that he invented humility, but Nolan Ryan kind of sets the tone in Texas these days. If he isn't full of himself, and he's about the most amazing pitcher who ever lived, then how can anyone let his hat size get out of hand?"

Also attending the affair that night to see her superstar son was Gloria Gruber. She, too, has a story.

"That state championship game, the one where the score changed near about every inning, his grandmother was at that one, of course. Well, every other inning of it, to be truthful about it.

"Maw-maw would chew her fingers to the bone every time Kelly played, but this was one of the worst times. She spent half that game sitting on a tree stump, near the concession stand out back. Back and forth the whole game. Everybody still talks about it."

At her home later that night, her husband ties the bow on a day full of reminiscences. As well as any, David Gruber's story signals the turning point Kelly Gruber took on his road to the major leagues.

"At eleven, twelve years of age, he had such velocity as a pitcher," he says at the kitchen table of the townhouse overlooking Lake Travis. "Everybody thought I was going to ruin him by blowing out his arm. What they didn't realize, and I'd been working with him all his life, is that most of that power came from his legs."

Gruber's "career" as a hurler came to an end the year he turned sixteen, but it had nothing to do with an injury. The decision was prompted by a quirk in results at the plate on days that he pitched. It is the same flaw in humankind that prompted the introduction of the designated hitter to the American League.

"When Kelly pitched, he couldn't hit," says his father, spreading his hands. "Ridiculous. We figured somebody must have told him pitchers weren't hitters and now he believed it. The next three games, he went 7-for-9. Two homers, three doubles, a couple of singles. The fourth game, 0-for-3. I told him he'd never have to pitch again."

CHAPTER 13

HITTIN'

Any fool can learn to bunt. It is the first thing a kid ought to be taught when he graduates from the school yard to organized baseball.

Square around to face the pitcher. Slide the top hand halfway up the bat, gripping it near the trademark with the tips of the fingers and thumb. Let the ball hit the fat part of the barrel in such a way that it dribbles down one of the baselines.

Run like hell.

Properly executed, particularly when it is combined with the element of surprise, the play can be a thing of beauty.

The third baseman darts in and scoops up the ball with his bare hand. In the same motion, in the same fraction of a second that he knows he is headed for a three-point landing in the dirt at home plate, he underhands a bullet at first base. Ball and runner arrive at the bag simultaneously and the umpire, caught up in the drama, does a dance. Safe-safe-safe! Out-out-out! Sometimes, there is a wonderful argument.

What a travesty it is that the high art of bunting, even as

a sacrifice to move runners into scoring position, is on the verge of becoming extinct.

At the forefront of the campaign to kill it have been none other than the Toronto Blue Jays. They will deny it, of course, but the fact is that until they embarked upon the 1991 season, they were among the "league leaders" in snubbing the bunt as a tactical weapon.

Since 1982, when Bobby Cox was hired to manage the club—"You get twenty-seven outs," he would bitch, "why give 'em one for free?"—the Blue Jays rarely, if ever, laid down more than a couple of dozen bunts in a season. The record low for sacrifice bunts (18) was set by the 1990 Blue Jays.

The chief high executioner, gone but not forgotten, was George Bell, who came to bat more than 4,500 times in nine seasons with the Blue Jays. Not once in all that time did he lay down a successful bunt. Only in his final term, when his bat began its inevitable drag through the last six weeks, did he even try one.

Everyone knows Georgie wasn't paid $2 million a year to bat a ball twenty feet, but, *Madre de Dios*, 0-for-4,500 is ridiculous.

The excuses for not bunting are all too inviting. With the coming of artificial turf, which stands up to the elements better than the green grass God intended for cud-chewing cows and playing the grand old game, bunted balls began reaching infielders as quickly as a jackrabbit jumps its mate on a balmy summer evening. Even in sacrifice situations, when a hitter would give himself up to push a runner into scoring position late in the game, the bunt on synthetic turf is an invitation to a double-play disaster.

The real reason for the fall from favour, of course, is that no hitter looks so foolish as when he fails once, twice, three times to turn a trick that even the klutziest Little League kid can perform on three of five tries.

On the rare occasions that Cox did call for a bunt, there seemed to be a commanding reason in specific circumstances: two men on base and none out, weak hitter at the plate, game on the line in the late innings. Since Jimy Williams and Cito Gaston were his understudies, they tended to follow the same philosophy when they followed Cox into the manager's chair.

This failure to execute one of baseball's most basic plays, Kelly Gruber believes, cost the team dearly at the plate and, something of a surprise, in the field.

"Automatic out? I don't know if that's a good enough reason to forget about it," he postulated one day after lunch in Baltimore in September 1990. "It's really a play meant to move a runner to second or third base so your more consistent hitters can bring him home. If you're prepared as a ball club, you shouldn't have any trouble getting the runner over and then getting him home. Not just now and then. All the time. Over the years, we've had a lot of problems doing it. We shouldn't."

The reason for this failure to execute is as clear to Gruber as it would be to any coach in Little League.

"These guys, who are expected to know how to bunt, should make a point of doing it in batting practice. Not just the first two fat pitches from a coach to remind you what a pitched ball looks like. Besides, the fifteen minutes in a cage that a block of five guys share is not meant for refining the niceties of the game. If a guy needs to work on his bunting, he should come out early or do it after the game. They should work on it in the cage beneath the stands. They should ask the coaches to help. I've never met one on this club who was too busy to help a player.

"Bunting should be as much a part of their game as swinging the bat. I don't think one guy from this club did it properly, or often enough, all this year. Me included. I'm guilty, too.

"Geez, but we had trouble doing it. 'He just gave me

the bunt sign. Gosh, I hope I can. Geez, I hope I don't screw up.' You could just see the words running through a hitter's mind when he got the signal. Right away, thinking like that, you're beat. Sure as the sun rises, you'll screw up. There's one way to overcome it. That's to do it so often it becomes second nature.

"Mookie Wilson set the example, but no one followed it. Bunting has been part of his game for years. He's no power-hitter, but he's fast. So he uses what God gave him and it kept him in the big leagues a long time. There were a couple of guys on this team, basically just like him, they didn't even try to bunt for a base hit. Swing for the fences, you know. That's fine if you've got some pop, OK? But pick your times. The guys I'm talking about, they're not power-hitters. These are guys that have great speed, who should be bunting."

A team that bunts well and often also reaps the benefit of unsettling enemy defences. Knowing full well the Blue Jays disdained this vital part of "the little game," Gruber says enemy infielders "cheat" the Blue Jays by setting up a step or two deeper for a hitter who shows little inclination to bunt. If this allows opposing teams to get to one more ground ball every game over a season, that's 162 outs or the equivalent of six nine-inning games. In division races often decided by the slenderest of margins, the "giveaway factor" becomes decisive.

"Use the bunt more often," says Gruber, "and some of these ground balls get through the infield. Make the defences take a step back and then use speed to beat out the slow bouncers. Put the ball on the ground. Get the runners over. There's no reason guys at the lower end of the line-up shouldn't be doing it.

"If nothing else, you want the thought of the bunt in the enemys' minds. It really does pull in an infield. If I've got decent speed as a third baseman and I know a guy isn't going to bunt, I'll play him a step back and maybe take another step on the side. That gives me a lot better range. If I know he can bunt, I've got to play in a step or two. That puts a lot of pressure on me."

As third man in the order, Gruber has been told by Cito Gaston that he is not being paid big money to lay down bunts. While Gruber professes to understand, he also argues that his place in the order loses some of its significance after the first pass through the line-up.

For instance, when he bats second in an inning late in the game and the lead-off hitter reaches base, Gruber thinks he should bunt the man into scoring position. "When that's the case, that's what I should be doing. That's baseball. I understand I swing the bat as well as anybody in the line-up and better than some, but I sure like hitting in a 'situation.'

"Cito says the number three hitter is supposed to take a shot at bringing the runner home. Drive the ball, score the guy from first and put myself in scoring position. Go for the big inning. What happens if I just miss—it's a game of fractions—and ground out to short? Double play. What good have I done? My instincts say to get the guy over. Make the next guy's job a little easier. All right, I'll drive the ball if you want, but I'll drive it to the right side. It still gives me a chance to get the guy over."

As vital as it might be to a well-rounded attack, in reality the bunt is the icing on the cake a player applies to his hitting game. No one ever bunted his way into the majors but, once there, a few hung onto their jobs because of that talent.

Mastery of the hitter's art begins in childhood. The first step in the process is developing a comfortable, workable stance in the batter's box. A visit to any ballpark from the tip of California to Baffin Bay confirms that there are as many stances as there are ballplayers. Being comfortable, then, is the first law.

"Unless you are," says Gruber, "I don't think you're going to succeed. Since each player is unique in this respect, a kid needs a coach's help to experiment. Still, there are some absolutes. As simple as it sounds, keep your eye on the ball. The tendency in kids, as they're swinging, is to turn their heads as the shoulder flies out when they're swinging. Keeping the shoulder tucked helps keep the head still. The ideal is to have the eyes in such a position that they see the bat head as it meets the ball."

Almost as important is the selection of a bat. Gruber, who goes through about fifty of them a season in practice and games, will accept or reject the ones shipped to him purely on the basis of "feel." At times, he will switch to one with a thinner handle and thicker head or vice versa.

"Length and weight depend on how strong I think I am," he says. "Early in the season, a lot of guys my size will use a bat 35 inches long that weighs 32 ounces. As the season drags on, they'll downsize to 34 inches and 31 ounces. For myself, the most likely combination is 34-31."

The trick is to apply, with considerable torque, the "sweet spot" of those 34 inches and 31 ounces to a similar sweet spot slightly below the centre of a ball three inches wide as it travels at more than ninety miles an hour. The bat's "sweet spot" is about the size of a nickel midway between the brand and the end of the bat.

It is a proposition much too late to tackle in the batter's box.

"Hitting is never far from your mind," says Gruber, "but in reality I begin the real preparation when I'm 'in the hole,' which means I'm the next guy in the on-deck circle. Pretty much, unless their pitcher is a rookie, personal experience tells me what he's got to offer before I leave the clubhouse."

At the beginning of his climb, acting on the example set by teammate Lloyd Moseby, Gruber began making entries in a notebook on pitchers that since has grown to two volumes of about 250 pages each. Each entry is headed with a pitcher's name in block letters and whether he throws from the right or left side. Each section also lists the pitch selection, the situation, such as outs, men on base, in which Gruber faced his opponent and the score at the time.

"Is his fastball average, above or below? Does it sink, tail or run true? Does he keep it away? Does he throw it for a strike on a first pitch? Does his curve drop? Is it slow, or does it break sharply? Same thing with his slider, change-up, forkball, whatever."

Nuts-and-bolts stuff, all of it. What is really interesting are the sections in which he outlines how certain pitchers tip off hitters with their body language.

There is one famous flamethrower, who shall remain anonymous to protect Gruber's advantage, who comes to the "set position" in the wind-up with his glove at different levels of his torso to signal what he is about to throw.

"High, it's a curve. At the belt, it's a change-up. Below the belt, fastball."

Gruber consults the book before each game, these days mostly to freshen his recollections, in the thirty-minute rest period before the umpire calls for the first pitch. The gamesmanship rises to another plateau in the moments before he leaves the dugout for the on-deck circle to await his turn at bat.

"What I'm watching in the minute or two before I face him is the sequence of pitches he's using on the guys ahead of me and reviewing my plan of attack. 'Am I still looking for the fastball low and outside, or will he try the curve he just threw? What pitches are working for him? Which one is his 'out pitch'?' He might be a breaking-ball pitcher, but if the curve is off the table there's no sense looking for it. If I don't get the pitch I want, I take it. If he throws me three pitches where I'm not looking for them, I just might have to go and sit down. It's a tough game.

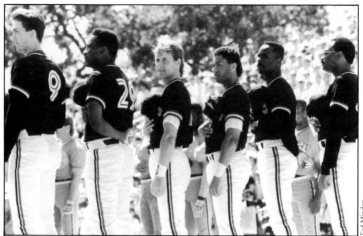

Ted Minden

Who's on First? *With all the changes the Blue Jays made over the winter of 1990–91, Kelly Gruber could have used a line-up card to identify his new teammates when they turned up for spring training.*

Toronto Star/Doug Griffen

At the Plate *Hitting instructor Cito Gaston, who took over as the Blue Jays' manager in 1989, shows a young Kelly Gruber the "sweet spot" on the bat. Hit the ball there, he says, and kiss it goodbye.*

Gruber collection

Home Cookin' *One of the best stops on the American League tour for Kelly is Arlington Stadium, home of the Texas Rangers. It's close enough to Austin that mom and pop (Gloria, David) can visit.*

Canada Wide/Paul Henry

In the Field *Never one to worry about getting his uniform dirty, Gruber will go flat out to flag down this line drive past third base. His efforts earned him a Gold Glove fielding award in 1990.*

Canada Wide

Surf's Up   *With padlocks on the gates at Dunedin Stadium, what's a guy to do? Kelly and Lynn Gruber headed for the beach to wait out the labour troubles that all but wiped out spring training in 1990.*

Ted Minden

Class Act *There are few players in Blue Jays' history who are as revered as Willie Upshaw. He left the Jays in the spring of 1988, but came back to the club in 1991 to coach in the minors.*

Canada Wide/Fred Thornhill

The Rookie *The new kid in town is Kody Robert Gruber, all of one day old when he settled down for his nap in his mom's arms. Providing the first family bear-hug is the proud papa Kelly.*

Toronto Star/Rick Eglinton

Hurtin' Time   *Working under the watchful eyes of manager Jimy Williams and the ump, trainer Tommy Craig (left) ministers to Kelly Gruber after he banged up his knee sliding into second.*

Manulife Financial/Rick Gomez

North and South   *Like the game Daddy plays, the Gruber family has an international flavour. Papa hails from Texas, Mom's from Toronto and baby Kody, born in Canada on July 4, 1990, enjoys dual citizenship.*

Canada Wide/Greig Reekie

The Cycle   *The only Blue Jay to do so, Kelly smoked a single, double, triple and homer to go for "the cycle" on April 16, 1989 against the K.C. Royals.*

Canada Wide/Fred Thornhill

Stopped Short   *A's Walt Weiss makes sure Gruber goes nowhere after he swiped this base in the fifth game of the 1989 play-offs. Oakland went on to San Francisco where they won the World Series after an earthquake.*

Canada Wide/Fred Thornhill

First At-Bat *Kody Gruber wasn't even a month old when he had his first at-bat before a capacity crowd at the splendiferous SkyDome. The occasion was the Blue Jays' annual family day at the park.*

Canada Wide

One Last Look   *Although Exhibition Stadium had long outlived its usefulness, Kelly Gruber felt a tug when the Blue Jays closed the history book on the park where he got his start in the major leagues.*

You go up there knowing your shopping list. You don't have that much time to adjust.

"When he gets two strikes on you, it's time to protect the plate. Put wood on anything that looks close and forget about putting any dents in the fences. A little flare into the outfield, a bleeder through the hole: either suits me just fine, thank you.

"Later in the game, adjusting to what you've seen for a few innings, you might change your approach. One thing's for sure, if I've had two good at-bats, I'm sure he won't give me anything decent. The stats might not prove it, but I think I'm a better hitter the third or fourth time up. Early in the game, more often than not it's a mistake I've made that gets me out. Later, it figures that I have a better idea of what he can do. Even if the relief has been called, I'm still better because I've had a chance to get into the flow of the game."

Among the things Gruber accomplishes in the on-deck circle is setting up what he calls his "pick-up point," the spot in the arc where the ball leaves the pitcher's hand.

"On each pitch, I make a mental note of the point in his arm's arc where he releases the ball. Some guys are over the top, eleven o'clock. A lot of guys are three-quarters, ten o'clock. A side-armer, which is rare, eight or nine o'clock. The ones who give me trouble, for reasons I'll get into later, are the submariners, six o'clock. Worse still are the guys who vary their release points.

"In the batter's box, the first thing I'll look at is the broad picture. The way the infielders set up can tip you off to how a pitcher intends to work on you. Close to the line suggests something on the inside of the plate, most likely hard. Further from the line, something low and outside, hard or soft.

"Then, as I'm digging in, I narrow my focus to the letters across the pitcher's shirt, eliminating any background that might disrupt my focus. This is when my concentration becomes really keen. When he leans in for the sign, I'll switch my focus to the little, bitty emblem on his cap. It's about the size of the baseball that will be coming at me in a couple of seconds.

"As he begins his wind-up, I call on that important note I made in the on-deck circle. The release point. Focusing on it, my eyes pick up the ball at the earliest possible moment. Now I have that vital split-second more to decide what the pitch is, if it's a strike and where it will cross the plate, and whether I want to offer at it."

What throws a hitch into this grand, elaborate plan, as Gruber observes, is that rare breed of pitcher who can vary his release point and still hit the strike zone. Having to alter one's focus at that last pivotal second in a pitcher's delivery, as minor a disruption as it might seem, can upset a hitter's concentration. Already the pitcher has won half the battle.

Only slightly less of a problem is the submariner. While his release point might be consistent, the pitch often is thrown with a great deal of body language and that, too, can be disruptive. A hitter switching focus from the emblem of a pitcher's cap to a point down by his knees also is asking for trouble.

Another pitch that tends to make a hitter look foolish is the knuckleball in that, thrown properly, it floats like a butterfly and can be a son of a bee to hit.

"To the fans, it looks like a batting-practice fastball," says Gruber. "Let me tell you, when guys like Charlie Hough [Chicago] and Tom Candiotti [Cleveland] have it working, there's nothing tougher. The ball is here for a tenth of a second, there for a tenth, back here for a tenth.

"It's a pitch that forces you to swing where you think it might be, except there's no telling where it will be. You often end up swinging through two square feet of thin air. It's embarrassing.

"And maybe it's my imagination, but they seem to have

a cruel streak. They'll toss a couple at you, have you chewing on the bill of your cap, then they bust a sixty-five-mile-an-hour fastball inside. Freeze. Strike. Listen to the catcher chuckle. Then, when they're really ahead in the count, they go back to the knuckler and throw it as hard as they can. It's like being on a rubber raft in the middle of a typhoon. Not only are you seasick but you know there's an excellent chance you're going to drown, too."

Paul Kilgus, a left-handed pitcher the Blue Jays traded to the Baltimore Orioles in December 1990, did nothing for Gruber's peace of mind when he told him about playing catch with Hough when the two were members of the Texas Rangers in 1987 and 1988.

"Hough would call the shot on which way it would move," Gruber relates. "Break right, break left, rise, sink. Mind-boggling. Not only does he already have the advantage, knowing what he's going to throw, but to do all those other things with the ball . . . it's mind-boggling."

At the other end of the scale is Roger Clemens.

"As if the guy didn't have enough going for him with the fastball and slider," says Gruber, "now he's got this wicked forkball down pat." What this means is that, in addition to being capable of delivering a pitch at ninety-five mph, he can make it sail, dart and drop at his choosing.

"The trick with Clemens is to try to make him keep the ball low. Upstairs, where a lot of hitters want the fastball, it tends to move a lot more. Basically, he doesn't try to fool you much. It really isn't all that necessary. 'Here it is,' he says. 'Try and hit it.' He's had a little success doing it, too."

Speaking of success, Gruber had quite a bit of it, relatively speaking, in his first couple of outings against Clemens in the 1991 season. In the home opener at Toronto, he went 1-for-4 with a squib single in the first inning against Clemens. In Boston a couple of weeks later, he was 1-for-3 with a double. The Jays, by the way, lost both games handily, and between the first and second meetings Clemens ran up a streak of thirty-one scoreless innings.

For all of Clemens's firepower, Gruber contends that major league hitters can hone their timing to the point that they eventually could learn to hit a golfball shot from a bazooka. "All the hard throwers," Gruber says, "sooner or later, you're going to catch up to them."

The key to survival, as any pitching coach from here to Paducah, Kentucky, will attest, is to "mix 'em up." For those who have not fallen victim to the black arts of "setting up a hitter," this is baseball code for changing pitches, and more importantly for varying the speeds and the spots to which they are delivered.

Nothing so promotes the cause of upsetting a hitter's timing as the relief pitcher. When lefthander Jimmy Key falters, when his curve loses its bite and his fastball slows from a canter to a crawl, manager Cito Gaston puts in a call to the bullpen coach, John Sullivan. Instead of the diet of stuff at variable speeds Key has been throwing, opposing hitters now face a flamethrower.

"Tom Henke or Duane Ward comes in with their 90 miles-an-hour fastball," says Gruber, "and in contrast to Key, it looks like it's doing 110. I'm not saying Jimmy Key throws slop. I've seen him throw the ball past people when he wants, but he's a control pitcher and his game is to keep the hitter off-balance."

In the unlikely event that he would be traded to another club, as had happened to "untouchables" Tony Fernandez and Fred McGriff in the winter of 1990–91, Gruber speaks for most hitters when he says he would prefer to face Henke rather than Ward.

"Henke knows where the pitch is going," says Gruber. "He's about as pinpoint as a pitcher who throws smoke can get. At times, that works against him because the hitters tend to dig in a little more than they would against

Ward. You get in against Ward, you think, ugh, he could just get on top of one and you'll be walking around for a week with the league president's autograph on your rump. He's been known to hit a few guys. Never on purpose, of course. His pitch is 'live' and therefore likely to have more than a little movement on it."

Managers being the keen intellects they are, they adopt a similar disruptive philosophy when they set up the club's rotation of starting pitchers.

"It was tough in '90 when Boston threw a Mike Boddicker at you one day, with his great stuff to keep you off-balance, and then countered with a Roger Clemens. It really upsets a hitter's timing. In Boston, I guess, they're saying the same thing about spotting Jimmy Key between Dave Stieb, Todd Stottlemyre and David Wells."

Although Gruber would not want it noised around to his bosses, the most effective way to undermine his notoriously fragile attention span is a ten-run lead—for either team.

"Ten runs down, you're embarrassed. Ten runs ahead, your mind wanders and your intensity level sinks like a stone. Hey, go up there hacking. 'Let's get out of here and go for a beer.' It's a bad enough attitude at the time, but the real danger is that you'll take it into the next game. For me, it's a big problem. Sounds corny, maybe, but it's true that you can't turn this game on and off—a sin to which I will sometimes have to plead guilty. So even if we're up or down ten I try to keep the intensity level up, even to the point of making it something personal between me and the pitcher."

There are times when a parade of pitchers is an indication of events of historic proportions.

Such was the case on April 16, 1989, when the Blue Jays pounded the Kansas City Royals 15-8. It would have been another eminently forgettable blow-out at

Exhibition Stadium, of which there had been a few over the years, but for a singular exception.

It was the day Gruber accomplished one of the rarest feats in baseball. He became the first Blue Jay to "hit for the cycle"—single, double, triple and home run.

Of course there's an inside story. Gruber, smarting from a 10-5 beating K.C. administered the day before, hit a home run in the first inning of the rematch. As he headed for home plate, he "kind of smirked" at third baseman Kevin Seitzer. "He kind of laughed," Gruber recalls. "'Big deal,' he was saying."

After doubling the next time up and advancing to third, Gruber says he mumbled something intelligent like "Uh-huh," which was intended to suggest the spike might be on the other foot this day.

"He kind of laughed," says Gruber.

After tripling and standing with his foot on the bag as if it were a prize whitetail he just bagged in the Texas out-back, it was Gruber's turn to laugh.

"I'm watching him," Gruber continues, "and he's peeved. So would I be. I admit I probably was doing it in spite for pasting us the day before. So after I slid into the bag, he comes over and says, 'Well, I guess all you need now is a single.' Now I'm peeved. This whole time, he hasn't said a word to me. And with each hit, I've seen his mood change. I've had a heck of an afternoon and this is all he can think to say to me? Three hits aren't enough?

"Well, I ended up scoring and I'm on the bench, still a little hot over what he said. And it hits me. Home run, double, triple . . . *single*! Geez, it took me long enough! If it hadn't been for him reminding me, I might not have hit for the cycle. Inspiration? Heck, no. The single I hit next time up might have been a double any other day."

It is more than a coincidence that Gruber, third in the order that day, got decent pitches to hit all that Sunday afternoon.

If all goes according to form, one of the benefits that ac-crues to the third man is that he comes to bat after the club's most consistent hitter and before its most powerful. On the one hand, there are "ducks on the pond" to be driven home. On the other, there is less chance the other team will "pitch around" him with the clean-up hitter due next. As a consequence, Gruber had a "career year" in 1990, even though a nagging series of hand injuries ham-pered production for six weeks in the middle of summer.

"If it weren't for Tony Fernandez, George Bell and Fred McGriff bracketing me in 1990, I wouldn't have got-ten nearly the RBIs I did get," Gruber admits. "As well as getting on base himself and being pretty quick to get home, Fernandez pushed a lot of runners up for me. With McGriff on deck, there was no way a pitcher could get too cute with me."

Another example of the benefits was evident in the weekend series against the Baltimore Orioles in September 1990 when Gruber cracked the century mark in RBIs for the first time.

The assault began inauspiciously, a 1-for-4 night at the plate on Thursday including a pop-up with two on in the seventh and his team behind 5-2. It concluded with a three-run homer in the bottom of the ninth to ice a 4-3 victory on Saturday and a 2-for-4 outing on Sunday in a ten-inning victory. In between, there was a Friday night that he would dearly love to have bronzed.

Good enough to cinch honours as American League player of the week—13-for-28 for a .464 average and 14 RBIs to raise his season's total to 107—but when he re-members the weekend years from now, it will be for a mo-ment in the seventh inning that Friday.

With two out, score 6-3 in favour of the Orioles, he bounced a pitch from Jeff Ballard off the wall in left-cen-tre to score Manuel Lee and Junior Felix. RBIs 100 and 101, delivered at a vital point in the season, brought

50,000 out of their seats to bawl a chorus of The Standing O.

Gruber was genuinely surprised.

"I waited for it to die down," he said afterward. "It was getting embarrassing. Then, the way I looked at it, if they thought it was something I guess I'd better be polite and tip my cap."

As he did so, he glanced at the Blue Jays' bench and nodded to the man who had worked long and hard to bring him all that way from Dunedin in the springtime of 1984 to the heights of fame in the autumn of 1990: Cito Gaston.

"You could see that this kid had all kinds of talent—speed, good arm, power—just not polished, that's all," Gaston said one morning back at Dunedin midway through spring training of 1991. "Yes, I could see then what he'd be today. It just took him a while to adjust to the things I was trying to teach him. Then, about three years ago here in spring training, the lights went on for him. He finally caught on to what I was talking about."

Which was?

"Just get an idea what you're going to do when you walk out there, so you're not walking up there with a blank mind, just looking for the ball. That's something I don't teach. Once in a while, he gets away from it. Sometimes he has no plan, probably swings at something he doesn't really want to hit."

Now that Gruber has achieved his measure of greatness, the Jays' new hitting coach, Gene Tenace, says there is now only one person who can stop Gruber from being all he can be.

"He's got to work harder," he says as he watches Gruber in the batting cage at Dunedin. "The problem with this game is that once you think you've got it made, you tend to slack off. The pitchers are still at work, though. Every at-bat, it's got to be like it was his last one."

Tenace, a catcher who played for three World Series champions in Oakland during the 1970s, says one of the most ferocious adversaries Gruber will have to confront is his own success.

"There's a sort of peace in failure," he says. "Nobody bothers you when you're hitting .220. Put that average up to .300, drive in 100 runs, be an all-star, now you've got people expecting you to do it every year. It can become an awful burden."

And if Gruber can slay that dragon?

"Hall of Fame," says Tenace. Seriously.

CHAPTER 14

 STARS IN HIS EYES

If there is a special place for Eric Lindros and Michael Jordan in a major set of baseball cards, no matter how brightly their stars now shine in other arenas, then there ought to be one for every player who suited up for the 1990 All-Star Game at Wrigley Field in Chicago.

Heralded as the second coming of Mario Lemieux long before he graduated from the ranks of junior hockey in the spring of 1991, Lindros made it into Score's 110-card "traded" set in 1990 wearing a Toronto Blue Jays uniform.

Jordan, the superstar guard with the Chicago Bulls of the National Basketball Association, turned up in Chicago White Sox linens on a featured card in the 1991 Upper Deck set.

These star-crossed athletes earned their place in baseball history through guest shots at batting practice.

As well as anyone, Kelly Gruber understands the niceties of the ancillary market and is not at all surprised that Score of Grand Prairie, Texas, and Upper Deck of Yorba Linda, California, would make good on a "celebrity visit" to the park. What upsets him is that the "celebrity visit" Gruber and his peers paid to Wrigley Field last July went largely unnoticed by the five major companies who control the booming North American trading card market (Donruss, Fleer, Score, Topps, Upper Deck).

"Sometimes they make cards of the players the fans vote in as starters," Gruber argues, "but never the ones the managers pick to complete the squad. Ridiculous. Highway robbery. It's just not right. All of us, whether we're elected or chosen by the managers, deserve to be recognized for making the all-star team."

In 1991, Gruber had to settle for what Topps did. The card company celebrating forty years in the marketplace, chose him as third baseman in its eleven-card team of American League all-stars, ignoring the people's choice, Wade Boggs of Boston.

These glossy bits of cardboard often are regarded as a source of consternation by ballplayers—"Hey, mister, sign my card!" is the polite chorus they hear the minute they step onto Civvy Street—but at the same time the cards are considered a trapping of professional success.

Gruber, one of the more patient signers, will autograph any of his cards but the one in the high-end 1990 Leaf set printed by Donruss. Not that he has any quarrel with the manufacturer. Far from it. It is just that the only Leaf card that will ever bear his signature is the one he is keeping for his infant son Kody. If Gruber had his way, he would one day be able to give the boy his dad's all-star card from each of the sets marketed in 1991, particularly since the two bases he stole in Chicago tied a record shared by the great Willie Mays.

Given a little luck, he was saying at his locker at the SkyDome a few days later, it could have been a record-breaking three. With Dave Smith of the Houston Astros pitching, American League manager Tony La Russa called Gruber off the bench to run for Boggs of the Boston Red Sox after he singled to right field in the sixth inning. With the count 3-1 on Jose Canseco of the Oakland Athletics,

Gruber was off, and had Smith's offering been a strike instead of a ball Gruber feels he would have swiped his first base of the night cleanly. As it was, he had to wait a few minutes. With the count 3-2 on Blue Jays teammate George Bell, he and Canseco pulled a double steal when Bell struck out swinging.

The next inning, after Julio Franco of the Texas Rangers singled to drive home the only two runs of the game, Gruber walked on a 3-2 pitch. On the first offering to Canseco, he swiped his second uncontested base of the game.

Even though he flew out sharply to centre field in his final at-bat, making him hitless for the two times he has been named to the American League's dream team, Gruber took great pride in his accomplishment and wishes there was a set of his all-star baseball cards he could hand down to his children.

The card companies could argue that adding full all-star squads would inflate their already inflated sets, but Score in 1991 included 125 rookie prospects, 25 draft choices who may never make it out of Double A ball, and special cards honouring Master Blasters, K-Men, Riflemen, a No-Hit Club and a subset for each team's franchise player.

Gruber thinks the wants of card collectors and ballplayers alike could be satisfied with a twelve-card subset of all-star highlights that would include the game's most valuable player and winning pitcher. At the very least, a stylized star could be posted on a corner of each player's regular issue.

"Years from now, I can see people asking if So-and-so was on the 1990 All-Star squad. 'Oh yeah, he was the MVP.' 'Really?' I have no stats to back this up, but I'll bet that at least half the time the top player in the game wasn't a starter. Look at the cards and you'd never know it. Now, to my mind, that guy, whoever he might be, made an important contribution to baseball that season. The card companies should be helping people remember those things."

Even more compelling is the argument that baseball's All-Star Game is contested far more fiercely by the participants than by their counterparts in hockey, football and basketball—contests in which the competitors are careful not to jeopardize a fellow athlete's career with anything remotely akin to hard contact. The tone for baseball was set long before, but it is epitomized by the body block Pete Rose of Cincinnati threw at catcher Ray Fosse of Cleveland in the twelfth inning of the 1970 game. In separating Fosse from the ball in that historic collision at home plate—Rose's was the deciding run in a 5-4 victory—Rose also separated the catcher's shoulder. Fosse, twenty-three and on the threshold of becoming a fine receiver, never became the player he was once fully expected to be.

If some of this suggests that Gruber's ego has outgrown his hat size, it should be noted that he says all the things a gracious also-ran ought to say regarding the fans' choice of Boggs as the all-star starter at third.

"He's paid his dues," Gruber says of the five-time AL batting champ and future Hall of Famer. "He deserved to be there. No doubt. Making the all-star team is one of the benefits he reaped for what he's done down through the years. I'm just hoping that my time will come before I grow too old."

Mid-season stats suggest Gruber was jobbed. After 75 games over the first three months of the season, Gruber was hitting .308 (92-for-299) with 20 home runs and 64 RBIs—the stuff in which MVP seasons are rooted. Boggs, after 70 games, was hitting .295 (80-for-271) with five home runs and 29 RBIs. Nor was it defence that turned the key for Boggs, since Gruber was on his way to winning the Gold Glove for his work in the field.

Gruber admits he would prefer that baseball come up

with a fairer way of selecting the teams that play the mid-summer classic. Since 1970, the year the vote was taken away from the sportswriters and given to the baseball fans, the selection of starters had been only a popularity contest.

Indeed, a player must have talent to be considered. At the same time, however, it helps to play for a team in a populous market. This means many deserving players must rely on the all-star manager who fills out the roster. Most of the ballots are cast at the twenty-six stadiums in the major leagues—vote early, vote often for the guy with the nicest set of buns—and tend to reflect bias for the home team. All well and good, supporters of the system assert, since each team plays the same number of games before a home crowd.

Sometimes, for reasons that have little to do with the product, a team that is drawing well has a larger voting base. The tendency of spectators is to vote for their own, so the system is open to abuses. This is why a singles hitter with a high average at the plate, never mind his tentative approach to work on the field, often outpolls a fencebuster whose face is forever in the mud knocking down certain singles before they find the outfield.

No question, too, there would be a glorious opportunity in Toronto to rig the vote in 1991, when the All-Star Game would be played at the SkyDome. Certain to challenge season attendance figures that set a major league record in 1990, the hordes who showed up at the SkyDome in 1991 were well aware that stacking the vote would put their favourites on the field that July. Gruber, for instance, drew close to 150,000 notes on the first count even though he played in fewer than half of his club's first fifty games.

At least one glaring injustice—in Gruber's opinion, if not that of the voters—was committed in 1990 when Mark McGwire of the Oakland Athletics got the call at first base instead of Cecil Fielder of the Detroit Tigers.

"Not taking a whole lot away from McGwire, but Cecil should have started at first," says Gruber. "Up to that point he had been the more productive player. McGwire got it because he was the more familiar face to the fans and Fielder had just come back after playing a year in Japan."

Gruber's analysis of the McGwire-Fielder situation was borne out at season's end when Fielder finished second to Rickey Henderson of the Athletics in MVP voting. Fielder, with 51 homers and 132 RBIs, finished with 286 votes, 31 fewer than Henderson—and a whopping 260 ahead of McGwire.

"If I know Cecil," says Gruber, "he'd say it didn't really matter as long as the manager filled out the All-Stars' roster with the right guys. To me, that's taking too much of a chance. Why entrust something so important to one man? It puts an awful lot of heat on one guy to make up for the mistakes the voters might have made. I'm sure he really doesn't want the pressure. First, he has to make sure every team has at least one player on the squad. If he fills in with one of his own guys, no matter how deserving, there's bound to be charges of favouritism. Then in every city on the road that season he's got an enemy who thinks he should have been picked instead of another guy."

Gruber believes there is a simple way to help keep everyone happy. "No real need to change the way things are done for the game. Keep it as a popularity contest. What I'd like to see at the end of the season is a second all-star team, based on what went on that entire year. That way, the guy who had a great second half gets recognition. Comparing the first and second squads would also give the fans something to argue about the whole winter."

Gruber thinks it would be most interesting if the managers of the four division winners made the end-of-season selections, and to keep the process impartial, forbid them from voting for players on their own teams. Another method, one that would fill a few columns on the sports pages in the off-season, would be to let the writers call the shots at the end of the season.

It might take the human element out of it, but another way of deciding the issues would be to hire one of the baseball statistical services that proliferate. They're the ones that can tell a fan, down to one thousandth of a point, why pitching Fred McGriff low and away on a hot, sunny afternoon is a lot smarter than running a fastball off his rump. (Answer: He's six foot three, 210 pounds of marble, carries a bat and can cover sixty feet real quick.)

Whatever methods were used to make the choice, Gruber says the resulting twenty-five man roster is one he would like to see take the field after the World Series has been put into the books.

"Make it a best-of-seven series between the two leagues," he says, "and if the cause was the right one—the baseball pension comes to mind, with an eye on the old-timers who started the union but got shorted out on the benefits—I think the players would love to play it.

"Then again, it might be too good of an idea. It might outdraw the World Series."

There is hardly an award handed out following the season, according to Gruber, that could not stand reviewing. As expected, since it is the most prized, chief among them is the Most Valuable Player Award.

It traces its history to the short-lived Chalmers Award, presented from 1911 to 1914 along with a car to the out-standing player in his league. The MVP Award was insti-tuted in 1922 when a committee charged by the American League honoured first baseman George Sisler of the St Louis Browns for a season in which he hit .420, drove in 105 runs and scored 134. The National League launched its award two years later by selecting pitcher Clarence

(Dazzy) Vance of the Brooklyn Robins for his 28-6 record (2.16 ERA).

The selection process was turned over to the Baseball Writers' Association of America (BBWAA) in 1931 and has been in their able hands ever since. What bedevils them in their task, much as it has those who have attempted to draft a new constitution for Canada over the past generation, is defining what is valuable.

Gruber sympathizes, and at the same time is willing to add his two cents' worth to the argument.

"You've got to have the stats to win it," he says, "but stats are not enough."

For the sake of argument, he offers the numbers that were put to the sportswriters in 1990. Rickey Henderson of Oakland led the league in runs scored, 119; on-base average, .439; and stolen bases, 65. Cecil Fielder of Detroit led in home runs, 51; RBIs, 132; total bases, 339; and slugging percentage, .592. Henderson, a splendid left fielder, also finished second in slugging percentage, .577; fifth in homers, 28; and fourth in walks, 97. Fielder, so slow of foot that he had yet to steal his first base in the majors, finished second in runs scored, 104, and plays first base, one of the least demanding defensive positions.

As the figures and Gruber suggest, the stats fail to cut a clear and compelling case for either man as MVP.

"It has to come down to something else. What does 'most valuable' mean? If we remove each guy from his team, what happens? Oakland struggles but still wins the West. Instead of finishing third behind us in the East, Detroit finishes fifth or sixth.

"Now say Detroit comes out of nowhere and wins its division. Why? Cecil Fielder, obviously. Now my vote goes to him.

"Part of the equation, obviously, is how important a role a player had in making a team a contender. Call it the Most Important Player and it might get a more accurate vote. To me, the player has to be a key part of a contender. Was he just involved, or did he do something that put them over the top?

"Put it this way, between Henderson and Fielder in 1990, it had to be Henderson—he's a little more versatile; he'll hurt you more ways—but the margin he won it by [317 to 286] tells you how close it was."

Fielder, for his part, appraised the vote candidly. He thought he had been screwed.

"Of course I feel I should have won; nobody wants to finish second," he said the night the award was announced. "I can't say that I didn't have an MVP type of season, because I did. I did everything I can do. I can't fill out the ballots. I did a lot more than people thought I could do. Including myself."

Had it not been for a frustrating stretch of injuries to his left hand, which tossed him into a six-week slump following the break for the All-Star Game, Gruber might well have taken it all. As it was, his efforts—.274 average, 31 homers, 118 RBIs—earned him fourth place in the voting with 175 points, 37 fewer than pitcher Roger Clemens of Boston.

Fielder has a point when he says that others have won it while playing with teams that were not contenders.

Andre Dawson, formerly of the Montreal Expos, captured the honour in 1987 when he hit 49 home runs and drove in 137 runs for the Chicago Cubs. So far and away was he the *best* player that there really was little debate about the choice. Making it easy was that Tony Gwynn, the other hot hitter in the league with .370, 218 hits, laboured for the San Diego Padres, who matched the Cubs for sixth-place finishes.

One choice that did bring the system into question was the selection of Robin Yount as the American League winner in 1989. There is no question that the Milwaukee Brewers outfielder will enter the Hall of Fame before this decade is out. However, his numbers that season were less than awesome. He finished fourth in batting average and hits (.318 and 195) to Kirby Puckett of the Minnesota Twins (.339, 215); second to Ruben Sierra of the Texas Rangers in total bases (344-314); third in slugging average to Sierra (.543-.511); fourth in runs scored to Rickey Henderson (113-101); and sixth to Sierra in RBIs (119-103).

"Sierra leads the league in five departments [RBIs, slugging average, extra-base hits (78), total bases, triples (14)] and it's not good enough for MVP," says Gruber. "Yount leads in none and he wins it. You've got to have some guys voting for one reason, others for another reason. Either that or there's a lot of politics involved."

Statsmaster Bill James, whose work has been used for years by Gruber's agents, Alan and Randal Hendricks of Houston, in salary negotiations, backs the choice of Yount in his 1990 edition of *The Baseball Book*.

Among the comparisons he cites that favour Yount is the percentage of runners scored from third base with fewer than two out: 85, third in the league, compared with Sierra's 62, not in the top 20; Yount's batting average with runners on second or third was .355, sixth in the league, compared with Sierra's .337, twelfth in the league; and Yount's performance on the road, where he hit .328 (.490 slugging) with 7 homers and 44 RBIs, compared with Sierra's .295 (.468), 8 homers and 46 RBIs.

On the subject of hitting, Gruber suggests that a batting average is not the measure of success it is cracked up to be. He would rather be remembered as a dangerous hitter, for instance, than one who wins batting crowns.

"A lot of times, a guy will win the title because he was smart enough to walk 80 times. 'Uhhhh, how many runs did he drive in?' 'Forty.' 'Uhhhh, how many times did he score?' 'Forty.' 'Uhhhh, how many homers did he hit?' 'Ten.' I think a lot of guys go up there thinking about walks, thinking about themselves. Is that what it's all about?

"What about the guy who hits .280, has 25 more hits and drives in 100 runs but draws 40 fewer walks? His average is lower, but who's the more valuable player?

"There are times you have to be patient, times you do things for your club. I'm up there for one reason: drive in runs. If that calls for going two or three inches out of the strike zone thinking I can hit it in the gap, instead of taking it for a walk, then I'm going to swing and try to drive in the run."

A prime example of what Gruber is talking about can be seen by comparing the statistics of Wade Boggs and Kirby Puckett.

"I was really impressed when Puckett won the batting title in '89. He hits .339, leads the league with 215 hits but—and this is the amazing part—has only 41 walks and 59 strikeouts. He's up there to hit, not to look."

It also made amends for the previous season when he finished second to Boggs (.366-.356) after leading the league with 234 hits and 657 at-bats. What cost him the title were the minimal 23 walks he took. Boggs, meanwhile, walked 125 times in 1988 and 107 times in 1989.

His backers will say that Boggs stroked 200 hits for seven seasons in a row, 1983 to 1989, but what separates the two players as hitters are the slugging averages Puckett has posted since he came into the league in 1984. Only in 1987, when he hit an unaccustomed 24 home runs, did Boggs' slugging average rise above .500 (to .588). In three of the past five seasons heading into 1991, while averaging 37 walks, Puckett has led the league in hits and posted slugging averages over .500.

All this talk about slugging may remind the reader that Gruber has yet to collect his first hit in All-Star competition. Not all that surprising, perhaps, considering that it took him a couple of All-Star Games to record one official trip to the plate.

His first trip to the game, in 1989, ended in the on-deck circle. After pressing flesh with President Ronald Reagan in the American League clubhouse at Cincinnati, Gruber was approached by the manager, Tony La Russa, to discuss the way he intended to employ him that night.

"He told me I was a valuable asset to the team because I could play so many positions," Gruber recalled. "'You're really the most versatile guy on the club,' he said. 'If somebody goes down, if we get into extra innings, that's where you might make all the difference.' If he'd told me all this later, I might have thought he was putting me on. But before the game? I took it as a compliment that he sought me out to tell me how it was going to be."

For what promised to be the most significant at-bat to that point of his career, the call to "get loose" came from La Russa in the bottom of the seventh inning with the American League clinging to a 2-1 lead at Anaheim Stadium in California.

"He told me I'd be the fourth guy up in our next inning," said Gruber. "I was like a bee in a hive. Find my helmet. Go to the rack and haul out my favourite bat. Put my batting gloves on. Take a few swings. Think about what Mitch ("I pitch like my hair is on fire") Williams, warming up for the Nationals, will throw at/to me (fastball the first two strikes, then *maybe* something off-speed) and which one will offer me my best chance.

"'All right!' I'm thinking. 'Fourth guy up. One guy gets a hit and I'm up there with a chance to drive in a big run.' What a way to make your all-star debut. Funny, but I wasn't a bit nervous. Look at my history, and that's the last thing you might have expected. I had good vibes, too. I felt really strong.

"First guy up, I don't remember who, he makes an out. Second guy, Ruben Sierra, gets a base hit. 'Yeah! That one's for me. Now I get my shot.' You can imagine how

excited I am when Sierra winds up on second base. All it
will take is a simple single to bring him home."

Williams, facing catcher Mickey Tettleton of the
Baltimore Orioles, catches Sierra leaning and picks him
off cleanly. Then he fans Tettleton. End of inning.

It took a while for Gruber to comprehend that the bat
has been taken out of his hands in the 1989 All-Star
Game. Dammit.

"I came back to the dugout. I laid down my helmet. I
look at a couple of guys. Pitcher Mark Gubicza of the
K.C. Royals looks at me, his face as long as an afternoon
in mid-July. 'Don't worry about it, Kelly,' he says. 'There'll
be other days.' What's he talking about?

"I sat down on the bench, wondering if they'd stick with
Williams in the ninth or pull another live one from the
bullpen. We get one out. I'm still fidgety. Ready to go.
Everybody else is getting excited, too, but I'm in my own
little world. Then we get another out. Now everybody in
the dugout is standing up. They're yelling stuff like 'One
more to go!' 'Yo, American!' 'C'mon, guys! Wrap it up!'

"Then it dawns on me: 'Wait a minute, Kelly. This
might be the home of the Angels, slowpoke, but you ain't
on the visiting team. One more out and this whole shooting match is history. Put away the bat, fool, and start
cheering.'"

Tony La Russa offered his regrets to Gruber, but there
could be no faulting his decisions in guiding the American
League through a squeaker to its second All-Star Game
victory in a row for the first time in thirty-one years.

"He told me I'd be back. Within a year, give him credit,
he kept his word. All last winter, knowing he'd be the All-
Stars' manager again this summer in Toronto, I promised
myself to take the matter out of his hands by making sure
I won the vote for the starting job at third base. What's
that line about the best-laid plans of mice and men? I
wonder if it was meant to include baseball players."

CHAPTER 15

 THE "INSIDE" STORY

Aside from the throwing of strikes, which is the first rule in the pitcher's law of survival, there is no dictate more vital to his well-being than taking the outer half of the plate away from a hitter. This is called "working inside," and the pitcher who fails to do it effectively will not work long in the big leagues. The reason for it is simple enough.

Whatever the pitch, the easiest ball to hit far and hard is the one that crosses the outer part of the plate at belt level or higher. It allows a hitter to extend his arms fully, imparting maximum force to the swing, and it places the heaviest part of the bat in the immediate vicinity of the baseball.

This is not to say that laying pitches on the outside corner need be a cardinal sin. Quite the contrary. What must accompany such a pitch, like peanut butter on the toast before the jelly goes on, is the process of keeping the hitter off-balance. A big part of it is "working inside."

Hitters, ever eager to pounce on any advantage, like to lean out over the plate and reap the harvest of offerings on the outside. Pitchers, naturally, try to make a mess of hitters by flaming the ball inside.

The device is known by all manner of names—"purpose pitch" and "duster," "brushback" and "the high hard one"—but the idea is the same. Keep the hitter on his toes, and if he still thinks he can take advantage by leaning, see if he gets the message when he's on the seat of his pants. Believe it or not, hitters understand.

"These guys have to pitch inside," says Kelly Gruber, who has done his fair share of leaning and of paying the laundry bills for the privilege. "If they don't work inside, you kill them."

Just how far inside is the not-so-grey area that concerns Gruber and his peers.

"You just hope the attitude isn't, 'Well, I'm going to pop one inside and if it gets away, well, tough salami. It hit him? Big deal.' They know where the hitter is. He's over there on first base, checking to see how many ribs he's got left. 'Could have been worse, eh? At least he didn't smoke one off the wall.'

"It might not be the right attitude, but there's a lot of pitchers who have it."

First inclinations prompt a victim to make a beeline to the mound and square the debt. Tactically, says Gruber, this is a mistake for a lot of reasons.

"For one thing, your chances of making it to the mound are slim," he was saying one night in July of 1990 before he delivered himself into the hands of the Blue Jays trainer Tommy Craig to correct a minor ailment. "Even if you're rolling around in the dirt, a smart catcher puts himself between you and his pitcher. The ump, who doesn't want the black mark of a brawl on his shift, also knows what you might be thinking even before you think it.

"Even if you're quick, even if you do get to the mound, you'd be doing well to get in a couple of pokes. And you're already hurt. He's had the first shot. If that isn't enough of an advantage, he sees you coming and knows a catcher and an ump are right behind. If he's smart, he low-bridges you, knocking you back into his catcher, just as you bounce your overhand right on the upper part of his back.

"Let's say you do get lucky and land a couple. Next thing you know, you're fighting for your breath under a pile of players. They toss you out of the game for starting a riot, and then a few days later the league president sends word that your next cheque will be light because you're taking three days off to mend the error of your ways. Now your manager is pissed because you screwed up his line-up. Maybe you lose a game you should have won, and because of it your team blows the pennant.

"Sure, I'm laying it on a little thick. Same time, tell me it couldn't happen."

Ask any hitter, from George Brett to Robin Yount, the best method for exacting true vengeance and their eyes glaze over when they mutter something along the lines of "hittin' 'im where it hurts most . . . on the scoreboard."

More often than management cares to know, Gruber says, frontier justice prevails.

"If I think someone is trying to hurt me, if someone's jacking around with the way I make a living, then I'll have my time to get him. 'Listen for the knock on the door, friend. It's you and me. Under the stands. In the street. Nobody else to break it up.'"

While some club-owners might lose their lunch at the idea, Gruber also says a few hitters have been known to settle the score in an instant by helicoptering bats towards the mound after the next pitch. "I've done it," Gruber said. "Problem is it didn't go anywhere near the guy. But I let it go. I've thought about picking up the ball, too, going out there and firing it as hard as I can from twenty feet. Eye for an eye. See how he likes it. It just doesn't seem fair to me that I'm up there like a sitting duck and some guy's got the right to pluck me."

Deciding on a course of vengeance is a matter far more

black-and-white than wading into the shady areas of who is and is not taking liberties with a hitter.

"First thing you do after you're hit, even before the pain sets in, is wheel around and see the guy's reactions," says Gruber. "Usually, those first ones are telling. Boom! I get hit. Forget the pain. Look at the guy. Don't give him time to put on his mask. Is he upset or satisfied with himself?"

An errant pitch can have profound effects. Two such "mistakes" may have cost Gruber the 1990 Most Valuable Player award in the American League. Coincidence of coincidences, both pitches were made within a ten-day period, hit virtually the same spot on his left hand, happened early in the openers of three-game series and involved pitchers from the California Angels, the first on July 3 at the SkyDome and the second July 12 at Anaheim Stadium.

With the veteran Rance Mulliniks in the wings, eminently capable of providing adequate defence at third base, it might have been better for the Blue Jays had Gruber's throwing hand been injured. The left hand anchors the bat and the right hand acts as a propelling force, so he would have been able to cope with such an injury at the plate. Working as a designated hitter would have given him time to heal his wounds while keeping his batting eye sharp.

Undoubtedly, it also would have kept him in the running for the MVP vote. Entering the break for the All-Star Game, Gruber was hitting .296 with 20 home runs and 66 RBIs. With half a season left, elementary math suggests, he was on track to hit 40 homers and rack up 132 RBIs. Put these numbers beside the name of the major contributor to a division championship and visions of an MVP award are bound to well up.

Instead of the steady beat his bat had maintained in

April, May and June—seven, six and seven home runs; 20, 20 and 24 RBIs—he connected for two home runs and 11 RBIs in July, one home run and 12 RBIs in August. His hand healed, he snapped out of his slump in September and October with a .333 average, eight home runs and 31 RBIs.

The first injury could not have come at a more disruptive time. Over the next three weeks, he would be all over the map. Literally and figuratively.

The night Blyleven's pitch got away, he and his wife of almost four years planned that she would enter hospital the next morning to have the birth of their first child induced, if doctors considered the procedure safe. Gruber then would skip the second game of the series, play the next day and in a three-game weekend series against Seattle. Depending on the well-being of his wife and new son, he would arrive late in Chicago to attend the All-Star Game. After a brief return to Toronto to visit his son, he would join the Blue Jays in California for an eleven-day tour of the West Coast with stops in Anaheim, Seattle and Oakland. He would arrive at his home in Toronto at dawn on July 23 after almost three weeks of living out of a suitcase.

To do all this while ministering to a banged-up hand was a big pain in the hip pocket.

Bert Blyleven, a veteran pitcher in the final stages of a career that might send him to the Hall of Fame, is noted for his pinpoint control. His curve rated as one of the best in the majors and his fastball, while lacking its former snap, clocked in at 85 miles an hour.

Gruber is well aware of the sweeping curve right-hander Blyleven likes to lay on the outer edge of the plate. "Leaning" a little to take advantage, it is easy to see how Gruber got caught by an inside fastball intended to brush him back.

"It looked like a pitch that got away," says Gruber.

"He'd been pitching me inside anyway."

Even if Blyleven had been aiming, he could not have caught Gruber more squarely or at a more critical point. Bruising was extensive and a large blood blister formed where the meat of the hand had been pinched up against the bat. For a while, the team's doctors worried that a bone also had been chipped.

To look on the brighter side of things, the timing of the first injury was opportune. After struggling through the weekend series with Seattle, Gruber did not have to press himself through the three-day break in Chicago. After his brief visit with his wife and baby back in Toronto, the hand had shown rapid improvement by the time he reported to the clubhouse at Anaheim Stadium.

"That afternoon in the clubhouse, I was feeling pretty good about what I had been able to do in the All-Star Game. 'Geez,' I'm thinking, 'maybe I am right to believe I belong in this league. I've got 20 homers, 66 RBIs, my average is right up there and I didn't embarrass myself in Chicago.'

"As I'm putting on the uniform, thoughts are racing through my head. 'This might be the season I put it all together. Only one real injury and I've had time to put it right. For once, I feel really healthy. I know I can be consistent. I won't let these little mental slumps get to me. I'll keep my intensity level up. I'll stay on the right track.'

"Batting practice was great. Even the stretching, which can be a bore in the middle of the season, seemed like fun."

Considering his frame of mind going into the first game of the second half of the season, it is no wonder he felt higher than a kite a few minutes later when, after Kirk McCaskill worked him for a couple of strikes, he smoked a crackling curve into right field for a single.

"As I'm going down to first base, I feel like I've hit a grand slam to win the pennant. I've just taken my first positive step in the second half. First at-bat. Didn't take any time at all. Not only am I healthy, I've also answered the biggest question facing me. 'Do I still have the stroke?' Right then and there I've answered the question. 'Yes, I've got my stroke.' I was some kind of happy."

Things were going so well, it made some sort of convoluted cosmic sense that they just had to go bad. Quickly.

"Next at-bat, Boom!" says Gruber. "I get hit on the same stinking spot on the same stinking hand! Fastball. Right away, paranoia. 'The S.O.B. did it on purpose! He wants to wreck the second half for me!' At this point, I'm a candidate for a straightjacket. As crazy as I am, as screwy as this sounds, my first rational thought is to see how McCaskill is taking it. When I look, he's doing a pretty fair impression of a guy disgusted with himself that he gave up a free pass. All the way to the base, I watch him, waiting for him to say something. He doesn't crack. I had to give him the benefit of the doubt.

"If I had to pick the worst minute of the season, this had to be it. I feel awful. 'God almighty, not another second half of being hurt! Here we go again. I just get this sucker well and now it's back to being all smashed up.' Not only does it inflame an old injury, but it adds something to it. And, unlike the last time, there are no days off ahead for it to get well. 'This one's really going to put me off track. I know it. Will I get my swing back? How long will it take? Why me?'

"My coaches might not be impressed with the all-for-one attitude, but that's all I could think of for the rest of the game."

There is little doubt that Gruber creased McCaskill on his first at-bat—an offering on the outside that was lashed into right field. After that, the Canadian-born pitcher intended to keep Gruber "honest" the second time up.

A few years back, McCaskill, who once owned a superior fastball clocked at 90 to 95 mph, was forced to resort to a more guileful game after suffering an assortment of arm ailments that included bone chips around his elbow. He rebounded with a 15-10 (2.93 ERA) record in 1989, but faded to 12-11 (3.25) in the 1990 season. Forced to compete with a diminishing arsenal, he must now survive on pinpoint control. Unable to "blow away" hitters, he does not pitch inside as often as he once did.

Given these factors, it figures that Gruber was looking for something outside again and McCaskill, "working inside" to keep Gruber off-balance, got too close.

"First Blyleven, then McCaskill," says Gruber. "It seems too much of a coincidence for it to be an accident, but how can you convince yourself they were able to hit the same, exact spot? If they could pick off a knuckle at sixty feet, hell, they wouldn't need to keep me honest in the first place. . . .

"Both of them smashed my hand right up against the knob on the bottom of the bat. A surgeon needs his hands, right? Same with a baseball player. He'd almost prefer anything else be hit except his hands. For a long while there, maybe a good six weeks, one of mine was next to useless."

As high on life as he had been, Gruber fell into a tailspin psychologically as well as physically after those two pitches. He can withstand his share of pain, but he is too frenetic an individual to be considered a "good patient."

There are any number of instances in his professional career that illustrate his high threshold for pain. When the pursuit of money was involved it was too easy to construe an ulterior motive. The best examples of his tolerance are to be found in his days as a high school football star back home in Austin.

"Most kids at that age like to lie in on Saturday morning," he was saying one night before a game last August. "I'm the same, but the difference was I couldn't get up. First thing I felt when I rolled over was that stinking sheet ripping away from all the scrapes I picked up the night before. Strawberries all over my legs and elbows. First thing you'd have to do was peel them suckers off. Some kind of hurtin'.

"I'd be a mess. Both ankles torn up. Bruises all over. For two days, it'd be a struggle to get around.

"Funny, but come that Friday night, I'd be ready to play those four quarters and never feel a twinge. I'd go sixty minutes, too. Quarterback on offence. Safety on defence. I'd carry the ball thirty times a game.

"The older I get, the more I look back and think, 'How could you not feel it in the game?' The answer, of course, is that the intensity level is way up. You don't feel the aches and pains. Until the next day."

Perhaps age has something to do with it, perhaps the different demands of a different game, but while the peaks of intensity are attained as easily in baseball, the reminders issued by various body parts are more acute.

"Same as football, once the game starts, you tend to forget about your hurts," Gruber agrees. "These days, though, you seem to pay for your sins as you go along. Like last year with the hand injury. You'd get fooled on a pitch, swing hard, try to hold up. Man, that's hurtin' time. So then you take the strike, let the bat go round, minimize the pain. Get back in the box and hope you don't get fooled again.

"Right away, the doubts start creeping up on me. 'Geez, Kelly, you're not seeing the ball well. Can't let this guy get a strike on you or you'll be in the hole.' You tend to swing through on more pitches because you don't want to check-swing with your hand hurting. So you swing over top of it to avoid the pain. Now you're deeper in the hole. And the one thing you've got to remember about pitching at this level is that when they've got you down, they'll put a foot in your face. Fair enough, too.

"Unlike football, there aren't the days off for healing.

The toughest thing, when you're ailing, is to come out every day. Batting practice, which can be fun, becomes a chore. It was an ordeal just to get the hand lubricated. And it gets tighter each day because you never give it a rest.

"I wasn't seeing the ball as well as I had. As a hitter, I'm right off the tracks. I'm out there turning the game on and off, depending on the score, and that means my batting average and that of the club are suffering because of it.

"It goes on. And on. And on. Until finally, the season's over or by some slim chance, it gets well.

"The worst part of it is that these things weigh on you mentally. Most likely you've slumped because of the physical problem. Now that you're down, your mind starts playing games on you and making things worse. My team needs me, but I'm not pulling the load. We're ready to make a move, but my foot's on the brakes. No matter how good the reasons might be for being unable to do your bit, they're cold comfort when you look in the clubhouse mirror before you head home.

"What makes it doubly difficult to snap out of it is that you're battling two kinds of slumps. Physical and mental. It's tough enough beating one of them, but two?"

If there was a benefit to be reaped, a silver lining to the clouds that descended on him, it had a lot to do with the old saw about necessity being the mother of invention.

"You get hurt. You compensate. I like hitting an inside fastball as well as anybody. It's a natural tendency for me, for any young guy who thinks he has power. Even though I can't hit it now, can't get around on it like I was able to before I got hurt, I still want to swing. So I adjust. Instead of waiting on the stuff that's hard and inside, I start to look for something away that's a little slower. It didn't take long before I was parking a lot of what hits I did get in right field, which is not all that normal for me."

For very good reasons on both sides, manager Cito

Gaston balked when Gruber told him he wanted to switch the emphasis on his swing from the bottom to the top hand.

"He didn't order me not to do it," says Gruber, "but he refused to teach me how to do it. Cito was doing the right thing because he was thinking long-term. He didn't want me getting into the habit of hitting with my top hand. It's a bad habit, because you roll your wrists when you make contact and that causes you to hit the ball on the ground. That's not my game. I drive the ball.

"As for me, my left wrist was hurt and weak. My right wrist was strong. I took it upon myself to learn how to hit with my top hand. I figured I had to do it to compete."

More of the same awaited him in the summer of 1991 after he returned to the lineup from a freakish injury that occurred on the night in May that Nolan Ryan of the Texas Rangers tossed a no-hitter against the Blue Jays.

Gruber, who had drawn a walk with two out in the first inning, broke for second base when Ryan bounced a pitch that squirted away from catcher Mike Stanley. Recovering quickly, Stanley soon had Gruber involved in a rundown. Although Gruber made it back to first base, saving an out would cost him dearly over the next couple of months.

During the play, Gruber fell and caused extensive damage to the thumb of his right hand. In addition to spraining ligament and causing considerable dislocation, he also fractured the base of the thumb. On the next two trips to the plate (fly to left, strikeout swinging) the pain was so severe that Gruber had to keep the thumb off the bat.

Three days later, after extensive tests at the University of Virginia Medical Centre in Charlottesville, Dr. Frank McCue told Gruber he would be out for as long as two months.

"With the changes that had been made and the way they were working out, I couldn't wait for the season to start," Gruber groused in Toronto a few nights later. "Now this. Now I'm a spectator. To be so useless now that we've got the club the way we want it, that's hard to take."

At the root of similar troubles in 1990 were the recurring rumbles about a pattern of Gruber going from boom to bust in the second half of the season.

"You hear the whispers," Gruber admits. "They hurt, but it's a part of the game you just have to eat. Still, you think, 'If only you knew.' When you're hurting, you have to keep a low profile to improve your chances of survival. Sounds dramatic but it's true. The trainer knows. The manager knows. Maybe a few coaches. Let it get around that you've got a weakness and it's like slitting your wrists in a pool full of sharks. A pitcher finds out you've got a sore hand, he's going to be feeding there. Who needs the sharks?

"Another reason for keeping your mouth shut is that complaining about injuries sounds like you're making excuses. You play this game 150 times a season or more, you're bound to play it hurt a lot of the time. So you shut up."

As if life did not already have its share of reminders about human frailty, Gruber awoke one day in mid-August with a muscle spasm in his upper back. It visited just as he thought he was emerging from his slump with a 3-for-4 afternoon in Minneapolis against the Twins.

"It just grabbed hold of me," he says. "It got to a point where I didn't sleep at all the next couple of nights. I'd keep looking for a comfortable way of spreading out, but none of them worked for long. It was like having a rib injury and somebody keeps planting a knife in you. A gripping pain. The kind of pain that takes your breath away."

No sooner did he recover than another pitcher, "working inside," added his signature to Gruber's much-abused left hand.

Fortunately, the damage done to Gruber's wrist by Walt Terrell of the Detroit Tigers early in September looked far worse than it was. The pitch struck Gruber between the bones on each side of the wrist, causing a severe muscle bruise and raising a bump the size of a walnut. The swelling and stiffness sidelined him for four days.

"I could fight the pain," said Gruber. "I couldn't fight the pain, the stiffness *and* the swelling. The biggest problem was trying to get the wrist lubricated and the mobility back."

The psychological effect was even greater.

"My stroke had been coming around and I was seeing the ball pretty good. I was hoping I'd miss only one or two games. A lot of times, a couple of days off will give you a good rest mentally and physically, but it won't blunt your sharpness. Four days without batting practice, four days of not seeing live pitching, that meant starting all over again."

For all of his problems, Gruber says it all could have been much worse had one of the season's first deviating pitches nailed him an inch or two from where it did. It was delivered by Nolan Ryan.

"We were in Texas for the season opener," says Gruber, "and it seems like Ryan had a couple of strikes on me. I'm protecting the plate, like I should be, but you still have to respect his fastball.

"Damned if he don't throw me a curve. Damned if I didn't know what it was when it came out of his hand. Only when it got halfway to the plate did I pick up the rotation that told me. Like a deer caught in the headlights of a pickup truck, I froze. It was all I could do to turn my head in the nick of time. It hit me solid on the back of the helmet. Thank God those things are built solid!"

After shaking his head to see that all the moving parts were in some working order, Gruber looked up to see Ryan approaching the plate with a look of concern on his face.

"He asked if I was OK."

It might well be the one occasion in his career that Gruber has looked upon a beanball as a compliment.

There is an epilogue.

"Back home," Gruber says, picking up the story, "Nolan has a commercial about these headache pills. 'Take two of 'em,' he says, 'and your problem is long-g-g gone.' Later that night, me and a couple of buddies happened to be having a few beers at a bar. Nolan happened to be there, too. I want over to him, asked him if he had a couple of those pills so my headache could be long-g-g gone.

"All the time, I was thinking that if it had been one of his 100-mile-an-hour fastballs that hit me, the last thing on my mind would be a headache. If I had a mind left."

CHAPTER 16

 A TALL SHADOW

With a single exception, says a man who has studied the matter for close to a decade, Kelly Gruber is every bit the player that George Brett has been on the journey that will take him one day to the doors of the Hall of Fame.

"Save for that one thing," says Rance Mulliniks, who has been forced to take a seat on the bench by both these superstar third basemen, "Kelly can do everything better. But who hits like George Brett?"

A couple of freshly bandaged pet bats lying nearby, Mulliniks made the comment as he waited his turn in the hitting cage at Grant Field one morning in the spring of 1991. Then, as Gruber took another cut, he spread his hands as if to say this is where comparisons become unfair.

"How many people have been able to hit like Brett? One, two at the most, each generation? He's won a batting title in the seventies, the eighties, the nineties. The only guy to do it in three different decades. You can be a good hitter, make enough money so the rest of life is one long day off, and still not be within spitting distance of George Brett as a hitter."

Mulliniks, a venerable thirty-five years old when he reported to camp a few weeks earlier, earned his credentials as an expert on Gruber and Brett while accumulating bench-time during fourteen years of major league service. He broke in with the California Angels in 1977. During the 1970s he had spent a four-season apprenticeship in the minors. Then the Angels shipped him and first baseman Willie Aikens to the Kansas City Royals in December of 1979 for outfielder Al Cowens and shortstop Todd Cruz.

They did him no favours. To win everyday work, all Mulliniks had to do was beat out Brett for the job at third, the speedier U.L. Washington at shortstop, or Hall of Fame prospect Frank White at second base.

He sat and watched a lot of baseball.

What impressed him, as Brett embarked on a hitting tear through the 1980s, was his teammate's ability to drive a baseball to all fields.

"A lot of guys, good hitters, are able to hit 'the other way,'" says Mulliniks. "A lot of guys can slap it for a base hit. Brett would drive these same pitches, put a charge into the ball, up the middle and to the opposite field."

Even more impressive, since Brett had never hit above .300 in the minors, was the commitment he made to becoming the finest hitter of his time—an accomplishment reflected by the eleven occasions he has hit better than .300 since coming to the majors to stay in 1974.

"Mental toughness," Mulliniks explains. "Other guys, they might not have slept, they might be torn up from the game yesterday, fight with the kids all day, and then when it's time to come to the park they'd say, 'Ahhh, fiddle, now I got to do this.' With George, it'd be, 'Ahhh, now I get to do this.'

"You just couldn't keep him down. Slump a little, the answer was easy. Work a little harder. Grind it out. No matter how tough. Rain, shine, 100 in the shade, Brett would be out there at 3:30 because his batting average had slipped five points to .330."

Mental toughness, insists Mulliniks, is a quality that can be developed in much the same way as a powerful set of forearms. Hard work. A day at a time. To match the ethic of George Brett, whose shadow Gruber liked to see when he played out his dreams in high school, Mulliniks thinks Gruber still has much work ahead of him.

"Becoming mentally tough is a process that has to be developed consciously until it becomes like second nature," says Mulliniks. "It becomes an attitude, in the middle of a slump and going up against the other team's ace, that 'this is the night I break out of it.' It's not, 'I'm struggling. I'm scuffling. I'm not worth a flip.'

"To play every day, to excel, to put up a .300 average over 162 games, six months of a season, you've got to be tough upstairs. You're gonna have days when you feel terrible at the plate, weeks when you go 2-for-26, but you've got to be tough enough to get through it.

"Shee-it, the whole world's struggling, but we've got to get it done somehow. When you go out there, you grind. Kick yourself in the ass. 'This is my day.'

"Maybe this year, I keep hoping, but Kelly hasn't developed that kind of mental toughness yet."

For Mulliniks, as it is with all those not born with exceptional physical gifts, dedication to the concept began in childhood—"ever since I was old enough to know that baseball was what I was going to do"—with hours of after-school and weekend batting practice with his father Harvey, who spent two years in the mid-1950s as a pitcher in the New York Yankees' farm system. "It started when I was seven or eight years old, so that makes more than twenty-five years I've been learning to hit. It started, literally, when I got big enough to swing a bat. I remember Dad throwing BP to me when my best bolt wouldn't leave the infield on a Little League diamond. That's how small I was.

"I made a lot of sacrifices I was willing to make because I wanted it so badly. It was a labour of love. I gave up goofing off with the guys. I was down at the yard putting in my shift. My dad and I, if kids came around who were a distraction, they were asked to play somewhere else. It was all business. Just like it is here.

"When people say it's just a game, that may be the only pet peeve I have. They don't know. I didn't grow up with the idea that I could be a major leaguer and make thousands of dollars. I wanted to wear the uniform. I wanted to play against the best of the best."

That Mulliniks won a two-year contract from the Blue Jays in the winter of 1990-91, after entertaining "come home to Texas" bids from the Rangers, is testimony that long ago he learned nothing would come to him easily.

"I'm not blessed with the greatest skills," he is not the least bit reluctant to say, "but I learned I could outwork, outlast, a lot of people."

It was a truth he began proving to the Blue Jays' faithful in March of 1982 when the Royals swapped him for pitcher Phil Huffman. Pat Gillick has swung many deals over the years, despite his former reputation as a conservative on the swap market, but this one ranks among the most one-sided in his favour.

Having appeared in only sixty games with the Royals the previous two seasons, Mulliniks launched a six-season platoon partnership with Garth Iorg that season. On three occasions since then, he has logged .300 averages and batted .275 or better three other times. Although he lacks the range of his early years, he has been a competent replacement for Gruber during down time caused by injuries.

His longevity is a surprise even to Mulliniks. Heading into the 1987 season, after Iorg was shuffled to the utility infielder role in which he closed out his career, Mulliniks fully expected Gruber to assume everyday duties as the club's third baseman.

A couple of days before camp broke in 1987, manager Jimy Williams called Mulliniks into his office at Grant Field and anointed him to start the season at third. "He didn't explain why," says Mulliniks. "I didn't ask. It's not my place to ask." The scenario, again to Mulliniks' surprise, was repeated the following spring.

Gruber, for his part, makes no bones about being upset by the move.

"Pissed off about not starting again?" he says, surprised that the question needed asking. "I was pissed off from Day One that I wasn't out there. I wanted the team to say, 'This is our man. This is where we're going. This is how we'll get there.'

"There had been a number of times in '86 and '87 that I pinch-hit, platooned, whatever, and did the job. Next day, if there was a right-hander pitching, I'd be on the bench. Like as not, I'd have a few days to think of reasons to get down on myself.

"Some people need to be broken in slowly and for some it's sink or swim. I was a platoon player and I guess they hoped I'd bounce off the bench one night and nail down the job for every day."

Lloyd Moseby, who played the decade of the eighties in centre field for the Blue Jays, sheds some light on the situation.

"Kelly was the kind of kid who couldn't play two days a week," he says. "A lot of guys take that job because the pressure's off. Kelly wanted the pressure, but we were still kind of leery because, again, he was a young player. He didn't talk a lot, but he talked enough to piss you off. 'Okay, let's see what you can do!'

"Then the light went on. One day you might get a couple of hits and go on for a spell. Then you get cold for a time. This kid never looked back. Incredible. It's not that I didn't think he could be a superstar. It's the way he did it. Overnight. Ba-boom."

There is a suggestion, difficult to prove, that manager Jimy Williams wanted Gruber in the line-up more often but was held back. Such power lies only in the hands of Pat Gillick, the éminence grise of the club's baseball operations and a man with firm opinions on the day's line-up.

"I tried to understand," says Gruber. "The club was on the verge of pennants and bringing in the kid might mess up the plans."

Upper management's assessment that Gruber was not yet ready for prime time was one with which the forthright Mulliniks concurred.

"To that point, Kelly had never been given a chance to play every day and, quite honestly, I don't think he had proved he could play every day. He had given no strong indication he was ready.

"The raw ability was there, all kinds of it. Great quickness. Great arm. Power. Good, quick bat. All these things. There also were a lot of things he could not do. He couldn't hit the breaking ball. I mean, he had no idea. He really didn't understand hitting or how to go about it. Honestly, at that point, I did not think he would have hit .250, .260 just platooning against left-handers."

To a degree, the statistics bear out Mulliniks' contention. Entering the 1990 season, after two years of success at the plate, Gruber had career averages of .258 against lefties and .266 against righties. The figures against the latter improved greatly in the breakthrough 1989 season, in which he hit .325 against lefties and .274 against righties. In 1990, despite six weeks during which he was hampered by hand injuries, the averages remained consistent but his mushrooming power stats were reflected by a .530 slugging average.

Mulliniks would not have dreamed it possible the day he trotted out to third base for the Blue Jays' home opener in 1988.

"Once they figured out what Kelly had trouble with,"

he says, "I thought they'd give him a lot of trouble. Kelly had shown no indication he could adjust. That's why it really did surprise people when he started coming through at the plate every day.

"He was strictly a dead-pull hitter. He had a lot of holes in his swing. He couldn't take the ball up the middle and the other way. Unless you're a rare exception, it's something you have to do to stay in the major leagues.

"Once his weaknesses became common knowledge, which would take no time at all, there would be a lot of ways to pitch him. Breaking ball away. Off-speed away. He would be theirs for keeps. It's simple. Show him a fastball or two once in a while just to make him think he was going to get a fastball or two once in a while. Then throw him nothing but breaking stuff away. Your mind tells you to adapt, but if you haven't been working on it, if you haven't got the feel for hitting the other way, all of a sudden you're forced to do it and can't. Pretty soon, the pitchers get to where they can throw a fastball and he can't hit it because he hasn't seen a decent one in such a long while.

"They throw you three or four breaking balls and you're out in front. Now you say I'm going to wait, wait, wait. That's when they pop the fastball past you. You either take it or you're so far behind, you dribble it to second base. Kelly just hadn't proved he could make this adjustment.

"It's a fundamental law of hitting in the major leagues, but it's not easy. If it were, the majors would be stacked with .300 hitters and they'd have to move the mound five feet closer to home plate. That's why there are only a few hundred people in the world who make a good living out of hitting a baseball."

The most telling statistics to support Mulliniks' claim are those of eight players, led by George Brett at .329, who batted .300 or better in the American League in 1990. In the National League, there were a dozen.

As corny as it sounds, Gruber's emergence as a super-star was no less sudden than any imagined in the Broadway fables about the understudy bringing down the house on opening night after the star shows up hoarse.

The afternoon of the 1988 home opener broke with Gruber on the bench after a springtime of rumours that the club would be open to deals to package him off for anything remotely interesting. After six seasons of unful-filled promise, he was coming off a year in which he had batted a mediocre .235 with a dozen home runs and 36 RBIs.

The play that turned his career around came in the first inning after Rickey Henderson of the New York Yankees got on base, stole second and was now hell-bent on swiping another.

"I took the throw and had my foot in front of the bag," Mulliniks recalls. "He slid into it. It just kind of hyper-extended the knee, stretched something called the cruciate ligament. The damage was slight, the way it turned out, but it was painful. I was on crutches for a couple of weeks. When I came back, it was to the bench."

As distressing as it is supposed to be when a comrade bites the dust, Gruber admits he felt the rush of adrenaline when it became clear he would be the next best thing to the starting third baseman for the home opener.

"I remember coming to the plate after that inning," he says, "and as much as I tried to shut them out, I could hear the voices in the crowd. They were saying good things. 'Show us what you got.' 'Go for it, Kelly.' 'Here's your chance. Make the most of it.'"

He went 4-for-6 that afternoon, including two home runs, and drove in five runs. In the blink of an eye, Rance Mulliniks had become a designated hitter and occasional third baseman.

"More or less, I went up the hump all in one day," says

Gruber. "Finally, I belonged. There was no more looking over my shoulder. I didn't have to worry about having the bat taken out of my hands if I didn't get a hit the first couple of at-bats. With Garth gone and Rance down, who was going to play third base? 'They must think a lot of me,' I was thinking, 'or else I wouldn't be here.' I could map out a game plan, put it into action and change it with the situation. For a while at least, it wouldn't be a hit-or-else proposition."

He used the opportunity to become the club's player of the month, batting .288 with three home runs and 11 RBIs, and won the same honour in June, batting .318 with six homers and 19 RBIs. By season's end, despite a second-half slump due in part to a hand injury, he hit a commendable .278 with 16 home runs and 81 RBIs. With men on base, he led the club with a .364 average (51-for-140). He also stole 23 bases in 28 attempts. In the field, his .971 average was fifth in the league, but he led in total chances with 477 and 349 assists and was second in putouts, with 114, and 31 double plays.

"Some guys respond to pressure and some cave," says Mulliniks. "We didn't have anybody else to run out there if he had a bad night, so Kelly had to play every day. In those first two weeks, he proved he should be out there every day. The rest of the season proved he was no fluke."

Mulliniks was surprised.

"There was only one thing that was keeping him from playing every day in the majors," he says. "Hitting. All of a sudden, overnight, he could do the things he couldn't do the year before. Something clicked. All of a sudden, he could hit that slider to right field. He could handle a lot more than just a fastball from the middle in."

"I've often wondered why it all came together on that one day," says Gruber. "Why was it different from the first time I picked up a bat in the big leagues? If I'd known why, it would have saved me a lot of grief. The only explanation I have is that I was ready. Maybe, I've often thought since then, it was my last chance and I had to be ready."

Mulliniks, a prime candidate to teach hitting once his reflexes finally fail him, offered Gruber some free advice now that he had proved he belonged.

"Work hard. Very hard. No rest. The minute you take the game for granted, get to thinking it's not all that hard, that's when you go from .320 to .250. To me, if you're hitting .320, you've still got to be out there hitting early so you'll stay at .320."

To this day, however, he wishes Gruber would find the key to distinguishing the difference between playing hard and playing reckless.

"He plays hard," says Mulliniks. "Sometimes, a little out of control. On the field, he gives all he's got, all the time. Runs everything out. Hard. Goes after everything. Dives.

"It's those petty little injuries, the ones that knock him out for four or five days. I tell him, 'Hell, what good does it do the club if you knock yourself out going into second base and we lose you for a week?'"

It took a three-year contract, one that will lighten the Blue Jays' vault by more than $11 million, to make Gruber see the light, but see it he did.

"There are times when I do play reckless and I am stupid," Gruber admits. "Now the club has put $11 million into me, I'm sure they'll want me to show a little care for their investment. I'll pay attention to a few more things, but at the same time I don't want to lose that edge. All my life I've played the game one way. Hard. I don't play it to pace myself through a season. I don't play it with the thought that I might wring a few more seasons out of myself at the other end.

"I've toyed with the thought that being careful might add 15 or 20 points to my average, that it might keep me on the field for a dozen more games in a given season, but these things really don't count. What matters is that I can rise to an occasion. For me, that's the true measure.

"July and August were dreadful months for me in 1990, but it became a good year when I was able to play at my best in September when we made our run. If it had been the other way around, the year would have been a bust."

Among the concessions Gruber made in the spring of 1991, at the behest of manager Cito Gaston, was a number of practise sessions in the sliding pit at the Engelbert Recreational Complex before the official opening of camp at Grant Field.

Over the years, Gruber has been thwarted by hand injuries and his bosses hoped to cut the risks by having him slide feet-first into bases more often instead of the preferred head-first method that allows a runner to slip a hand through or past an infielder's tag on close plays. Still, Gruber has his doubts that he will be able to apply the new techniques at the crucial moment. "It's one thing to wet down some grass at the side of a field and play at tucking a foot under a bag," he says. "When it's for real, something inside tells you to give every ounce."

At the same time, Gruber admits that some of the most debilitating injuries to his hands might well have been left them brittle from his days as a high school football player.

"Your knuckles can take a beating," he says. "Put an arm on someone and all you come up with is a fistful of jersey. There were a lot of times between plays when you had to pop the knuckles back into place. It's like any joint; it can break down."

For all of his good intentions, it was a thumb injury that sidelined him for 36 games a month into the 1991 season.

Although he worked diligently to stay in condition—lots of running, taking his regular turn in fielding practise—there was no way he could keep his "edge" as a hitter.

This was all too apparent when he returned to action on

June 12 against the Indians at Cleveland. He was 0-for-4 against knuckleballer Tom Candiotti, striking out three times. He was 0-for-2 the next night and committed an error.

He was superb in the opener of a series against the Baltimore Orioles, going 3-for-4 with a two-run homer before 50,287 at the SkyDome. The following afternoon, he "stunk out the joint." In addition to committing two throwing errors, he was 0-for-4 at the plate and hit into a double play.

"It's like spring training all over again."

Which reminds him . . .

There have been a number of such mishaps, but his first hand injury in the majors dates from the time he tried to steal a base towards the end of his first spring training with the Blue Jays in 1984. Since he kept the injury to himself and because his memory for such details is fuzzy, it is difficult to reconstruct the situation now. What remains clear, however, is the specific action and his reactions to it.

"As I slid, I reached far to my left to grab the bag," says Gruber. "I caught the middle finger and, without breaking it, pulled it as far to the side as possible. It was so bad I couldn't even pick up a bat and shadow-box with it. I carried that one around with me the whole season, even took it down to Syracuse."

As coincidence would have it, the same thing happened at spring training four years later when Gruber, sliding into third base against the New York Mets, made a mess of the knuckle again.

"I could feel it swelling inside the batting glove. By the time I peeled it off, it was half again its normal size. Put a little mustard and relish on it and I could sell it for half a buck in the stands behind third base. To be truthful, I'm a little pissed off with myself. You're not out to prove anything in spring training. The idea is to work on things, get ready for the real season. That's one area where I think I'll turn it down a notch. If I can."

The seeds for that particular injury had been sown the summer before.

Gruber, dancing off second base with Ernie Whitt at the plate and two out late in a game at Exhibition Stadium against the Chicago White Sox, slid back into the bag when catcher Carlton Fisk faked a throw to shortstop Ozzie Guillen. In the exchange that followed between the infielders, Gruber got the idea that Guillen had issued a challenge. He was happy to oblige.

"If Fisk had thrown it," Oz told me, "I'd have been hung out to dry. I was young at the time, so it didn't take much to light the fuse. If he was that sure, I told Oz, then get Fisk to give up the ball this time. I was a little sore, and to make sure Fisk would try I took an extra step on the lead. Never mind stealing, I was going to put Oz on his butt."

On the next pitch Fisk took the bait, and as Gruber dove back to the bag he was more intent on burying Guillen than impressing the umpire ready to make the call.

"At the last second, Oz steps out of the way. About the time I realized I'd miss him by a Texas mile—as you might expect, that's a far piece—I looked down and saw I was directly over the bag and due to make a three-point landing any second now. Oops. I reach back for the bag with my left hand and hook onto it.

"The finger pops. Same one I banged up in Vancouver three years back. The only difference is it hurts worse this time. I also tore my pants on one of Ozzie's cleats. As if that wasn't bad enough, Ernie Whitt had gone down swinging for the third out of the inning."

The consolation, if it can be so called, was that he would have been safe on the play. All the way.

Some consolation.

CHAPTER 17

 THE HENDRICKS BROTHERS

There is a story Alan Hendricks likes to tell, every word of it the truth, that says much about the agent-eat-agent recruiting wars waged far from the fields where boy-men play their children's games for huge sums of money.

The tale takes shape on a Saturday morning early in 1984 with Hendricks desperate for an excuse to weasel out of a trip to the supermarket that his wife has arranged for him.

He got lucky.

Mike Konderla, then pitching in the Cincinnati Reds farm system, calls his agent to say he and a pal from Austin are running late and will not be able to make their 10 AM appointment at Hendricks' home in the Memorial district of Houston. Would noon be all right?

No sooner does Hendricks hang up than Rayner Noble, a client who had just finished his first season in the Houston Astros' farm system, is on the line with word that he and a pal from Victoria are in town a couple of hours early for their 1:30 PM appointment. Would noon be all right?

So much for Saturday morning shopping expeditions.

"The five of us go into the back yard, have a few beers and I tell the two new guys what my brother Randy and I might be able to do to help them make a living," says Hendricks. "I just kind of wing it, let 'em get a feel for who we are. I can't remember if they agreed to sign on the spot or a little down the road, but I must have said something right. We bagged both guys."

Kelly Gruber and Doug Drabek.

Not to be crass about it, but considering that the player agent's standard commission on a contract is between three and five percent, that one Saturday afternoon spent "recruiting" bought $462,500 worth of groceries for the Hendricks brothers one week in February of 1991. The rewards were the result of Gruber signing his three-year, $11 million deal with the Blue Jays and Drabek, fresh from capturing the Cy Young Award in the National League, winning a record $3.35 million in salary arbitration against the Pittsburgh Pirates.

"It's a story I love telling people who recruit their ass off in football and basketball," says Hendricks, leaning back in a chair by the desk of the study in his home in one of Houston's tonier neighbourhoods. "Fly all over America, hoping like hell they can get ten minutes to make their pitch to some kid fresh out of college. 'Here's how it works in baseball, guys.'"

There is more to it, of course.

A week after Alan Hendricks tells his story, he and brother Randal have embarked upon their annual spring pilgrimage through Arizona and Florida to touch bases with all the players they represent in the major leagues.

Tonight in Plant City, Florida, winter home of the World Series champion Cincinnati Reds, Randy Hendricks is ready to flop into yet another strange bed in yet another strange hotel room after eighteen hours on the go since daybreak. At least the arithmetic is familiar.

"There are 26 teams in the major leagues and 31 days

in the month of March," he says. "We have the equivalent of two and a half to three teams of players. Every team is another town, sometimes another state. Up at six, in bed by midnight. For a month, it's pack and move, move and unpack.

"Sure, you spend a lot of time in the sun—I'm not saying it's all that dreadful a way to make your money—but a vacation? Hah! It's tough pitching when you're forty-five years old. And I'm no freakin' Nolan Ryan. I've got kids older than a lot of the people we represent."

If it were easy, the brothers agree, everybody and his, well, brother would be doing it.

This pair has been at it, hard, since 1971 when first-round draft choice Elmo Wright, a two-time All-American wide receiver from the University of Houston, signed them to handle contract talks for him with the Kansas City Chiefs of the National Football League. They cut a three-year deal for $150,000, which was in keeping with the times, and one of the brothers' tactics turned out to be significant for sport in Canada. As a lever in the talks with the Chiefs, the brothers entertained offers from the Toronto Argonauts of the Canadian Football League. It was the first of many forays the brothers made into Toronto on behalf of a pro athlete.

After five years of representing professional football players, a pursuit that formed only a small part of the real estate investment business they were also building, the brothers decided to branch into baseball.

Through Hendricks Sports Management, a division of the Hendricks Management Co. Inc., the recruiting began in earnest. The timing, tied to the demise of generations of baseball slavery, could not have been better.

Before the 1973 season, the U.S. Supreme Court ruled that baseball's "reserve" system did not contravene the anti-trust laws of the land. In so doing, it confirmed the owners' control over the game without regard for the traditional legal consequences pertaining to the owners' treatment of their on-field employees.

Eminently aware that revolt was at hand—there had been a thirteen-day players' strike in 1972—the bosses reluctantly agreed to put in place a mechanism to settle salary disputes. Decades after it had been established as a bargaining tool in the factory, binding arbitration became a fact of life in baseball.

The lid started coming off after the 1974 season when pitcher Jim "Catfish" Hunter of the Oakland Athletics claimed owner Charles Finley had screwed him out of money spelled out in his contract. He suggested to arbitrator Peter Seitz of New York that the contract had been breached and thus voided the agreement. Hunter won the case and became a free agent. The only warning that management recognized, however, was that they would have to be scrupulous about the terms of the deals they signed.

The workers took another view. After playing the 1975 season without signing the contracts management had imposed on them, pitchers Dave McNally of the Montreal Expos and Andy Messersmith of the Los Angeles Dodgers appeared before Seitz. They contended the automatic renewal of a contract was valid for only one year, not for perpetuity, as baseball tradition had maintained for generations.

Seitz agreed.

When a federal court confirmed the ruling, the players considered it the clarion call to emancipation. Thereafter, all players were entitled to become free agents after a one-year renewal of their contract. Collective bargaining in 1976 generated a new basic agreement between the owners and the players' union. Henceforth, players with at least six years in the major leagues could elect to sell their services to the highest bidder.

Randy Hendricks, having fought the restrictions on free agency in the National Football League, appreciated what the new system would mean in baseball. Thus, in 1976, the two brothers took a new direction and began to represent baseball players.

Before the decade went into the books, the Hendricks and others like them had helped boost the average major league salary from $24,909 in 1970 to $185,000 in 1980. Ten years later, that average had soared to $597,357. To put a slightly more familiar spin on the spiral, the same Blue Jays team that gave Kelly Gruber a $1 million bonus to sign a three-year contract in the winter of 1990–91 paid its entire team $800,000 for their inaugural voyage in 1977.

As astute as the Hendricks brothers have proved to be—*The National*, a respected daily sports newspaper in the U.S., ranked them among the top ten most influential men in baseball—there was still no way they appreciated fully the financial harvest that would fall to the players and those who helped them reap it.

"We were getting into a business where one in every ten players had an agent, the average salary was $30,000 and the minimum was $13,000," Randy Hendricks says in recalling those early days. "Did we envision that within five to eight years the players would be making $300,000, $400,000? Certainly. But did we think that by 1991 there would be players making $3 million, $4 million, $5 million? Sure we did. And we also thought we'd have a man on Mars by 1990, the Dow-Jones average would be 6,000, and bubble-gum cards we bought in the fifties would put our kids through college."

Having noted the Pyrrhic victory inherent in free agency, Randy Hendricks turned to his brother Alan and told him their future was no longer in football.

"We concluded that the football union was not that competent, not that well-organized—it still isn't—but that the labour movement in baseball was strong and getting stronger," says Randy Hendricks. "As conscious decisions go, it might have been the smartest I've ever made."

Luck, as it often is, happened to be a side effect of design.

A former real estate partner who had moved back to Cleveland invited the brothers to speak to an investment group during the winter of 1975. Among those who attended was Fritz Peterson, a pitcher with the Cleveland Indians.

"C'mon down to Tucson and talk to our buddies,'" Alan Hendricks remembers Peterson telling him. "Stayed for nearly a week. Had a good time, too. A handful of players signed with us and it kind of grew from there. That was spring training of 1976. Lo and behold, by that August we had a new collective-bargaining agreement in place that established the free agency and arbitration systems as we know them."

Still, as promising as the future suddenly had become, there was no way of grasping how much money was out there to be had.

Remember Dave LaRoche? Those who do probably recall a left-handed reliever with the Cleveland Indians, California Angels and New York Yankees whose sixteen-year career wound up in 1983 with a 65-58 record, 126 saves and a 3.53 ERA after he appeared in 647 games. He also participated in one All-Star Game, one American League play-off game and one World Series game.

Mention LaRoche's name to Alan Hendricks and the effect is something akin to how Ali Baba must have felt when he rose on his Arabian charger and hollered "Open Sesame!" at the door to his desert hoard. "We did a deal for him in '77 that took him from one year at $40,000 to five years totalling $1 million," says Hendricks. "We thought we had just knocked over Fort Knox."

To mark the occasion of hammering out their first seven-figure contract, the Angels owner, Gene Autry, autographed a picture for the brothers with the title of his signature tune, "Back in the Saddle Again."

The third and fourth of five sons in a family of six children, the brothers grew up in Westwood, a town of about 2,000 just on the Kansas side of Kansas City. Their father put food on the table during the Depression by selling Fuller Brushes door-to-door after he was laid off by the Kansas City Power & Light Co.

"There was no such thing as personal disposable income," says Randy Hendricks. "If you wanted something special, you went out and got yourself some kind of job. Johnson County was a wealthy county, highest per capita income in the United States, and we were on the lower end of the social and economic scale, which tends to shape its own set of attitudes. Whatever it was we were going to do we were determined to be successful."

Clint and Edith Hendricks were as strong on religion as they were on education. He was an elder in the Disciples of Christ church, a made-in-America offshoot of the Presbyterian faith. In the latter respect, the Hendricks family was fortunate to reside in the Shawnee Mission school district of Johnson County, where an astounding ninety-plus percent of high school grads in the late fifties and early sixties went on to college or university.

Alan Hendricks, working summers in banks and insurance companies, put himself through universities in Missouri and Texas and graduated with a bachelor's degree in finance and a minor in economics. Randy Hendricks took a similar route, working for computer firms while majoring in finance, with minors in accounting, economics and history. He graduated from law school at the University of Houston, never having missed an honour roll or a dean's list in his life.

After that he went to work for a blueblood firm of lawyers, but the experience proved too confining for a free spirit. He and his brother decided to become their own bosses.

Perhaps Randy Hendricks, the brother most likely to wax poetic, has a handle on the "variations" in their personality profiles.

"Alan is the social person, Randy the loner," he says. "The stereotype is that Alan is the nice guy, the guy everybody likes and can deal with. Randy is the guy who is hard and demanding, but when it's high noon, time to go into the street, it's always been Randy. That's my lot in this family. Always has been, always will be.

"Randy has never belonged to a club in his life. Didn't even join a fraternity in college. Iconoclastic, individualistic, but at the same time he'll talk your ear off on a given night. Alan is more reserved, even guarded, allocates his time in a very precise way. I call him the world's greatest dispatcher. He organizes the baseball division—we have a diversified company—and he's much more involved with the players on day-in, day-out matters. I sort of flow in and out of different departments in our company while he sticks with one."

The thread, of course, is that the brothers genuinely love the game of baseball. Alan Hendricks, now six foot three and 230 pounds, was asthmatic as a child and therefore was forced into the role of spectator. No matter. Randy Hendricks, devoted brother that he is, brags enough for both of them.

"It's a night game and I'm warming up," he says, recalling his most memorable moment as the twelve-year-old pitcher on the sandlots outside Kansas City. "I'm going, 'Boy-y-y, I've got it. I'm going to bury these guys.' I had a real good fastball, threw either a cut fastball or a slider, which I've been paying for ever since, and had exceptional control. Give me a little backing, and generally I'm a winner. This night, we're playing the best team in the league, so I'm even a little more pumped. The reason they're leading the league is because, a couple of nights earlier, I beat the team that used to be in first. I'm thinking cocky, but I'm smart enough not to be talking cocky. Who's kidding who? Anyone who's any good, that's the way they are.

"Except for one bleeding ground ball between first and second, which went for a single, except for the same guy hitting a ground ball out to the same spot for an out, I struck every batter out.

"It's easy for me to relate to ballplayers. Even in Little League, the feelings are the same, or were for me, as they are at the highest level of the game. I've never forgotten those feelings."

The dream brushed up against reality a few years later, and, torn between his passion for sport and his considerable academic abilities, he made the smart move by taking up the study of law at the University of Houston.

The Hendricks' record on the fiscal field of battle has been such that they now have "somewhere between sixty and seventy" major leaguers in their stable—"I really haven't sat down to count them lately," says Alan—and it was on their behalf over the winter of 1990-91 that the agents racked up in excess of $100 million in contracts in less than 100 days.

Among them, of course, was the $11 million they arranged to divert from the Blue Jays' coffers into Gruber's account over the 1991, 1992 and 1993 seasons. It was not a hard sell. Its structure was based on artistic and financial comparisons with outfielder Bobby Bonilla of the Pittsburgh Pirates, before his setback in an arbitration hearing. Even though Bonilla had been converted from a third baseman to a right fielder last year, there was much in his and Gruber's 1990 performances and their careers that covered common ground.

After five full seasons and 761 games in the majors, Bonilla had a .279 hitting (.467 slugging) average, 430 RBIs, 98 home runs, 157 doubles and 31 triples. The figures for 1990, a season in which he was runner-up for the

MVP Award, were .280 (.518), 120 RBIs, 32 homers, 39 doubles and seven triples.

Gruber, in 668 games over the past five seasons, posted a .267 batting (.422 slugging) average, 326 RBIs, 77 home runs, 107 doubles and 18 triples. In 1990, a season in which he finished fourth in MVP voting, the figures jumped to .274 (.512) 118 RBIs, 31 homers, 36 doubles and six triples. Any deficiencies that might have been perceived in Gruber's statistical package were offset by the Gold Glove and Silver Slugger awards he won as the American League's best defensive and offensive third baseman in 1990.

Also noted by the Hendricks brothers and negotiators for the Blue Jays, chiefly President Paul Beeston and Assistant General Manager Gord Ash, was that each player earned $1.25 million in base salary in 1990. Gruber also collected bonuses of $100,000 for making the All-Star team, and for winning the Gold Glove and Silver Slugger; Bonilla's contract did not contain such clauses.

Still, as Randy Hendricks recalls the details, it was a "yes and no" situation.

"Is our rapport with Kelly Gruber exceptional? Yes. Is our rapport with the Blue Jays excellent? Yes. The 'no,' simply, is that we saw Kelly at somewhere in the neighbourhood of $12 million. They saw him at around $9 million.

"What makes it enjoyable with the Blue Jays is that the repartee is good. We play like friends play poker. To win. To do it right. There is no animosity, but neither side gives an inch without getting an inch."

Beeston, a rare bird in major league baseball's aerie in that he was born and reared in Canada, agrees that it can be an enlightening experience to toss around millions of dollars with the Hendricks clan.

"Everybody brings something different to the party," he says, "but I think what makes them best is their abiding passion for the well-being of the game. They understand the game. They understand management's side of it. They want the best deal for their clients, but they understand management has to be responsible. You can talk to them about the weaknesses of a player and they understand. They don't use the press and, particularly, they have an abiding passion for the game."

In the spirit of cutting a fair deal, Randy Hendricks and Beeston agreed that market conditions would be a decisive factor in negotiations. If either side were faced with overwhelming evidence of value, the other would adapt to it. When contract talks for Bonilla and Gruber lagged, Bonilla filed for arbitration at $3.475 million and Gruber at $3.3 million. The Pirates countered with $2.4 million and the Blue Jays set their price at $2.25 million.

"As the negotiations with Bonilla progressed, there were stories in the papers that the Pirates were offering $15.5 million and then $16 million over four years," says Randy Hendricks. "At the same time, they offered him $3.1 million to settle his arbitration case. On the face of these numbers, in the spirit of the promise to bargain in good faith, it became clear the Blue Jays had to come to our side of the ledger."

Gruber, paid $1 million for signing the deal, earns $2.7 million for the 1990 season, $3.3 million in 1991 and $4 million for 1992. He also is eligible for bonuses of the type he cashed for the 1990 season. The moment he applied his signature to a sheaf of papers, he became the highest paid third baseman in the history of baseball.

Within hours, as the fates would have it, the arbitrator in the Bonilla case sided with Pittsburgh. Bonilla's 1991 salary was pegged at about $1.3 million less than Gruber will earn.

Gruber trusts his bosses will appreciate how he got himself into such a fix in the first place. He saw it as a moral imperative that he relieve them of all that cash over the next three years.

It was much more than a simple case of economics in the workplace. Gruber, by far the best third baseman in the American League in 1990, swears he would have been content with a couple of bucks less were he still playing follow-the-leader in the salary sweepstakes that occupy his profession in the off-season.

"I'm not the follower any more, waiting for this guy or that guy to sign and give me an idea what I should ask when my turn comes," says Gruber. "Now everybody's waiting on what I do.

"Just as the guys who went before me, guys like Eddie Mathews and Brooks Robinson and Mike Schmidt, made all this possible for me, it's my turn now to make sure good things will be happening five years down the line for some kid starting out today. It's my duty."

Some tycoons out there blame that sort of thinking for bumping off the golden goose, but Gruber is quick to defend the notion that big business did not become big business by spending itself into debtors' prison.

"There has been a lot of bitching and moaning about the increase in salaries to the players," he says. "It happens only because the owners can afford it.

"They do it because they know that people don't come to the park to watch them sit in their private boxes, smoke their big cigars and count their money. We're what generates the dollars. We deserve to be compensated. It's called free enterprise. That's what makes our way of life in the States and Canada so much better than anyone else's way of life."

If Gruber sounds like a second-storey man who lucked onto the Crown jewels rather than the happy-go-lucky kid with the dirty uniform at third base, it is probably because this particular bit of speechifying came from the front seat of a long, white, chauffeured Cadillac as it sailed down the Don Valley Parkway in Toronto one night in January of

1991. He had spent the afternoon signing cards, photos and baseballs at a collectibles store that includes him among its owners. The business of doing business was uppermost in his thoughts. However, he has not lost sight of what it is that got him this far.

As the rusted lacework of the Bloor Street viaduct flashes by overhead, he says the Toronto ball club has certain "home court" advantages.

"I have ties here," he says. "My son, my wife, her family, they're Canadians. I like the Blue Jays organization. First-class. Room to improve, of course, but still first-class. You couldn't help but like the city. The fans, too. It's a great place to play.

"I'm not going to cry about the extra taxes. I'm not going to complain about customs at the airport. They're doing a job. The only thing I don't like about Toronto is the winter. Does that make me different from a lot of Canadians?"

In admitting as much, Gruber all but set aside the most decisive weapon in his arsenal. If he had played out the 1991 season and had a summer anything like the one he put into the books in 1990, is there a club that would not give the keys to the vault to an all-star third baseman?

He swore that was not what he wanted.

"I think the Blue Jays know I'm no troublemaker," he said. "I don't think they look upon me as a difficult guy when it comes to talking about money. When the deal was done, I wanted them to feel as good about it as I did. We're in this together after all. I wanted them to wrap me up for three years. I've worked hard. I've paid my dues. This is where I wanted to go. Now that I'm here, let's talk security. Ten million dollars? Yeah, that's some kind of security. On the other hand, how much would they be paying me if I crapped out in Triple A?"

In keeping with his international capacity to turn a dollar, Gruber is one of the few Blue Jays to employ an agent solely to take care of his business interests north of the border. It is a direction more athletes should consider, suggests Elliott Kerr, thirty-nine, president of The Landmark Group, a made-in-Canada agency with offices in four Canadian cities and New York.

In the two years it took Gruber to soar from everyday player to superstar status at the outset of the 1991 season, Kerr lined up half-a-dozen "blue-chip corporate relationships" for Gruber and boosted his fee for an "appearance" of two to three hours to $10,000. This is a far cry from the times, not so long ago, when the professional athlete considered Canada a wasteland as far as endorsement opportunities were concerned.

"In part, they have themselves to blame," says Kerr, who holds a master's degree in business administration. "Many of the young players were working for a lot less than the 'fair market' would dictate. What hurt them, in part, was that for a long time the older players had been doing deals on their own that undercut the market for everyone else. With thorough, informed professionals to represent them, the picture has improved considerably."

The new way of doing business also occasioned something of a backlash from a corporate sector that had grown accustomed to buying athletes' names and their time at bargain-basement prices.

"I've had quite a bit of grief about Kelly's appearance fee," says Kerr, "but I think it's fair. If you want him, he'll do it; but you have to pay. And he's worth every penny. He's magic with people."

Kerr, whose firm also represents close to twenty-five players in the National Hockey League as well as golfer Dawn Coe, decathlete Michael Smith and equestrian Ian Millar, has watched his business grow from a kitchen-table operation in the middle 1980s to a firm with a staff of twenty-five on the verge of doing $5 million gross business annually. In addition to representing athletes,

Landmark also manages sports events and acts as a corporate consultant on the use of sport for commercial purposes.

While the revenue the company generates for Gruber does not approach the money reeled in for him by the Hendricks brothers, Landmark is laying the foundation for Gruber's commercial opportunities in Canada when his playing days are finished.

"His wife and son are Canadian," Kerr says, repeating the obvious, "so he'll be spending a certain amount of time here long after his playing days come to an end."

For their part, the Hendricks brothers are also doing their bit to see that Gruber's stay in Toronto is lucrative. The agents are proud of their relationship with sport managers.

"Sounds hokey and corny and old-fashioned," says Alan Hendricks, "but you treat an individual with respect and things tend to work out fine. Integrity and honesty never hurt anything. I don't mistake the fact that I can get along with a lot of people and enjoy them and their company. That doesn't mean anyone has to compromise the task at hand."

Fine sentiment, but not the kind of stuff that tends to make a hard-nosed bargainer see the good sense in parting with some of the box office proceeds.

"Wel-l-l," he says drily, "all the Xs and Os on the blackboard always turn into touchdowns, don't they? But you still have to go out and execute, don't you? It's that old story of actions speaking louder than words. Good thought to live by."

The profession they chose has its ticklish moments. Late at night in a hotel room at Plant City after a day with the Cincinnati Reds, Randy Hendricks remembers how he once thought he might have to do battle with the Blue Jays over a pittance of $5,000. It happened a couple of years back when Kelly Gruber set a firm price for his services to the Blue Jays.

Randy Hendricks clears his throat, reaches for his imaginary lawyer's hat and puts it on.

"It was the judgment of our client that, based on all the available evidence, the very least he could accept was $475,000. However, in the interests of maintaining a cordial relationship with management, he was willing to accept $465,000. It was the assessment of his employers that $450,000 was fair recompense for his services. In the interests of good labour relations, however, they were willing to increase their offer to $460,000."

The hat comes off.

"We have a policy that we never do a deal our guy doesn't want to do," he says. "Let's assume I think the client's wrong. My job is not to tell him he's wrong. Or to make him feel weak. Or that the team's gonna get him the next time. My job is to educate him with respect to the facts so he will modify his position voluntarily. Then he makes an informed decision."

Even so, neither party wanted to budge over the $5,000 difference.

"This was almost at the point of absurdity," says Hendricks. "Finally, and we don't know whether to laugh or cry, Beeston and I come to an agreement. Split the difference. The hitch is that if anybody else on either side balks, the deal is off and we go to arbitration.

"Arbitration! It'll cost each of us more than $2,500 to fly our guys up there, put them in hotel rooms and feed them. Fortunately, both sides were happy that the other gave a little."

As wealthy as they have become, it is surprising that few in management regard the Hendricks as grasping. Their fee structure here is significant. Naturally the brothers prefer to attract clients as they embark upon their careers; Gruber and Drabek being classic examples. The firm charges nothing for its services until a player reaches the major leagues. At that point, a sliding fee scale takes effect—5 percent up to $500,000, 4 percent up to $700,000, 3 percent thereafter.

Hendricks, who knows a thing or two about statistics himself, can divine where baseball is headed in the salary tug-of-war that will be waged throughout the 1990s.

"Management is going to have to come to grips with the overall revenues of the industry and how they can't act like poor old Seattle when the New York Yankees are getting rich. On top of that, they need to have the union and players give them some market stability, so they can count on labour costs no matter what happens. That's something that can be jointly addressed.

"As for the rest of it, I've never had a cheque bounce and we haven't seen a team go belly up yet.

"People have been screaming bloody murder for years on salaries. I tend to turn a deaf ear to all that stuff. Salaries are a function of the overall revenues of the industry."

In other words, boss, keep the cheque books open, the pens poised and the inkwells full. It's only money, after all.

CHAPTER 18

 ## TEMPTATION

In the good old days, before plastic grass and designer drugs and megabuck contracts made life so darned complicated for a ballplayer, there were two ways a good-time guy could find trouble off the field.

Whisky and women.

A taste for either, or both of them, was not at all frowned upon. Indeed, as oldest-of-the-oldtimers Jimmy Reese remembered before a game in Toronto a few seasons back, it was more or less expected.

Babe Ruth is a prime example. For two seasons with the New York Yankees in 1930 and 1931, where he rode the bench as an understudy to second baseman Tony Lazzeri, Reese was The Great One's designated roommate.

"I guess I did spend a lot of time keeping his suitcases company," he was saying one evening as the California Angels, his current teammates, took batting practice before a game against the Blue Jays at Exhibition Stadium. "He'd come in and change shirts once in a while, though. 'Hi ya, kid,' he'd say. 'See ya a little later.' Then he'd be gone."

Nor did his appetite stop there.

"Rye and White Rock soda, he'd have four, five of them before dinner and eat like he just got out of the orphanage. Doubles on everything. Then he'd sit back and puff through a couple of those big, black Cuban cigars.

"In the mornings, he'd go through a couple ham steaks, half a dozen eggs, a stack of hotcakes, three or four glasses of orange juice and lots of coffee. Then he'd start thinking about how he'd get to the ballpark for the game that afternoon."

Jimmy Reese stops the narrative to pull a pouch of Red Man chewing tobacco from his hip pocket, dips two fingers inside it and hauls out a wad that would choke an umpire. From his place on a bench in the bullpen in right field, he takes a long moment to survey the pre-game rituals that have changed so little over the sixty seasons he has been involved in baseball.

"Things," he says, "they were a lot simpler back then."

Indeed they were.

"Choices," Kelly Gruber was telling a group of twelve-year-olds one February evening not long ago in a meeting room at a community centre near his winter home. "That's a word all of you understand. It's not a ten-dollar word. It's not a word that will make you run to the big dictionary in the school library. It's a simple word, but at this time of your life it's a word that can send you in a lot of directions."

Most in the audience of about sixty youngsters are wearing baseball caps, precious few of them with the stylized Blue Jay of Gruber's club. Clutched in their hands are baseballs, autograph books and stacks of bubblegum cards to be signed after the guest of honour finishes talking to them. Curiously, for a collection of such blithe spirits, they are awfully quiet.

"Back when I was going to Westlake High," Gruber

says of the place nearby that he left a little more than a decade ago, "we knew where we could get beer. We knew there was stuff you could smoke, too. And if we looked, we could find it, too.

"I'm not saying we always made the right choice, but we always knew what the right choice was. It was a lot simpler back then than it is now. It's more frightening today because there are more choices, more ways to go wrong, more ways to be tempted.

When I was going to school, the only kind of crack I knew about was the one I got to run through with a football when the blockers on the line did their job. Today, it's a word that scares me. Scares your teachers and your parents, too. Do it just once, people tell me, and it can take over your life.

"You don't want to live in chains. That's not what your mom and dad have in mind for you when they make sacrifices to dress you, feed you and send you to school. Don't say no to drugs just for them. You've got a choice to make, for good or for bad. Say it for yourself."

The monologue drifts on for ten minutes and then there are questions. Familiar ones. Who's the toughest pitcher? "Any of them, on the day they're right, can be your worst nightmare." Will you ever come home to Texas to play for good? "I always play for good." Is a Gold Glove really made of gold? "Hmmm. Have to check that one out."

An hour later, after a pit-stop for hamburgers and Dr. Pepper with a couple of pals from his school years, Gruber is piloting his grey and white Ford F-150 pickup over a maze of Texas pavements toward his home in the hills near Austin.

Suddenly, he comes to another of his crossroads.

"There," he says, braking. "Zilker Park."

To the casual observer, it looks no different than a thousand other green spots in a thousand other cities that punctuate the urban landscape between the Rio Grande and the line of permafrost that marks the gateway to the Canadian wilderness.

To Gruber, however, Zilker Park is the place where his life turned around one winter night seven years before.

"I'd just come home from Colombia, had to go to camp with the Blue Jays in a couple of weeks and I'd been out with the boys for a few beers," he says, country music on the radio. "For whatever reason, I stopped the car, parked it, got out and set on the hood.

"I was looking at the stars and I got to wondering what it was all about. I started to think there's got to be more to life than what I'm experiencing. 'There's more'n a couple of pieces missing here,' I told myself. 'I'm lonely. I want a wife, but there's no girl in my life. I've travelled all over hell's half-acre and who knows how far I'm away from the major leagues? I'm living my life in a way that doesn't particularly please me.' It was time to make a few commitments."

Couched in any number of terms over the past decade, what Gruber is talking about is tossing himself into the wave of Christian renewal that broke over the major leagues during the 1980s. In many respects, it was a movement that caused as much dismay among ruling management classes as the wave of drug abuse that seemed to be crashing down on the game at the same time.

The faithful were shaken to their very roots in 1980 when two of the game's young stars entered treatment centres for "substance abuse." They were catcher Darrell Porter of the Kansas City Royals, who was just coming off what might have been the best season of his career; and Bob Welch of the Los Angeles Dodgers, who would win a Cy Young Award a decade later with the Oakland Athletics.

How widespread was the use of cocaine? In an inter-

view with the *New York Times* in 1985, president John
McHale of the Montreal Expos said without reservation
that cocaine used by eight of his players cost the team the
1982 division race in the National League. One of the
players, outfielder Tim Raines, admitted later that he often slid into bases head-first so he would not crush the
vial of cocaine he kept in his hip pocket.

These were not isolated incidents. First baseman Keith
Hernandez of the New York Mets, whose seventeen-year
career coasted to a halt in 1990 after a trade to the
Cleveland Indians, testified under a grant of immunity in
1985 that forty percent of all players in the major leagues
in 1980 had used cocaine. One of eleven players to testify
at the trial in Pittsburgh of seven men accused of dealing
drugs to ballplayers, Hernandez referred to the drug as
"the devil on this earth."

Rarely a winter went by that decade in which a mar-
quee name did not turn up in print connected with a
treatment program he was undergoing for "substance
abuse." If those in baseball's ivory towers were surprised
by off-the-field developments, they were simply ignoring
reality.

Only a few months before the "me decade" of the
1980s began, Bill (Spaceman) Lee of the Montreal Expos
said something about sprinkling marijuana on his
Wheaties every morning. No one took him all that seriously. On January 15, 1974, the day boozing buddies
Mickey Mantle and Whitey Ford were elected to the Hall
of Fame, restaurateur Toots Shor of New York said something about the honour showing what a man "can accom-
plish if he stays up all night drinking whisky all the time."
On July 12, 1970, Dock Ellis of the Pittsburgh Pirates
pitched a no-hitter against San Diego—after what was
widely rumoured to be a hard night on the town (Cito
Gaston, the Padres' all-star outfielder, was among the vic-
tims). Not so, Ellis corrected the record a few years later;

he had popped an LSD tablet before the game.

So engrained is the problem of "substance abuse," in fact, that the institution of spring training in the southland has been attributed to it. It may have been part of a management campaign more than a century back aimed at combatting the use of the demon rum by baseball players.

The sporting goods tycoon, A.G. Spalding, owner of the Chicago White Stockings in 1886, was so worried about the effects alcohol was having on his charges that he sent them that year to train in Hot Springs, Arkansas, where they could sweat out their poisons. In short order, Hot Springs became the winter home of many a team in the majors.

"For the longest time, right or wrong, there was this image of the everyday ballplayer," Gruber says as he pulls the pickup truck back onto the road for home. "Drink hard. Cuss hard. Chase hard. The owners more or less got used to it. It got so that if you played it another way, if you didn't drink and chase women, people wondered if something was wrong with you.

"To me, that's stereotyping. To me, it ought to be each to his own way. I'm not judging anybody by what they do off the field. I don't want anybody to judge me. Isn't that why we've fought all those wars? Freedom of choice."

The influence of Christianity on a player's life is in its way equally controversial. As much as management, sometimes moreso, players complain that it can nurture the passive qualities in a player and suppress the aggressive instinct vital to any athletic pursuit. "We lost. It was God's will"; "I struck out. Christ has something better in mind for me"; "If it is Thy will, we will win."

Gruber himself admits that religion can be a crutch.

"To be honest, when I turn to God it is often when things aren't going right. And I shouldn't. If I was a true Christian, the way God intended, I would seek Him all the time. Then again, if I was perfect . . ."

Perhaps coincidentally, on many afternoons in 1985, one could count six proud-to-be born-again Christians out of the nine positions when the Blue Jays took the field. That number was down, way down, within the club that left the dugout on the first day of the 1991 season.

For the defence, Gruber contends the Blue Jays were never more successful than they were in the 1985 season. That was the year when they came within one victory over the Kansas City Royals of going to the World Series against the St Louis Cardinals.

"We had a lot of Christians on the team when we were winning," he says. "At the same time, and I can say this honestly, there was nothing like a drug problem. Why people would be upset because there were so many Bibles in the room, I don't know. One thing Christians say is that God created us to have a good life, to succeed, to be all we can be. Why would we accept defeat? Why give any-thing less than everything? I can't see God being pleased with anybody if they slacked off."

Just the same, some highly placed members of the Blue Jays' brass as well as Gruber's family and friends worried that he was in danger of getting too close to heaven to be any earthly good to the team.

"We were very concerned," Gruber's father David says of the period following that 1985 championship series. "These guys [the Blue Jays] were going in the wrong di-rection. They thought they were being holy but they were being very passive. They weren't setting any examples for Christianity. Who would want to follow them?

"Kelly got into some of that and they had to question him. They were afraid it would affect him on the field.

"I take my Christianity seriously and I think God wants us to have things, not so many that we put Him second, but I think he wants us to be successful. All his life, Kelly has had people pushing him to excel. Myself. His coaches in high school. All kinds of people in pro ball. To bring out the best, he has to be extended."

Howard Bushong, coach of the Westlake High Chaps, recalls the change he noticed in Kelly Gruber during his visit to Syracuse one summer to see how his former short-stop was making out with the Blue Jays' top farm club.

"He was big in the Baseball Chapel and that's good," said Bushong, "but there were times when I thought he was overdoing it a bit. I felt he was expecting the Lord to just take care of things. If Kelly just believed, he figured everything was going to be OK."

Bushong, a former catcher whose talent never exceeded his desire, was surprised at the laissez-faire attitude his star pupil showed towards his work when he was but one step removed from the major leagues.

"I'd make him go to the ballpark early," says Bushong. "Then the other guys would look up when he got there and say, 'Hey, Kelly, what the hell are you doin' here at this time?' I jumped his ass for not working hard. He had a tremendous talent, but I think he'd have been in the major leagues a couple years earlier if he'd have put more effort into it.

"His manager at the time, Jim Beauchamp, said something about the religion thing to me and I agreed with him. 'The Lord's gonna give you some talent,' he said. 'Now you gotta go out and do something with it.' Basically, I kept telling Kelly, God doesn't give a dam about a game of hardball."

Having sharpened the focus of his commitments by the side of the road that night in Austin, Gruber says he was influenced profoundly by the true Christians he met at his first spring camp with the Blue Jays in 1984. Among the most prominent were outfielders Jesse Barfield, Lloyd Moseby and Ron Shepherd, shortstop Tony Fernandez, first baseman Willie Upshaw and pitcher Roy Lee Jackson. Mormons Garth Iorg, at third base, and pitcher

Jim Gott did nothing to lower the tone of the neighbourhood.

"They helped me make a decision," says Gruber. "I
would stand up and be a Christian. They helped make me
feel like I had a relationship with God, that Christ died on
the cross for me. I also admit I wanted what they had, a
job in the big leagues."

When Gruber landed steady work—the process took a
couple more years—he also discovered that the temptations, varieties both old and new, were of major-league
calibre. Steroids, for instance.

"You meet a guy in the minors one spring," Gruber says
vaguely. "Say he's six feet, goes maybe 180 pounds. Next
winter you see him and he's beefed up thirty to forty
pounds and it's in all the right places. 'Liftin' weights,' he
says. 'Sure. Tell it to the bull out back. He needs something to help make him go.'

"After that you hear he's ripping the ball and the big
club's called him up. Next spring, when you see him again,
he's got muscles on his muscles. 'Liftin' weights,' he says.
'Sure. The bull's still out in back.'"

Gruber, who has spilled his share of sweat in training
rooms every step up the ladder to the major leagues, admits that taking the quick route a pill provides can be an
awesome temptation. At the same time, he says, the long-
term effects cannot be ignored in favour of the short-term
gain.

"'Oh, that won't happen to me,'" Gruber mimics. "Well,
it can happen to you. And when it does, it is not a pretty
sight."

A bigger threat by far, although it has become much
less so in recent years as ballplayers have become ac-
quainted with the risks, is cocaine. In earlier times, when
its effects were not as fully documented, it was considered
the drug of choice for the devil-may-care athlete. It made
perceptions razor-sharp, imbued the user with a supreme

sense of well-being and, not to be dismissed, it was considered a trapping exclusive to the rich and famous. It was
also perceived as physically non-addictive. The hangover
it left was nothing that couldn't be banished with another
dip into the snow.

Just how critical the cocaine threat to North America
has become was driven home to Gruber when kids with
whom he went to school were sent to Central America
with the army to flush out the despot, Manuel Noriega,
and put a crimp in the drug pipeline that empties into
neighbourhoods across the United States and Canada.

"Kids not even in their teens taking crack," he says.
"Hooked. Frightening. The kids, they're the future and
they're dying before they can read their first book. Rich,
middle-class, poor. Any kid can find drugs easily today.
The school yard, it's like a supermarket. The tragedy is
that even the survivors don't walk away clean. What do
these things do to brain cells? What do they do to the
value system of our society? What do they do to the fami-
lies of the victim?

"It might sound harmless, and I'm not saying you're
condemned for doing it, but getting drunked up with the
boys makes it impossible for you to be your best the next
day. Multiply that ten times and you get a hint of how
enormous the problem can be."

His employers might not approve of his stance, but
Gruber rates the abuse of marijuana and alcohol as
equally harmful in their physical and mental effects on
users.

"What's the difference between smoking a couple of
joints and killing half a bottle of Jack Daniels? They're
both drugs. One's legal. One's not. That's all. In baseball,
they'll look the other way if they catch you doing one, try
to take your livelihood away on the other."

The temptations to use one, some or all of these drugs
at one critical time or another are severe.

"The 'up side' is that they offer a quick, easy way to put your mind at peace," says Gruber. "Dad and Mom come out with the kids, see an exciting game, go home and go to sleep. That's the way it should be. Going to the game is supposed to set your problems aside for three or four hours. At the same time that family is in dreamland, though, the ballplayer might be walking the floor. Taking a drink, a hit of something, it can be a quick trip into what seems a better world without having to unpack the baggage in this one."

Gruber takes very seriously the belief that major league ballplayers, held in special esteem by children, have a duty to live up to expectations set for them.

"I know the decisions facing them, the choices they have to make," says Gruber. "The kids put me, people like me, on a pedestal. They're looking for ways in life to live it better. If I live in such a way that it will influence some of them to reject these terrible things, then the world will be a little bit better place. If I can help, that's far more important than any game of baseball."

CHAPTER 19

 AND KODY MAKES THREE

The cynic who lives inside all of us suggests that Lynn Seguin knew a good thing the instant she trained her sights on Kelly Gruber. He was young. He was handsome. He was famous. And, one day soon, he would be rich. Really rich. So she chased him until he caught her.

"I'm sure that's what some people think," she says softly as her husband of five years nods off to sleep on a black leather couch across the living room of their winter home in Austin, Texas. "Believe me, it's not the way it was."

The lady will admit Gruber was easy on her hazel eyes the moment she saw him across a crowded auditorium one Saturday afternoon early in May of 1986.

At the time, she had been to only one Blue Jays game, when she and a bunch of pals from her high school days were among the 43,587 who froze their assets at the home opener in Exhibition Stadium a few weeks before. She knew next to nothing about baseball or any of the guys in the funny blue hats who played it.

As for the charge of gold-digging, she prefers to let the facts speak for themselves. If she had known the heights her mate-to-be might scale, this former cheerleader for the Toronto Argonauts football team could have easily become rich in her own right searching out diamonds-in-the-rough for any of the other twenty-five clubs in the major leagues of baseball.

Her marriage to Gruber less than six months after she met him was simply the act of a young woman blinded by love. At that point it was a colossal gamble.

When they exchanged vows on October 18, 1986, before 500 friends and relatives at Central Christian Church in Austin, Gruber was coming off a season that well might have put him and his new bride on a bus to the boondocks the following spring. In 143 at-bats over 87 games, mostly as a sub in the late innings for his platoon partners Rance Mulliniks and Garth Iorg at third base, Gruber's professional batting average bottomed out at .196 while his power stats fizzled to 10 extra-base hits and 15 RBIs.

"If she knew where I was going that day, if she knew when I'd get there and how much I'd be worth," confirms Kelly Gruber, "then she knew a lot more about this game than I did. If she wanted a 'prospect,' a 'meal ticket,' there were far better ones to be had."

The Blue Jays did think enough of him to expand his role in 1987, promoting him to Mulliniks" platoon mate while Iorg was shifted to utility duty, but Gruber did little to firm up his bride's sense of security. His batting average rose to a mediocre .235 (12 homers, 36 RBIs) in 341 at-bats during 138 games. There were few signs that he would become the rock upon which the Blue Jays' infield would be founded a couple of seasons later.

For all that Lynn Seguin knew when she was making her vows, she could have been marrying a player who would flirt with promise for a season or two and then "wash out of the game." While the nest egg he would have accumulated might keep them comfortable for a few years, Gruber's best chance of competing in the "real world" would have been to return to university and hope to graduate before he was thirty. Lynn Gruber, in the meantime, would be raising the family of an "almost there" ballplayer in Texas, thousands of miles from the Canadian city in which she grew up.

And there were warnings.

"I had one of the cheerleaders come up to me one day and say, 'How's your bench-warmer?'" she recalls. "I remember hearing people in the stands. 'Hey, Gruber, why'd you get dressed today?' It hurt. I was twenty-one and in love. I wasn't thinking of the drawbacks. I didn't think of having to spend the rest of my life in the middle of Texas. I didn't think about waking up one day and hearing on the radio that my husband had been traded to Pittsburgh, or Cincinnati, or Seattle.

"Honestly, I didn't know a baseball player made any more money than a plumber. Naive, I guess, but I didn't read the sports pages. All I knew was that baseball players were popular, that there weren't very many of them."

While some couples seem destined to cross paths, Kelly Gruber and Lynn Seguin had to work at their "chance meeting" on May 3, 1986.

Flipping through the pages of a morning newspaper the previous day, Gruber had noticed a photo of a chorus line of Toronto Argonauts football cheerleaders with a caption announcing that they would be appearing at a fitness show near Exhibition Stadium that weekend. To suggest Lynn Seguin caught Gruber's eye from the pages of a newspaper would be stretching the truth, but she does cut an impressive figure in person. A trim 120 pounds on a five-foot-six frame, she appreciates the work involved in maintaining glowing good looks. Gruber would have forgotten all about the event had it not been for a reminder during the game that Saturday afternoon.

"We're sitting on the bench, my roomie Mark Eichhorn and me, when this plane dragging a tail circles the park around the sixth inning," says Gruber. "The sign says something about the fitness show and I turn to Ike and I tell him, 'Hey, we got to go there after the game.' I was thinking, 'Geez, I'd like to see some of those girls who were in the paper.'

"So we went over and I saw Lynn up there on the stage. I told Mark, I said, 'I'm gonna meet her.' That's really about all I remember."

Lynn Gruber's recollections are far more precise. Part of the dancers' routine, which was built around fitness glad guy Richard Simmons, involved the Argo cheerleaders seeking out old folks and children in the audience to join them on stage for exercises. As Seguin searched the sea of faces, she noticed Gruber standing with Eichhorn.

"My God, he's cute," she remembers thinking.

She hoped he would stay around long enough after the act so that she could bump into him, "accidentally on purpose, sort of," when the cheerleaders went into the audience to hand out souvenir sweat-bands.

That proved to be easy.

"He saw me give a sweat-band to another guy, which happened to be my last one," she says. "Then he came up and asked for one. I told him to hold on a second. I ran back behind the stage to see if there were any left. Nuts! There weren't. 'Now what do I do?'

"Sorry," she told him. "That's the last one."

"How 'bout the one on your wrist?"

"Sure," she said, slipping it off.

"How 'bout putting your phone number on it?"

"No way," she said, although she admits today the thought crossed her mind the moment he gave voice to it. They ended up touring the booths at the fitness show instead. The small talk, as Eichhorn eased himself into the background, included Gruber's fib that he and his buddy were businessmen visiting Toronto for a convention.

If the tour of the booths accomplished nothing else, it helped set the terms of their first date. That night, at the apartment Gruber and Eichhorn shared in midtown Toronto, all three watched the tape of *Star Wars* the roomies had rented at the corner video store.

From that point on, whatever else the Grubers might say now that they have become an "old married couple," neither could see enough of the other.

"It all seemed to happen so fast," says Gruber. "One minute you're alone, the next there's someone there who cares about you. From the beginning, I respected her. Other times when I was involved, I'd be telling myself what it is about the girl that I could live with and what I couldn't. That part of it was missing this time. From the moment we met, it was all so natural, as if we always knew what way we were going."

A minor hitch at the beginning of the relationship, however, was another man in Lynn Seguin's life. Nothing serious, she told Kelly that Saturday night between the pyrotechnical scenes of *Star Wars* when he asked if she would be free Sunday evening, but she had given her word to keep the other date. Later she decided to break it.

Unable to clear her mind of Gruber all that Sunday afternoon, Lynn called Kelly to ask if he still were interested in seeing her.

"Of course," he said.

"I was pretty taken with him," she admits.

The second occasion, dinner at a swank little steakhouse in downtown Toronto, was slightly more formal.

"He was neatly dressed, but very casual," she remembers. "I don't remember anything 'ooh-ahh' about him. He wasn't the kind to press. Looking back, the unnatural thing about it all was that it all seemed so natural. There was a newness about it, no question, but it was as if we had known each other for a long time but just discovered each other."

At his apartment later she made several points very clear. "I told him that if it was true what they said about baseball players, that they had a girlfriend in every city, that if I was just somebody he wanted to sleep with him, then to forget me. The team was about to leave on a two-week road trip to California and I told him that if I was his idea of a fling, not to call when he got back to Toronto.

"I'd had three relationships in my life. Each one of them lasted about two years. I wasn't the type who went in for a fling. I wanted to make sure he didn't expect something like that from me."

In no time at all, she says, they were seeing each other every day that the Blue Jays were at home, calling each other long-distance when the team was on the road. She says she knew the relationship had reached the "serious" stage when Kelly cut her a key for the apartment.

"He'd phone me, wherever he or I happened to be, and ask me to be there when he got home from the game," she says. "He would tell me to come over in the mornings and let myself in so I'd be there when he woke up. When a guy says those kinds of things, it gives you a fairly big clue as to what he thinks."

Despite all the hints Kelly dropped, Lynn was taken by surprise when he proposed one night early in August. It took her a minute or two to understand that he had asked her to marry him.

"We were sitting on the floor of his living room," she says, "and he says, 'Do you think you could spend the rest of your life with me?'

"To me, when you're dating, that's just conversation. You talk about marriage first before you actually pop the question, right? Then he asked me why I thought I might be able to spend my life with him. 'Let's talk about why we'd be compatible,' he said.

"I told him I loved him. I told him I knew I could be his wife. What else is there?"

Pause.

"He kind of looked at me as if he was embarrassed,

kind of confused."

Longer pause.

"I kind of looked back at him. Like, why are you stopping the conversation? He stood up. I looked up at him. 'What?'"

"You're not going to answer me?" he said.

Her turn to pause.

"I'm asking you to marry me," he said.

Longer pause.

"You're asking me to . . ."

"Uh-huh," he said.

"I was shocked. 'Oh. Okay.' No ring or anything. He must have known, deep down in his heart, that I'd say yes. He doesn't like embarrassing himself. He would not have asked me if he thought I'd turn him down. Gee, from what the wives told me the next day at the stadium, he'd told everybody on the team!"

There is some dispute on this point between them. She maintains that any number of players' wives will attest that Gruber sought their husbands' advice on the etiquette of proposing. For his part, Gruber says he asked only a couple of the guys.

One of the first concessions Lynn Seguin made was to forgo a month-long dance tour in Europe that she and a number of the Argonauts' troupe had planned for the autumn of 1986. And make no mistake, a baseball wife is expected to live a life of sacrifice while her husband works/plays to make their after-life secure.

"I was really excited about it," she said, "but Kelly asked me not to go. He promised that, one day, he would take me to all these places. He wanted to be married that October. I agreed. I was young."

Her second major sacrifice was connected to the first. In spite of the tradition that decrees the groom put himself at the disposal of the bride on *her* day, Gruber persuaded her to marry him before his friends and family in

Austin.

"If it was now, at my age now," she says, "I would have said, 'No way. I'm getting married in Toronto.' Here I'm the bride and I hardly know anybody at the wedding. Sure, I had my bridesmaids, my maid of honour and I had my family, but the rest of the people were strangers to me. I had a lot of friends, a lot of relatives, but it would have been too much to expect them to come all the way from Canada to Austin."

As happy as she was, as inviting as the future must have seemed when she and her husband returned from a honeymoon in Acapulco, the winter of 1986–87 proved to be the longest of her twenty-one years. Culture shock.

"That first winter was terrible," she says. "I was so homesick. It was like moving from Toronto to the North Pole. Little things, things you'd never guess, would get to me. If I wanted to go anywhere, I had to drive this big pickup truck. It's exactly what you want for a place with a lot of highways, but I felt like a construction worker driving it. When I did go out, it was a struggle not to get lost. At home, I could go to a mall and there would be an off chance that I might bump into someone I knew. Nobody knew me here. Nobody. I had Kelly. I had his family, and as warm as they were to me, they were strangers, too, because I'd just met them.

"I missed my dad and mom, Robert and Suzanne, and my sister Chris so much. We're so close. It was terrible. I called them all the time, mostly in tears. Kelly didn't understand. How could he? Austin is one of the most beautiful cities in North America, but I'm going to feel closer to the place that was home to me. Austin was so far away and I was so young."

Their first Christmas, the one supposed to be among the most enchanting for a couple, did turn out to be one they will never forget.

Freshly settled in their apartment in Austin after the

honeymoon in Hawaii, Kelly Gruber got the call to report to the Licey team in Santo Domingo, Dominican Republic, for two months of winter baseball. The money is always handy, but more important, Kelly Gruber wanted the opportunity to prepare for spring training with the Blue Jays.

Fighting off a case of the 'Dominican flu' and bouts of loneliness as Christmas week dawned in the Caribbean, Lynn tried to think of a way to add a touch of Yule spirit to their hotel room.

"Of course, you couldn't buy a Christmas tree in Santo Domingo," she says, "but on every corner of the city they were selling these, I'd guess you'd call them 'decorations.' A bunch of twigs, painted or dyed white, stuffed into a can weighted down with sand. Three, maybe four feet high."

Evergreen it might not have been, but Lynn wasn't about to quibble with Christmas only a few days away.

"I brought it into the hotel room and set it up," she says. "I decorated it as best as I could. I cut some pictures out of magazines and hung them around the place to help remind us of home."

By the following morning, their room was infested with ants.

"We got rid of the tree."

There were other examples of how profound culture shock can be.

"One of the newspapers, it must have been American, had a full-page ad for Big Macs," says Lynn Gruber. "A lot of the players cut it out and were showing it around like it was something they just pulled out of the family album. We were dying to get home for American food."

The "hunger" reached a peak on the flight back to Miami after the Dominican season was over. Also on the plane and fighting similar yearnings were Oakland A's teammates Terry Steinbach and Eric Plunk and their wives.

"As soon as we cleared customs," says Lynn, "we ran to a big McDonald's there. We gobbled up about two Big Macs apiece."

Five years later, she considers herself the most fortunate of the Blue Jays' wives because she is the one who gets to spend the summers in her hometown.

For all the obvious benefits of her life now, it is not one of leisure. In addition to doing the lioness's share of the parenting, she also organizes at least three major moves each year, shifting households from Austin to Florida for six weeks in spring, to Toronto for the summer, then back to Austin for the winter.

Toronto, of course, makes the most stringent demands on her time. In addition to a phone that always seems to be ringing, the boom in her husband's popularity has turned his wife into his part-time appointments secretary, accountant and office manager.

"There are times I think he married me because I worked in a bank and could help him balance his books," she says.

Escaping to Texas for the winter relieves the pressure on her of having to be "up front and on top of things" the moment she leaves the door of the family's condominium on the outskirts of Toronto.

"Austin is the time to relax," she says. "When you go to a game in Toronto, it's a fact that people are aware of what you eat, what you wear, how you act. You don't want to look like you just fell out of bed and couldn't find a comb. People know who you are and what you do reflects upon your husband."

Like the wife of any Blue Jay, a select circle that sits as a loosely knit group in the section behind the plate at home games, Lynn is acutely aware that a remark of hers blurted out in the heat of a game can have far-reaching effects on team morale.

"You have to watch what you're saying," she says. "Anything I say could be taken as coming from Kelly. In the clubhouse, with the players, I'm sure it's the same way. All of them have their bad days, and in the stands you might think things when somebody makes a mistake, but you've got to be supportive. Besides, you never know when it's going to be your turn."

As identifiable as the group becomes in the course of a season, its members sometimes are forced to bear the brunt of the criticisms of disenchanted fans on their husbands' performances. One of the most memorable incidents occurred at Yankee Stadium, where the inmates tend to air their innermost thoughts in the late innings, after a dozen watered beers.

"Kelly and I had been married less than a year, so I might have been a little protective," she says. "Anyway, a ball went through his legs and this guy said something that doesn't bear repeating. I turned and looked at him. Hard. Froze him.

"The next inning, he sent down a beer. Maybe he was from Toronto."

Like her husband, she had learned over the years to pretend not to hear what hurts. Similarly, she says, she lives by the credo of the veteran ballplayer. "Never get too high when you're high, never too low when you're low. It's a long season."

Since the summer of 1990, she has had far better things to occupy her thoughts than a husband's conduct on the field.

She stopped practising birth control the previous autumn in the hope of conceiving by the following spring. That would have allowed her to give birth during the relative tranquility of the off-season.

"Nobody gets pregnant right away, right?" she says. "Wrong-g-g. It was planned, but it wasn't planned so soon."

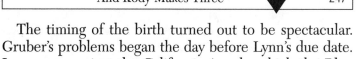
The timing of the birth turned out to be spectacular. Gruber's problems began the day before Lynn's due date. In a game against the California Angels, which the Blue Jays won 5-2, starter Bert Blyleven ran a fastball off his right hand.

"All I could think about was the next day, July 4," he says. "Lynn was going to have the baby. That was the due date, but the doctors told us a pregnancy can run a couple of weeks late the first time. I didn't want that to happen because I'd be away with the team. If the doctor says it's totally safe, I told her, then let's go in on July 4 and have the birth induced.

"I probably shouldn't have, but I played the rest of that game. I was in a lot of pain and my thoughts were nowhere near the ballpark. My next two or three at-bats were dreadful. Just as well for the club, maybe, I would be taking the next couple of days off."

Like most modern fathers, Gruber wanted to witness the birth of his child. Like all mothers, Lynn remembers her moment of fear in the agonizing moments before the child took its first breath.

True to his family's roots in two nations, Kody Robert Gruber was born at The Credit Valley Hospital in Mississauga, just west of Toronto at 6:25 PM on July 4, 1990. Mother and baby, eight pounds, one and one-half ounces, were fine, grateful thanks to doctors Mathias Gysler and Donald Black. The new father was a mess.

"'Here he is,' they said," Lynn Gruber recalls someone in the delivery room saying. "And he didn't say anything. 'Is he okay? Is he okay? Is he breathing?' It took him a second. Finally . . ."

Kody Gruber took a deep intake of breath, and let out a howl. Gruber took his son into his arms and brought him to his mother's side. As he and Lynn greeted him, Gruber felt the nape of the infant's neck. At the base of the skull, just as there is on Kelly Gruber and just as there had been on his grandfather Archie Hunt, there was a small arrow-shaped growth of bone.

Kelly Gruber, a new life his to help mould, said a prayer of thanks to Maw-maw and Paw-paw.

The circle was complete.

Kelly Gruber—By the Numbers

Year	Club & League	AVG	G	AB	R	H	2B	3B	HR	RBI	HP	BB	SO	SB-CS
1980	Batavia (NYP)	.217	61	212	27	46	3	2	2	19	3	15	46	6-3
1981	Waterloo (Mid)	.290	127	458	64	133	25	4	14	59	6	24	85	15-7
1982	Chattanooga (Sou)	.243	128	441	53	107	18	4	13	54	3	21	89	11-6
1983	Buffalo (East)	.263	111	403	60	106	20	4	15	54	5	23	44	15-7
1984	Syracuse (Int)	.269	97	342	53	92	12	2	21	55	7	23	67	12-2
1984	Toronto (AL)	.063	15	16	1	1	0	0	1	2	0	0	5	0-0
1985	Syracuse (Int)	.249	121	473	71	118	16	5	21	69	7	28	92	20-8
1985	Toronto (AL)	.231	5	13	0	3	0	0	0	1	0	0	3	0-0
1986	Torono (AL)	.196	87	143	20	28	4	1	5	15	0	5	27	2-5
1987	Toronto (AL)	.235	138	341	50	80	14	3	12	36	7	17	70	12-2
1988	Toronto (AL)	.278	158	569	75	158	33	5	16	81	7	38	92	23-5
1989	Toronto (AL)	.290	135	545	83	158	24	4	18	73	3	30	60	10-5
1990	Toronto (AL)	.274	150	592	92	162	36	6	31	118	8	48	94	14-2
ML	Totals	.266	688	2219	321	590	111	19	83	326	25	138	351	61-19

Championship Series Record

Year	Club & League	AVG	G	AB	R	H	2B	3B	HR	RBI	HP	BB	SO	SB-CS
1989	Toronto (AL)	.294	5	17	2	5	1	0	0	1	0	3	2	1-0

All-Star Game Record

Year	Club & League	AVG	G	AB	R	H	2B	3B	HR	RBI	HP	BB	SO	SB-CS
1989	AL at Calif.					DID NOT PLAY								
1990	AL at Chi (NL)	.000	1	1	0	0	0	0	0	0	0	1	0	2-0

Kelly Gruber—By the Numbers

	1990					Career				
	AB	**H**	**HR**	**RBI**	**AVG**	**AB**	**H**	**HR**	**RBI**	**AVG**
Season	592	162	31	118	.274	2219	640	83	326	.288
Toronto	305	89	23	62	.292	1107	297	45	165	.268
Road	287	73	8	56	.254	1112	293	38	161	.263
vs Baltimore	54	19	4	16	.352	174	57	10	34	.328
Boston	55	9	4	13	.164	188	41	10	33	.218
Cleveland	53	23	7	17	.434	186	54	9	32	.290
Detroit	35	9	2	10	.257	159	45	7	30	.283
Milwaukee	48	12	2	7	.250	195	56	4	22	.287
New York	49	14	0	6	.286	191	46	6	27	.241
AL East	294	86	19	69	.293	1093	299	46	178	.274
vs California	34	7	0	3	.206	166	42	1	12	.253
Chicago	47	15	3	9	.319	153	43	7	24	.281
Kansas City	50	11	1	9	.220	155	45	3	21	.290
Minnesota	41	14	3	9	.341	157	40	6	21	.255
Oakland	45	10	3	6	.222	156	39	8	23	.250
Seattle	36	7	1	5	.194	166	38	6	20	.229
Texas	45	12	1	8	.267	173	44	6	27	.254
AL West	298	76	12	49	.255	1126	291	37	148	.258
Pre-ASG	321	95	20	66	.296	1251	360	49	190	.288
Post-ASG	271	67	11	52	.247	968	230	34	136	.238
vs RHP	426	113	23	84	.265	1472	391	61	224	.266
LHP	166	49	8	34	.295	747	199	22	102	.266
Pinch Hitting	2	1	0	3	.500	36	8	2	8	.222
Designated Hitting	1	1	0	3	1.000	12	2	1	4	.167
in April	83	27	7	20	.325	263	82	15	51	.312
May	100	30	6	20	.300	415	114	13	55	.275
June	116	35	7	24	.302	434	133	21	73	.306
July	89	15	2	11	.169	376	82	11	38	.218
August	102	21	1	12	.206	341	75	6	38	.220
Sept/Oct	102	34	8	31	.333	390	104	17	71	.267

Career Highs

Season			Game		
Average	.290	(1989)	Home Runs	2	(6 times)
Home Runs	31	(1990)	RBIs	6	(vs. K.C. Royals, at SkyDome, Sept. 8, 1990)
RBIs	118	(1990)			
Hits	162	(1990)	Hits	5	(vs. Tigers, at Detroit, June 12, 1989, and vs. New York, at Exhibition Stadium, April 11, 1988)
Steals	23	(1988)			
			Steals	1	(61 times)
			Hitting streak	15	1989
			Cycle		(April 16, 1989, at Exhibition Stadium)

CHRONOLOGY

February 26, 1962	- Kelly Wayne King born in Bellaire, Texas.
October, 1966	- Adopted by David Gruber, a year after he marries Gloria King.
April 7, 1977	- Toronto Blue Jays play their first game at Exhibition Stadium, Toronto.
1978 to 1980	- Kelly plays shortstop for the Westlake High School Chaparrals, Austin, Texas.
June 3, 1980	- Chosen by the Cleveland Indians in the first round (tenth player overall) in the free agent draft. He receives a $100,000 signing bonus. The Toronto Blue Jays, drafting second overall, choose Garry Harris, second baseman, of San Diego.
Summer 1980	- Gruber plays shortstop on the Batavia Trojans in New York-Penn League in Batavia, New York, having been passed over by the Blue Jays.
December 5, 1983	- Toronto Blue Jays draft Gruber when Cleveland leaves him off its 40-man winter roster.
December 10, 1983	- Vita Evelyn Watkins-Hunt, Kelly's grandmother, dies when Kelly is in Barranquilla, Colombia, playing with the Café Universale.
April 20, 1984	- Kelly's major league debut with the Blue Jays at Exhibition Stadium, Toronto.

May 16, 1984	- Gruber is sent to the Blue Jays farm club, the Syracuse Chiefs in New York.
September 1, 1984	- Gruber returns to the Blue Jays for the pennant drive after the season in Syracuse.
January 27, 1985	- Archie Joe Hunt, Kelly's grandfather, dies in Austin, Texas.
August 31, 1985	- Kelly returns to the Blue Jays for the pennant drive.
May 3, 1986	- Gruber meets Lynn Seguin, twenty-one, in Toronto.
October 18, 1986	- They marry in Austin, Texas.
July 4, 1990	- Kody Robert Gruber born in Mississauga, Ontario.
February 12, 1991	- Gruber signs three-year contract with the Blue Jays for $11 million, making him the highest paid third baseman in history. He also wins the 19th annual Super Stars Competition in Cancun, Mexico, sponsored by ABC TV's Wide World of Sports.